Citizen of the World

Cycles

Series Editors
Andrew LaZella, The University of Scranton
Richard A. Lee Jr., DePaul University

Critical perspectives on the history of philosophy, from Ancient Greece to the nineteenth century, expanding traditional approaches to Western Philosophy

Cycles shows how the history of philosophy is a living tradition, influencing and determining our thinking in the present while maintaining its deep and rich roots in the past.

Books available
Aristotle on the Matter of Form: A Feminist Metaphysics of Generation by Adriel M. Trott
The Unconscious of Thought in Leibniz, Spinoza, and Hume by Gil Morejón
Kantian Ethics and Environmental Philosophy: Pursuing the Good in an Age of Crisis by Fiacha D. Heneghan
Aristotle and Tragic Temporality by Sean D. Kirkland
Citizen of the World: Al-Fārābī's Cosmopolitanism by Josh Hayes

Books forthcoming
The Theory of Incorporeals in Ancient Stoicism: Logic, Expression, Materialism by Émile Bréhier, translated by Jared C. Bly and Ryan J. Johnson, with essays from Michael James Bennett and Thomas Bénatouïl
Difference and Alterity in Early Modern Philosophy: La Boétie, Montaigne, Spinoza, Mendelssohn by Willi Goetschel
The Idea of the Instant in Descartes's Philosophy by Jean Wahl, edited and translated by Alan Schrift
Ontology and Politics in Hobbes' Civil Science: A Materialist Agenda by Andrea Bardin
Hobbes' Bodies Politic by Meghan Robison

Citizen of the World

Al-Fārābī's Cosmopolitanism

Josh Hayes

EDINBURGH
University Press

Edinburgh University Press is one of the leading university presses in the UK. We publish academic books and journals in our selected subject areas across the humanities and social sciences, combining cutting-edge scholarship with high editorial and production values to produce academic works of lasting importance. For more information visit our website: edinburghuniversitypress.com

Edinburgh University Press Ltd
13 Infirmary Street
Edinburgh EH1 1LT

First published in hardback by Edinburgh University Press 2025

Typeset in 11/13 Foundry Sans and Foundry Old Style by
IDSUK (DataConnection) Ltd, and
Printed and bound in the UK using 100% Renewable Electricity by
CPI Group (UK) Ltd

A CIP record for this book is available from the British Library

ISBN 978 1 3995 3054 5 (hardback)
ISBN 978 1 3995 3055 2 (paperback)
ISBN 978 1 3995 3056 9 (webready PDF)
ISBN 978 1 3995 3057 6 (epub)

MIX
Paper | Supporting responsible forestry
FSC
www.fsc.org
FSC® C013604

This book is printed using paper from well-managed forests, recycling and other controlled sources

Contents

Acknowledgements

There are numerous friends, colleagues, and associates who are responsible for assisting with the gestation, composition, and production of this monograph. I would like to especially thank Carol Macdonald, Judith Mackenzie, Souhaila Jouhar, Muhammad Ridwaan, Kate Kent, and the entire editorial team at Edinburgh University Press for shepherding this project along through multiple iterations and Richard Lee and Andrew LaZella, the Cycles series editors, for their patience, who first invited the proposal and presented the impetus for the initial draft. Parts of Chapter 2 were first published in *Aristotle and the Arabic Tradition* and *The Edinburgh Critical History of Medieval and Renaissance Philosophy*. I would also like to thank Glynis Fitzgerald, Leamor Kahanov, Mary Ellen Wells, Elizabeth Matteo, Corey Harris, and the Development and Research Committee at Alvernia University for funding to support my research and sabbatical request. I am grateful to Owen Goldin for hosting the annual Aristotle and Aristotelian summer workshops at Marquette University and to Eli Diamond, Richard Taylor, Dirk Baltzy, and Thornton Lockwood for their questions and comments. To my expansive circle of friends at the Ancient Philosophy Society, I would be remiss if I did not mention Emanuela Bianchi, Sara Brill, Jill Gordon, Marina McCoy, Adriel Trott, Marjolein Oele, Michael Shaw, Tom Tuozzo, Jeffrey Gower, Jeremy Bell, and Justin Humphreys. Parts of Chapter 3 were subsequently published in *Epoché: A Journal for the History of Philosophy*. I would also like to thank the Philosophy Department at Boston College, especially Richard Kearney, John Sallis, Jeffrey Bloechl, Gregory Fried, and Vanessa Rumble for their invitation to present the Arthur J. Fitzgibbons Lecture on themes related to cosmopolitanism and Islam. I am indebted to Kristi Sweet for her invitation to participate as a seminar leader for the Cosmology and Cosmopolitanism program of the Collegium Phaenomenologicum and to Ted George, Janae Sholtz, and Sharin Elkholy at the North Texas Philosophical Association annual conference for their hospitality. Several members of my medieval philosophy reading group were also tremendously supportive during my virtual presentation of a working draft of Chapter 6, especially Ian Alexander Moore, Jason Aleksander, Karmen McKendrick, Sean Hannan, Sean Erwin, and Daniel Selcer. An earlier version of Chapter 6 was published in *The Iranian Yearbook for Phenomenology*. I am also sincerely thankful for the friendship of Ahmed Alwishah and Philip Sidney Horky, which germinated during our time together in the Philosophical Research Group (PRG) at Stanford University under the indefatigable guidance of Hans Ulrich (Sepp) Gumbrecht and Robert Pogue Harrison. Finally, I am foremostly indebted to Jacques Derrida, Fred Dallmayr, Charles Taylor, Idit Dobbs-Weinstein, and Claudia Baracchi, who mutually inspired this project from its inception, and to Katharine Loevy, a fantastic friend and reader *sans pareil*.

‘Then he won’t be willing to take part in political life,’ he said, ‘if that’s what he is worried about.’

‘By the dog,’ I said, ‘he will in his own city, anyway, and in a big way, though maybe he won’t in his fatherland, unless some divine luck comes his way.’

‘I understand,’ he said; ‘you mean he will in the city we’ve now gone through founding, the one set down in speeches, since I imagine it’s nowhere on earth.’

‘But maybe it’s a pattern laid up in heaven,’ I said, ‘for anyone who wants to see it and for the one who’s seen to establish in himself. It makes no difference whether it is or will be present anywhere, because his actions will be those that belong to this city alone, and to no other.’

‘Likely so,’ he said.

Plato, *Republic* 592A5–B6

To family and friends, near and far.

1
Al-Fārābī's Plato

Introduction

Diogenes of Sinope, the early Greek Cynic, when asked where he came from, simply declared: *kosmopolitēs* – 'I am a citizen of the world.'[1] Although the idea that all human beings, regardless of civic or geographical affiliation, are citizens of the world appears to originate with Diogenes, cosmopolitanism as an ethical and political paradigm receives its most robust defence with Greek and Roman Stoicism.[2] Cicero's *On Duties* (*De Officiis*) proposes that cosmopolitanism arises in the innermost sphere of family and friends expanding to the intermediate spheres of the city, the nation or a people of the same 'race, tribe and tongue, through which all are bound strongly to one another' before arriving at the outermost sphere affirming the universality of humanity in 'a bonding which consists of reason and speech, which reconcile all humans to one another, through teaching, learning, communicating, debating and making judgements, and unite them in a kind of natural fellowship

[1] Diogenes Laertius, *Lives of the Eminent Philosophers*, II.6.63, 64–5. Cf. Baker, 'Cynical Cosmopolitanism'; Robineau, *The Dangerous Life and Ideas of Diogenes the Cynic*, 26–7; and Largier, *Diogenes der Kyniker*, 19–77. The themes of ostracism and exile subsequently reappear in the eighth-century Arabic poetry of 'Abd al-Raḥmān I, the Umayyad ruler of al-Andalus, who had been forced to flee his Syrian homelands during the 'Abbāsid conquest, 'A palm tree stands in the middle of Rusafa / Born in the West, far from the land of palms. / I said to it: How like me, you are, far away and in exile, / In long separation from family and friends, / You have sprung from soil in which you are a stranger / And I, like you, are far from home'; see Monocal, *The Ornament of the World*, 61; and more generally, Euben, *Journeys to the Other Shore*, 20–45.

[2] Jaspers's *Origin and Goal of History* identifies the inception of humanism with the Axial Age (*Achsenzeit*), 1–6.

or friendship'.[3] Cosmopolitanism is commonly assumed to have reached an impasse in the Middle Ages only to resurface in the Enlightenment period with the political philosophies of Erasmus, Grotius, Pufendorf, Smith, and Kant.[4] However, the Pauline-Christian heritage of Augustine and Dante, the Jewish heritage of Ibn Gabirol and Maimonides, and the Islamic heritage of al-Fārābī and Ibn Rushd also contributed to the expansion of cosmopolitanism by creatively re-imagining the universal bond conjoining human fraternity and political community on a global scale.[5]

We shall dedicate our particular attention to the rise and expansion of cosmopolitanism within the medieval Islamic milieu. Beginning with the 'Abbāsid caliph al-Manṣūr and extending to the subsequent caliphates of al-Ma'mūn and al-Mu'taṣim (813–42 CE), a monumental translation movement ensued which focused upon the transmission and dissemination of many of the most important works of ancient Greek philosophy and science. The reception of seminal texts from Plato, Aristotle, Euclid, Archimedes, Ptolemy, Hippocrates, Galen, and Theophrastus was often made possible by Syriac intermediaries who were employed as translators by the Baghdad caliphs.[6] The pervasive influence of Greek philosophy and science informed the argu-

3 Cicero, *On Duties*, I. I. 50, 53–4, tr. Miller. The Stoic notion of affiliation (*oikeiōsis*) is prominent in Hierocles (Stobaeus 4.671.7–673.11), who describes the expansion of the human community by recourse to concentric circles; see Long and Sedley, *The Hellenistic Philosophers*, 349. Cf. al-Kindī's 'Epistle . . . Showing That the [Four] Elements and Outermost Body Are Spherical in Form' (*Risāla . . . fī Anna al-'Anāṣir wa-l-Jirm al-Aqṣā Kurriyyat al-Shakl*), which also aims to establish the structure of the universe as a nested series of concentric spheres by retrieving Ptolemy's *Almagest* and Aristotle's *Physics* and *De Caelo*; see *Rasā'il al-Kindī al-Falsafiyya*, 1:48.9–53.13; and Rescher, 'Al-Kindī's Epistle on the Concentric Structure of the Universe'.

4 Nussbaum's *The Cosmopolitan Tradition* begins with ancient Cynicism and Stoicism to foreground Grotius, Smith, and Kant and thereby occludes the ecumenism of Judaism, Christianity, and Islam and its medieval iterations. Cf. Appiah, *Cosmopolitanism*, 1–12.

5 'There are, it may be, so many kinds of voices in the world and none of them is without signification. Therefore, if I know not the meaning of the voice, I shall be unto him that speaks barbarian, and he that speaks *shall be* a barbarian unto me' (Paul, 1 Corinthians 14:10–11). Augustine's *De Civitate Dei* introduces two universal cities, a city of God and the earthly city. The city of God is limited to those who love God and the earthly city is limited to those who love the self (XIV.i). Dante's *De Monarchia* revives Augustine's *De Civitate Dei* in the form of a universal monarchy (I.vi–ix). Ibn Gabirol and Maimonides also employ the metaphor of a king in his palace to describe the rule of God over all humankind; see Gluck, 'The King in His Palace'. Both al-Fārābī and Ibn Rushd recuperate a distinctively Platonic and Aristotelian variant of cosmopolitanism.

6 See especially Watt, 'The Syriac Aristotelian Tradition and the Arabic Baghdad Philosophers'; and Griffith, *The Church in the Shadow of the Mosque*, 106–28.

ments and doctrines of Mu'tazilite theologians (*mutakallimūn*), who constituted the predominant school of *'ilm al-kalām* during the first half of the ninth century. The inception and formation of philosophy (*falsafa*) was in no small part attributed to the rise of the Mu'tazila, who were supported by the caliph al-Ma'mūn's declaration of an inquisition (*miḥna*) defending the createdness of the Qur'ān among religious scholars and judges.[7] The Qur'ānic commentary tradition (*tafsīr*) also vitally transformed the comprehension of Greek philosophy. Among those theological pre-commitments inherent to the interpretation of the Qur'ān, the principle of divine unity (*tawḥīd*) and the principle of the One (*al-wāḥid*) promulgated by theology (*kalām*) and philosophy (*falsafa*) contributed to the formation of a distinctively cosmopolitan paradigm.[8] With the revelation handed down to Muḥammad proclaiming the oneness of God, which in turn came to be rationally defended by the Mu'tazila as the primary proponents of divine unity and justice, the unique correspondence between the oneness of God and the singular unity of the religious community (*umma*) established in the Qur'ān undoubtedly resonated with the Arabic transmission, translation, and reception of the *Timaeus*, one of the most widely disseminated texts throughout late antiquity and the early medieval period.[9] In his tenth-century *Catalogue* (*Fihrist*), the celebrated

[7] See Gutas, *Greek Thought, Arabic Culture*, 79–83. For the most comprehensive account of the early *kalām* tradition, see Van Ess, *Theologie und Gesellschaft im 2. And 3. Jarhhundert Hidschra*; and Wolfson, *The Philosophy of the Kalam*.

[8] The principle of divine unity (*tawḥīd*) is first presented in the Islamic profession of faith (*shahāda*), 'there is no divinity but the Divine (*lā ilāha illā Allāh*)' (Qur'ān 37:35). Seyyed Nasr presents the microcosm-macrocosm analogy in light of the Qur'ān, 'It is quite significant that the phenomena of Nature, the events taking place within the soul of man, and the verses of the Qur'ān are called *āyāt*, the human soul and Nature, being respectively the microcosmic and macrocosmic counterparts of the celestial archetypes contained in the Divine Word' (*An Introduction to Islamic Cosmological Doctrines*, 6). Cf. El-Bizri, 'The Microcosm/Macrocosm Analogy'.

[9] See Qur'ān 2:213 and 10:19. Plato describes the cosmos which impels one to imitate the beautiful order of the heavenly bodies, 'God devised and bestowed on us vision to the end that we might behold the revolutions of Reason in the Heaven and use them for the revolvings of the reasoning that is within us, these being akin to those, the perturbable and imperturbable; and that through learning and sharing in calculations which are correct by their nature, by imitation of the absolutely unvarying revolutions of the God we might stabilize the variable revolutions within ourselves' (*Timaeus* 28c). Citing Simplicius's third argument that physics has moral pertinence, Remi Brague demonstrates that what makes the cosmological physics of the *Timaeus* interesting from a moral and political perspective is 'in a word: we should imitate nature; more precisely, what is the most highly worthy of our imitation, which is the majestic order of the army of the skies, so as to put order into our lives' (*The Legend of the Middle Ages*, 84).

bio-bibliographer Ibn al-Nadīm reports that the *Timaeus* was first translated by Ibn al-Biṭrīq, a member of al-Kindī's circle, before being either retranslated or corrected by Ḥunayn ibn Isḥāq and Yaḥyā ibn 'Adī.[10] Given their access to Galen's paraphrase and Proclus's commentary on the *Timaeus*, it is not surprising that the pseudo-*Theology of Aristotle* (*Uthūlūjiyā Arisṭūṭālīs*), an adaptive translation of Plotinus's *Enneads* IV–VI, importantly appears to conjoin the Platonic Demiurge with the Aristotelian Prime Mover.[11] Alongside the *Timaeus*, the *Metaphysics* became a veritable sourcebook for investigating first principles and ranks among the first Arabic translations of Greek philosophy to be produced in the middle of the ninth-century by al-Kindī's circle (*majlis*) in Baghdad.[12] With the composition of al-Kindī's *On the Definitions and Descriptions of Things* (*Fī Ḥudūd al-Ashyā' wa-Rusūmihā*), Greek philosophical terminology was inevitably refined and transformed by its encounter with *falsafa*.[13] Although al-Kindī and those scholars affiliated with his inaugural circle were acutely attentive to *kalām* debates concerning the essence of God and divine attributes, the createdness of the Qur'ān, and free will, the pedagogical model of study adopted by the *falāsifa* ultimately came to reflect the philosophical curriculum attributed to the *Corpus Aristotelicum* beginning with Logic, followed by Rhetoric, Natural Science, Psychology, and Metaphysics, before concluding with Ethics and Politics.[14] Among those scholars and intellectuals who travelled from foreign regions to form circles of translation and commentary dedicated to the study and dissemination of Greek science and philosophy, bonds of friendship came to be forged which transcended both cultural and religious association. Abū Muḥammad, an itinerant tenth-century poet, aptly captures the sentiment of those who travelled to Baghdad to study the ancients: 'I have wandered seeking an equal to Baghdad and its people / Attempting thereby something hopeless / Baghdad is to me

[10] Ibn al-Nadīm, *Fihrist*, 246.4–5, 11–12, ed. Flügel, 593, tr. Dodge.

[11] Ibn Nā'ima translated the pseudo-*Theology of Aristotle* from Syriac in 835 CE for al-Ma'mūn's successor and student of al-Kindī, al-Mu'taṣim; see Ibn al-Nadīm, *Fihrist*, 244.5, ed. Flügel, 587, tr. Dodge. Cf. D'Ancona, 'The *Theology* Attributed to Aristotle', 10; 'The *Timaeus* Model for Creation and Providence', 211–24, 228–31, n18–24.

[12] Ibn al-Nadīm notes that the first Arabic translation of the *Metaphysics* was produced by Usṭāṯ 'for al-Kindī', *Fihrist*, 251.25, ed. Flügel, 606, tr. Dodge. See Endress, 'The Circle of al-Kindī'; and Gutas, *Greek Thought, Arabic Culture*, 52–8.

[13] Al-Kindī, *Fī Ḥudūd al-Ashyā' wa-Rusūmihā*, in *Rasā'il al-Kindī al-Falsafiyya*, 1:163ff. Cf. Stern, 'Notes on al-Kindī's Treatise on Definitions'; and Kennedy-Day, *Books of Definition in Islamic Philosophy*, 19–31.

[14] See D'Ancona, '"Arisṭū 'inda l-'Arab", and Beyond', 25–7; and Peters, *Aristoteles Arabus*, 7–54.

the world entire / its inhabitants all humankind.'[15] The rise and expansion of the 'Abbāsid Caliphate contributed widely to the flourishing of Baghdad as the capital for the transmission of Greek science and philosophy into the Islamic world. Although the House of Wisdom (*Bayt al-Ḥikma*) in Baghdad was reputed as a major library and cultural centre likely established during the reign of al-Manṣūr to support translations from Persian into Arabic, philosophers, commentators, and scholars who were affiliated with the translation movement travelled widely throughout various regions from one royal court to another.[16] Therefore, the life of the itinerant philosopher was undoubtedly confronted with the prospect of political agitation. A strategy of prudent dissimulation (*taqiyya*) utilising both exoteric and esoteric techniques came to be adopted reflecting the dialectical interplay between explicit (*ẓāhir*) and implicit (*bāṭin*) forms of interpretation.[17]

Among those philosophers who travelled to Baghdad was Abū Naṣr Muḥammad ibn Ṭarkhān ibn Awzalagh al-Fārābī, a foremost disciple of Aristotle, universally revered as the Second Teacher (*al-mu'allim al-thānī*), who purportedly read the *De Anima* 200 times and the *Physics* 40 times.[18] The esteemed Maimonides is said to have compared al-Fārābī's works to the finest flour.[19] Al-Fārābī was born around 870 CE in the easternmost region of 'Abbāsid rule in present-day Kazakhstan.[20] His father was likely of Persian

15 Kraemer, *Philosophy in the Renaissance of Islam*, 24. From the early to the middle of the tenth century, the Christian commentator and translator Mattā ibn Yūnus, a teacher of al-Fārābī, along with his student Yaḥyā ibn 'Adī, rank among the most prominent proponents of Islamic humanism. The cultural nexus between the three scholars conjoins Islam with the Nestorian Christian tradition; see especially Tannous, *The Making of the Medieval Middle East*, 201–21.

16 Dimitri Gutas contests the romanticization of the House of Wisdom by scholars who overestimate its cultural importance; see *Greek Thought, Arabic Culture*, 53–60. In contrast, Joel Kraemer assiduously documents the cultural revival in Baghdad throughout the ninth and tenth centuries of the 'Abbāsid Caliphate, which sparked the Islamic Renaissance advancing the arts and sciences and promoting a critical humanism identified with the study and practice of philosophy; see *Humanism in the Renaissance of Islam*, 1–26. Cf. Balty-Guesdon, 'Le *Bayt al-Ḥikma*'; and Ishanoğlu, *The Abbasid House of Wisdom*, 1–33.

17 See Strauss, *Persecution and the Art of Writing*, 24–5; and 'How Fārābī Read Plato's *Laws*'. Cf. Harvey, 'Did Alfarabi Read Plato's *Laws*?'.

18 See Ibn Khallikān, *Wafayāt al-A'yān*, 5:154. Cf. Netton, 'A Tale of Three Cities', 89; and *Allāh Transcendent*, 100.

19 Maimonides' *Guide of the Perplexed* (*Dalālat al-Hā'irīn*) is undoubtedly influenced by al-Fārābī's account of prophecy in the *Virtuous City* and *Political Regime*; see Melamed, *The Philosopher-King in Medieval and Renaissance Jewish Political Thought*, 44–5.

20 See David Dipasquale's preface to *Alfarabi's Book of Dialectic* (*Kitāb al-Jadal*), x. For the most comprehensive historical reconstruction of al-Fārābī's biography retrieving the previous accounts of Ibn al-Qifṭī, *Tārīkh al-Ḥukamā'*, Ibn Abī Uṣaybi'a, *'Uyūn al-Anbā' fī Ṭabaqāt al-Aṭibbā'*, and Ibn Khallikān, *Wafayāt al-A'yān*, see Gutas, 'Fārābī i. Biography'.

descent having served as a soldier for the Sāmānid governors who ruled the ethnically and religiously diverse region of his birth. Al-Fārābī was initially educated in Bukhara where he studied music and jurisprudence, two fields which significantly influenced his philosophical disposition. In his later youth, al-Fārābī travelled to Marv where he came to study with the Nestorian Christian cleric and disciple of the Alexandrian school, Yūḥannā ibn Ḥaylān, who likely introduced him to Aristotle's Organon.[21] Subsequently, al-Fārābī travelled from Marv to Baghdad (sometime after 908 CE) to study logic, medicine, and sociology with Ḥaylān. While in Baghdad, al-Fārābī was introduced to the celebrated Nestorian Christian Aristotelian and translator, Abū Bishr Mattā ibn Yūnus, and the Arabic philologist, Ibn al-Sarrāj.[22] Although al-Fārābī's native tongue was Sogdian, an Eastern Iranian language common among inhabitants along the Silk Road, his travels from Baghdad to Byzantium contributed to the development of his extraordinary linguistic abilities which were said to include over seventy languages.[23] Around his fortieth birthday, al-Fārābī travelled with Ḥaylān to Harran where he dedicated eight years to studying Greek philosophy and science. Upon his return to Baghdad, al-Fārābī became revered for harmonising the works of Plato and Aristotle.[24] In 943 CE he travelled to Syria and possibly Egypt. Al-Fārābī died near Damascus in December 950 CE or January 951 CE. The circumstances of his death are reported by one source in the following terms:

[21] For the seminal influence of the Alexandrian school, see Vallat, *Fārābī et l'école d'Alexandrie*, 34–83.

[22] David Dipasquale observes al-Fārābī's relative notoriety as a scholar of logic and music; *Alfarabi's Book of Dialectic (Kitāb al-Jadal)*, xi.

[23] Dimitri Gutas contests the polyglot attribution as spurious; see 'Fārābī i. Biography'.

[24] Cf. al-Fārābī's *Harmonisation of the Opinions of the Two Sages, Plato the Divine and Aristotle* (*Kitāb al-Jam' bayn Ra'yay al-Ḥakīmayn, Aflāṭūn al-Ilāhī wa-Arisṭūṭālīs*); and *Philosophy of Plato (Falsafat Aflāṭūn) and Philosophy of Aristotle (Falsafat Arisṭūṭālīs).* The remarkable breadth of al-Fārābī's corpus is documented in Friedrich Dieterici's *Alfārābīs Philosophische Abhandlungen.* In works replicating the *Corpus Aristotelicum*, al-Fārābī addresses psychology, *Epistle on the Intellect* (*Risāla fī al-'Aql*), metaphysics, *Book of Letters* (*Kitāb al-Ḥurūf*) and *On the One and Oneness* (*Kitāb al-Wāḥid wa-l-Waḥda*), epistemology, *Enumeration of the Sciences* (*Iḥṣā' al-'Ulum*), logic, *Book of Utterances Employed in Logic* (*Kitāb al-Alfāẓ al-Musta'mala fī al-Manṭiq*), *Book of Demonstration* (*Kitāb al-Burhān*), *Book of Dialectic* (*Kitāb al-Jadal*), rhetoric, *Book of Rhetoric* (*Kitāb al-Khaṭāba*), poetics, *Epistle on the Canons of Poetry* (*Risāla fī Qawānīn Ṣinā'at al-Shi'r*), and music, *Great Book of Music* (*Kitāb al-Mūsīqī al-Kabīr*). His most influential political treatises include *Attainment of Happiness* (*Taḥṣīl al-Sa'āda*), *Aphorisms of the Statesman* (*Fuṣūl al-Madanī*), *Political Regime* (*Kitāb al-Siyāsa al-Madaniyya*), *Principles of the Opinions of the Inhabitants of the Virtuous City* (*Kitāb Mabādi' Ārā' Ahl al-Madīna al-Fāḍila*), *Book of Religion* (*Kitāb al-Milla*), *Book of Letters* (*Kitāb al-Ḥurūf*), and the *Summary of Plato's* Laws (*Jawāmi' Kitāb al-Nawāmīs li-Aflāṭūn*).

> Al-Fārābī was journeying from Damascus to Ascalon, and was met by a company of thieves called 'the Lads' (*fityān*). Al-Fārābī said to them, 'Take what I have of riding animals, arms and clothing, and let me go.' But they refused and determined to kill him. Seeing that there was no escape, Abū Naṣr (al-Fārābī) dismounted and fought till he was slain, with his friends. This greatly displeased the rulers of Syria (sc. the Ḥamdānids), who pursued the thieves and buried Abū Naṣr, and crucified them on tree-trunks close by his grave. It is reported that the Ḥamdānid, Sayf al-Dawla, and fifteen of his courtiers performed the funeral prayers for al- Fārābī.[25]

Although we cannot be certain about the manner of al-Fārābī's purported demise, his life as an itinerant philosopher was certainly guided by the search for truth and the preservation of friendship at the risk of persecution, exile, and death. His enduring legacy as the veritable founder of Islamic political philosophy has undoubtedly contributed to this hagiographical tradition. If we are to distinguish his biography from his philosophy, his political writings are rightfully acknowledged for introducing the Muslim community (*umma*) as a pre-modern predecessor to the nation. Alexander Orwin's *Redefining the Muslim Community* assiduously documents how this notion of the *umma* is historically rooted in both religious and ethnic identity.[26] Despite

[25] The story is recounted by Douglas M. Dunlop in his introduction to *Aphorisms of the Statesman*, 14–15, and attributed to Ẓahīr al-Dīn Bayhaqī's *Tatimmat Ṣiwān al-Ḥikma*, 19. Dunlop, 15, remarks that his last words address the contested state of Baghdad under the caliph al-Muttaqī, who sought military assistance from the Ḥamdānids of Mosul. Dimitri Gutas subsequently dismisses the story, 'Bayhaqī finally, has the romantic story of Fārābī being killed by highway robbers on his way from Damascus to Ascalon. As A. Adnan Adıvar suggests (*İA* V, 453a), this would appear to be in imitation of the story of the death of the poet Motanabbī' ('Fārābī i. Biography').

[26] Alexander Orwin ambitiously retrieves the neglected relevance of the *umma* and thereby resolves a long-standing lacuna in al-Fārābī's political philosophy, 'The Umma, which appears dozens of times in the Qur'ān, had long since become the term of choice for Muslims in defining their own religious community. The religious meaning of the Umma may be all too easily forgotten when reading Alfarabi, who appears to employ the term mainly in the ethic sense' (*Redefining the Muslim Community*, 2). Abdulaziz Sachedina accordingly highlights the religious sense of the *umma* as fundamental to the Islamic conception of pluralism by invoking Qur'ān 2:213, 'The people were one community (*umma*), then God sent forth the Prophets, good tidings to bear and warning, and He sent down with them the Book with the truth, that He might decide the people touching their differences' (*The Islamic Roots of Democratic Pluralism*, 22–3). Katrin A. Jomaa also brings necessary attention to individual differences in the initial formation of the *umma* in Medina, 'The guidance during that period was addressing them as individuals, not as an *ummah* with common laws . . . From an Aristotelian perspective, the immigrant Muslims had to be predisposed to law to form a political community . . . which is depicted in the Qur'ānic verse 2:213' (*Ummah*, 225).

the apparent religious and ethnic origins of the *umma*, al-Fārābī's political philosophy is also clearly motivated by a cosmopolitanism portending the existence of a global community (*ma'mūra*) extending across the entire inhabited world (*oikoumenē*).[27] By presupposing a certain solidarity among all humanity, al-Fārābī's *Virtuous City* (*al-Madīna al-Fāḍila*) ambitiously introduces three kinds of perfect societies ranging from cities and nations to a global community.[28] The controversial status attributed to the realisation of this global community may be framed within the purview of the Platonic corpus as a contest between the city in speech of the *Republic* and the second best city of the *Laws*. Beginning with the remarkable influence of Leo Strauss upon the contemporary reception of al-Fārābī, the second-best city is presented as the pragmatic paradigm of the virtuous city.[29] Strauss explicitly privileges al-Fārābī's *Summary of Plato's* Laws (*Jawāmi' Kitāb al-Nawāmīs li-Aflāṭūn*) as the veritable Rosetta Stone for distinguishing between esoteric and exoteric knowledge throughout the Platonic corpus:

> Our purpose in making this introduction is this: the wise Plato did not permit himself to present and uncover all kinds of knowledge to all people. Therefore he followed the path of using symbols, riddles, obscurity, and

[27] See *Attainment of Happiness* (*Taḥṣīl al-Sa'āda*), *Aphorisms of the Statesman* (*Fuṣūl al-Madanī*), *Political Regime* (*Kitāb al-Siyāsa al-Madaniyya*), *Principles of the Opinions of the Inhabitants of the Virtuous City* (*Kitāb Mabādi' Ārā' Ahl al-Madīna al-Fāḍila*), *Philosophy of Aristotle* (*Falsafat Ārisṭūṭālīs*), *Book of Religion* (*Kitāb al-Milla*), and *Book of Letters* (*Kitāb al-Ḥurūf*).

[28] al-Fārābī, *Virtuous City*, V, 15, §2, 229. For the controversy surrounding the translation of the title, see Rudolph, 'Reflections on al-Fārābī's *Mabādi' Ārā' Ahl al-Madīna al-Fāḍila*', 2–13, who notably identifies the *Mabādi'* as a work of theology. I have deliberately modified the translation of the title adopted by Walzer, *On the Perfect State*, to the *Virtuous City*; cf. Parens, *Metaphysics as Rhetoric*, 18.

[29] See Strauss (*The Argument and Action of Plato's* Laws, 1), 'The *Laws* is the most political work of Plato. One may even say that is his only political work, for in it the chief character, the Athenian Stranger, elaborates a code for the city about to be founded, i.e. he engages in political activity. In the *Republic*, Socrates founds a city in speech, i.e. not in deed, accordingly the *Republic* does not in fact present the best political order but rather brings to light the limitations, the limits, and therewith the nature of politics (Cicero, *Republic* II, 52)'; and 'How Fārābī Read Plato's *Laws*', 134–44. The second-best city of the *Laws* is espoused by several scholars who defend al-Fārābī's political realism; see especially L'Arrivee, 'Discrimination and Violence in Alfarabi's *Virtuous City*'; and Orwin, 'Can Humankind Deliberate on a Global Scale?'. This thesis is proposed by Parens, *Metaphysics as Rhetoric*, 62–7, and recapitulated by Butterworth, 'Alfarabi's Goal'; and 'What Might We Learn from al-Fārābī about Plato and Aristotle with respect to Lawgiving?'. In contrast, Steiris, 'Al-Fārābī's Ecumenical State and Its Modern Connotations,' and Bakhsh, '*The Virtuous City*', defend the cosmopolitan potential of al-Fārābī's political philosophy.

difficulty lest knowledge fall into the hands of those not deserving of it and be deformed or into the hands of someone who is not cognizant of its worth or uses it improperly. In this he was correct.[30]

The *Summary*, which is divided into an introduction, nine chapters, and a conclusion, culminating in *Laws* IX, importantly omits *Laws* X, 'Plato's theological statement *par excellence*'.[31] Strauss conceives the *Summary* as appealing not merely to the educated elite who can bear 'the toil of study and meditation' to inquire into the theological foundations of the law but ultimately to those mixed audiences who cannot bear that hardship.[32] Here Strauss associates such mixed audiences with those 'men on horseback' who reflect a certain practical unity between the rational and the irrational by virtue of wisdom and moderation.[33] Strauss brings particular attention to 'the general statement' within the *Summary* alluding to the utility of Plato's message for philosophers and sovereigns, 'Let us call "men of judgement" such men as have acquired the habit of discerning and attaining what is useful . . . by acting sometimes in a given manner, they induce the public to judge falsely that they will always act in that manner, so much so, that it will escape the public if they act differently on occasion, the deviation will be thought to be a repetition.'[34]

Strauss subsequently recalls al-Fārābī's story of the abstemious ascetic reputed for his probity, propriety, and piety who had become fearful of the unjust sovereign and wanted to flee from the city. A command had been issued

[30] al-Fārābī, *Summary of Plato's* Laws, vol. 2, 130, tr. Butterworth.

[31] Strauss, 'How Fārābī Read Plato's *Laws*', 134. Butterworth observes that *sharī'a*, denoting the 'Law' or 'divine law', occurs only four times in the *Summary*. However, *sunna* (pl. *sunan*) and its connection with *nawāmīs* denoting 'traditional laws' is pervasive; see al-Fārābī, *Summary of Plato's* Laws, vol. 2, 131n3. Therefore, the exclusive focus of the *Summary* is not upon enquiring into the purpose and cause of the divine law but rather the use or purpose of the traditional laws. As Butterworth attests, 'For the Athenian Stranger, who plays such a central role in the *Laws*, that query quickly gives way to the more important one of what purpose different lawgivers sought to achieve by means of their legislation. Alfarabi also moves from the question of who made the laws to the purpose they serve, passing over in silence that both are aspects of causality' (ibid., 109).

[32] Ibid., 130, tr. Butterworth; Strauss, 'How Fārābī Read Plato's *Laws*', 137. Moreover, Butterworth alludes to the omission of religion and divine revelation, 'In the *Summary*, Alfarabi refers not once to the Quran, Islam, prophetic missions, or Muhammad. Much as that silence prompts the perspicacious reader to wonder how revelation does affect lawgiving or what distinguishes divinely inspired lawgiving from that which is not, those topics are not addressed' (al-Fārābī, *Summary of Plato's* Laws, vol. 2, 108).

[33] See Strauss, 'How Fārābī Read Plato's *Laws*', 138; and Namazi, *Leo Strauss and Islamic Political Thought*, 179–80.

[34] Strauss, 'How Fārābī Read Plato's *Laws*', 135.

by the sovereign to search and arrest the ascetic. Therefore, the ascetic sought out a garment worn by vagabonds and came early at night to the gate of the city pretending to be drunk and playing a lute. When the gatekeeper said to him, 'Who are you?' He jokingly replied, 'I am so-and-so, the ascetic.' The gatekeeper presumed he was poking fun at him and left him alone. The ascetic was able to save himself without having to lie about what he said.[35] Akin to the man of judgement, Strauss contends that the ascetic 'acts appropriately with a view to what is most useful for himself'.[36] Although the identity of Plato is not conjoined with the piety of the ascetic, both share something in common, 'since they are both men of judgement, they act in such cases in the same way: they state the dangerous truth by surrounding it properly, with the result that they are not believed in what they say. It is in this manner that Plato has written about the laws.'[37] Al-Fārābī's focus upon the laws, namely, their origin and application, throughout the *Summary* may be contrasted with the *Philosophy of Plato* (*Falsafat Aflāṭūn*), which claims that 'the necessary and sufficient condition of happiness, or man's ultimate perfection, is philosophy'.[38] Given the relative silence about the role of philosophy in the *Summary*, Strauss concludes that al-Fārābī intended to supplant philosophy with rational theology (*kalām*). The art of *kalām* thus becomes the most accessible avenue for the common believer to be informed by the laws.[39] Therefore, the *Summary* should be prefaced by the privilege accorded to the practical utility of *kalām* for comprehending the content of the laws as the veritable blueprint by which the second-best city might come into existence.[40]

[35] al-Fārābī, *Summary of Plato's* Laws, vol. 1,130, tr. Butterworth.

[36] Strauss, 'How Fārābī Read Plato's *Laws*', 136.

[37] Ibid., 137.

[38] Ibid., 138.

[39] In his reconstruction of al-Fārābī's *Book of the Letters* (*Kitāb al-Ḥurūf*), Muhsin Mahdi underscores the practical importance of *kalām* to the political community, 'Theology, on the other hand, discovers the "theoretical and universal practical affairs" not declared, or other than the ones declared, by the giver of the religion, following his intention. It is stated emphatically that this is "another art." (sec. 145, 153.4). Theology also defends the religion. This latter function is contingent on the presence of a group who try to refute the religion. It comes in the second place, "The art of these two faculties" (jurisprudence and theology) is "only possible through the common methods, that is, the rhetorical". This means that in the religion legislated by philosophers, jurisprudence and theology dispense with dialectical and poetic methods, which are also "common" (cf. sec. 143, 152.4, and sec. 111, 132.21-22)' (*Alfarabi and the Foundations of Islamic Political Philosophy*, 215–16).

[40] Butterworth presents a more nuanced approach to weighing the theoretical emphasis of the *Political Regime*, *Virtuous City*, *Attainment of Happiness*, and *Book of Religion* against the practical emphasis of the *Summary*, 'This does not mean that Alfarabi jettisons the paradigms

Among those scholars of al-Fārābī inspired by Strauss, Joshua Parens defends the practical value of the second-best city (or nation) of the *Laws* against the city in speech proposed in the *Republic*.[41] Parens contends that the establishment of a virtuous political association existing throughout the entire inhabited world is a virtual impossibility since such a political association would presuppose a multiplicity of virtuous cities at any one time.[42] If the city in speech of the *Republic* remains merely a utopian paradigm, then the idea of a global community must be subsequently dismissed. Although the *Summary* does not aim to replicate the *Virtuous City*, which specifically introduces the notion of global community, the *Summary* entertains the possibility that the second-best city of the *Laws* might be more charitably comprehended beyond mere territorial and geographical limitations. Parens even alludes to al-Fārābī's references to 'temples' (*hayākil*) rather than 'mosques' (*masājid*) thereby 'broadening his view beyond the limits of his regime to include "the earth (*al-arḍ*)" as a whole'.[43] Hence, there is no harm imposed in extending the

set forth . . . which all point to good rulership as centering on philosophers or kings imbued with philosophic wisdom, but that the focus here on actual political life takes precedence. Consonant with this different emphasis, he draws attention throughout the treatises to the solidly human character of lawgivers and the shortcomings of those receiving their laws. He thus appears especially intent on identifying the components of a good, rather than a best, regime' (*Summary of Plato's* Laws, 108).

41 Parens assumes that al-Fārābī is a political realist who favours the second-best city of the *Laws*, 'If we assume that Alfarabi (following Socrates in the *Republic* [592a5-b5]) believed that the virtuous city is politically impossible, then it follows a fortiori that his two larger regimes are even more probably politically impossible. Consequently, when inquiring into the politically practicable, Alfarabi, like Plato, is compelled to look to a second-best city (or nation) ruled by written law' (*Metaphysics as Rhetoric*, 51).

42 Muhsin Mahdi cites the *Virtuous City* IV. 15.3 to explicitly discount the practical possibility of a virtuous association of the inhabited world, 'A virtuous nation is not a group of cities ruled by a virtuous or perfect city, but the nation "all of whose cities *cooperate* regarding the things by which happiness is attained"; and the association of all men in the entire inhabited world is virtuous "only when the nations in it *cooperate* to achieve happiness". The virtuous community of all men presupposes virtuous nations, and the virtuous nation in turn presupposes virtuous cities' ('Alfarabi', 223). Cf. Parens, *Metaphysics as Rhetoric*, 51, 166n2; and Galston, *Politics and Excellence*, 151–3.

43 'Then let him devote most of his concern to the issue of temples and esteemed places on earth so they do not change. For changing them will corrupt people's hearts, and corrupting their hearts will, in turn, throw the affair of the city into disorder' (al-Fārābī, *Summary of Plato's* Laws, 8.7, 169, tr. Butterworth). Cf. Parens (*Metaphysics as Rhetoric*, 65), who further corroborates the whole earth thesis by introducing another reference to '"governors of sea and rulers on land" (disc. 8.8). By speaking of temples rather than mosques, does Alfarabi mean to imply the existence of a multiplicity of religions? In addition, his discussion of boundaries focuses on the obvious impediments to rule over the whole earth, at least such rule by one governor.'

virtuous city to a virtuous association of the entire inhabited world. Georgios Steiris similarly concludes that 'the virtuous world-state, according to al-Fārābī, is not a reality, but it is possible to be realized in the future when all nations shall struggle for happiness. Al-Fārābī aspires to that specific type of ecumenism because it will maximize the common good and facilitate the realization of human nature.'[44] If the *Republic* presents a utopian vision of the virtuous city, then the *Laws* at least recognizes the possibility of its attainment within a specific city before expanding to alliances between cities and hence to the formation of nations and unions between nations.[45] Therefore, the ultimate aim of cosmopolitanism may be the existence of a future global community for all human beings which transcends any relative geographical location.[46] In contrast to the Athenian Stranger who establishes clear territorial limits to the second-best city, al-Fārābī's deliberate omission of a limited virtuous city in the *Summary* might lead us to conclude that such a political association of the entire inhabited world may be realised.[47]

The rise and expansion of the 'Abbāsid Caliphate inspired by the Hellenistic notion of the entire inhabited world (*oikoumenē*) and the unity of one religious community (*umma*) contributed immensely to this cosmopolitan realisation.[48] The historical contributions of the 'Abbāsid Caliphate to the

[44] Steiris, 'Al-Fārābī's Ecumenical State and Its Modern Connotations', 255.

[45] Alexander Orwin's *Redefining the Muslim Community* does not explicitly develop either the theological or political implications of the principle of divine unity (*tawḥīd*) for the sake of expanding the *umma* in the direction of a global political community.

[46] For the allusion of a general kind of justice which applies to all people, see al-Fārābī, *Aphorisms of the Statesman*, 59., 55, 143–44, tr. Dunlop; and al-Fārābī, *Selected Aphorisms*, 63. [74.15], 42. Al-Fārābī remains only partially aware of the political implications the *oikos* given his lack of access to Aristotle's *Politics*. The home (*oikos*) as a microcosm of political community reappears in the Stoic notion of affiliation (*oikeiōsis*) where the entire inhabited world (*oikumenē*) is incorporated into the cosmopolis. Richard Walzer attributes al-Fārābī's references to a *ma'mūra* to the expansion of Hellenism into the Near East, to include Persia and the Islamic Caliphate (al-Fārābī, *Virtuous City*, 433). Georgios Steiris surmises that al-Fārābī's biographical and historical experience with these empires led him to conclude that the perfect society should be realized in a political association larger than the city ('Al-Fārābī's Ecumenical State and Its Modern Connotations', 254).

[47] This admission of the existence of a global political community is attributed to a rather robust pseudo-Aristotelian tradition inspired by the Hellenizing influence of Alexander the Great. The pseudo-Aristotelian treatise *Aristotle on the World State* alludes to 'a future age when humans (*in-nās*) will unite under a "single command (*amr*) and single king (*malik*)", give up war and devote their time to pleasure and study' (Stern, *Aristotle on the World State*, 7–8; see also 10). Stern concludes that this single command and single king refers to a 'world state' (ibid., 35ff.).

[48] Here we should exercise caution to directly identify the territorial expansion of the Abbāsid Caliphate as a continuation of the political outlook and organization of the Roman Empire.

translation of ancient Greek philosophy and science into the medieval Islamic world was an unrivalled intellectual and cultural achievement. Multiple works were translated from Greek and Syriac into Arabic contributing to the inception and formation of the cosmopolitan paradigm of *falsafa*.[49] Although *falsafa* undoubtedly reflects its Hellenic character and influence, *falsafa* was also historically conjoined with several epistemic practices indigenous to the cultural heritage of Islam, to include *ḥadīth* (the historical transmission of the deeds and sayings of the Prophet Muḥammad), *adab* (the humanistic disciplines of poetry, rhetoric, linguistic theory, oratory, and grammar), *ḥikma* (the sciences of mathematics, astronomy, alchemy, medicine, logic, and rational theology), and *siyāsa* (the principles of governance and law).[50] If we are to comprehend the inception and development of *falsafa* throughout the early ʻAbbāsid period (750–900 CE), the notion of a global community (*maʻmūra*) may be said to arise from the dialogical intersection between these distinct epistemic practices and multiple knowledge cultures in the cosmopolitan milieu of Baghdad. In what follows, we shall aim to investigate the cosmopolitan character of *falsafa* and its contributions to the formation of al-Fārābī's own paradigm of a global community. Moreover, we shall seek to demonstrate how the influence of al-Fārābī's cosmopolitanism expands to his immediate associates, Yaḥyā ibn ʻAdī, al-Sijistānī, al-ʻĀmirī, and al-Tawḥīdī, and more distant disciples, Miskawayh, Ibn Rushd, al-Ṭūsī, and Ibn Khaldūn.

Given the unparalleled influence of Strauss upon the contemporary reception of al-Fārābī's political philosophy, Chapter 1 interrogates Strauss's adoption of Platonism as a pervasive hermeneutical strategy for interpreting al-Fārābī's political corpus. Al-Fārābī is the first Islamic philosopher to effectively conjoin metaphysics and political science into a unified political philosophy by explicitly retrieving the creation myth of the *Timaeus*. The confluence of Platonic and Neoplatonic cosmology is decisive to the inception of his cosmopolitanism. Beginning with his exposition of the principles of the One (*al-wāḥid*) and divine unity (*tawḥīd*) in *On the One and Oneness* (*Kitāb al-Wāḥid wa-l-Waḥda*), the harmonisation of Platonic and Neoplatonic

Orwin brings necessary philological attention to how *maʻmūra* denotes life and prosperity to reflect a uniquely Arabic form of eudaimonism, 'The Arabic term most closely related to the notion of a single, universal human community is *maʻmūra*. In this term, the Arabic root *ʻmr*, meaning "to live, to prosper", is cast in the form of the passive participle. The English expression "inhabited world" contains a similar participle and thus represents a reasonably good translation' ('Can Humankind Deliberate on a Global Scale?', 830).

49 See especially Daiber, *Islamic Thought in the Dialogue of Cultures*, 43–64; and Gutas, *Greek Thought, Arabic Culture*, 11–27.

50 See Khalidi, *Arabic Historical Thought in the Classical Periods*, 1–16.

cosmology with rational theology (*kalām*) portends the unity between the cosmos and the global community.[51]

Chapter 2 examines the historical reception of Aristotle's *Nicomachean Ethics* to the development of al-Fārābī's cosmopolitanism. The *Nicomachean Ethics*, widely disseminated throughout the Islamic world, inspired a rich commentary tradition throughout the first century of the 'Abbāsid Caliphate. In contrast to Neoplatonism, which explicitly promotes a hierarchical conception of the cosmos derived from the principle of the One and the constitution of a political community guided by a philosopher-king, Aristotle adopts a definition of happiness or flourishing (*eudaimonia*) which may be realised within each and every citizen. If eudaimonism is the ultimate aspiration of the political community, then al-Fārābī's *Attainment of Happiness* (*Taḥṣīl al-Sa'āda*) presents a vision of happiness attained by citizens of cities and nations. The intellectual virtues of practical wisdom and deliberation disclose the long-standing unity between metaphysics and ethics. Ethics complements metaphysics if only to accentuate the partial and limited character of metaphysical inquiry. Contemplation alone cannot accomplish human perfection. Rather, the citizen is called to engage with other citizens to attain happiness in the political community. Hence, the practice of metaphysics aspires towards the fundamental communality of ethics and political science. It is only by way of this communality that such perfection can be attained. The perfection achieved by contemplation is infused with the practical labour of the political. Therefore, philosophy as the contemplation of first principles comes to be conjoined with the philosopher who resides within a political community.[52] Since the composition of the political community spans both the metaphysical and ethico-political domains, the association of citizens

[51] The principle of divine unity is conveyed by reference to the First (Cause), 'Rather, it exists for its own sake (*li-ajl dhātih*); that something else exists from it attaches to, and follows from, its substance. Therefore, that existence (*wujūduhu*) emanates from its existence (*al-wujūd*) to something else is in its substance (*fī jawharihi*); and the existence by which it becomes substantiated in its essence (*fī dhātihi*) is the very existence by which something else attains existence from it. It is not divided into two things so that by one of them its essence becomes substantiated and by the other something else is obtained from it' (al-Fārābī, *Political Regime*, 28. [48.19–25], 43, tr. Butterworth).

[52] Al-Fārābī illustrates how the four metaphysical principles, *what* and *by what* the thing is, *from what* it is, *for what* it is, are essential to the task of political science, 'Then they should investigate all the things by which humans achieve this perfection or that are useful to them in achieving it. These are the good, virtuous, and noble things. They should distinguish them from things that obstruct their achieving this perfection. These are the evils, the vices, and the base things. They should make known *what* and *how* every one of them is, and *from what* and *for what* it is, until all of them become known, intelligible, and distinguished from each other. This is political science' (*Attainment of Happiness*, 1.20 [15.3–16.2–4], 24, tr. Mahdi, mod.).

in cities and nations reflects the association of physical bodies constituting the totality of the world.[53]

Chapter 3 presents the ethical foundations of al-Fārābī's cosmopolitanism as oriented by the civic virtues of benevolence, friendship, and concord. Following Aristotle's definition of the human being qua political animal as innately disposed to live in community with others, al-Fārābī's *Aphorisms of the Statesman* (*Fuṣūl al-Madanī*) distinguishes between different kinds of civic dispositions beginning with benevolence (*tafaḍḍul*), which is directed towards the good of fellow citizens. The exercise of benevolence informs the cultivation of friendship (*ṣadāqa*) and concord (*i'tilāf*) within the virtuous city. Friendship ranks among those virtues most useful for achieving perfection within the civic and cosmic order. Friendship is accordingly distinguished by a love (*mawadda*) arising from a spontaneous innate disposition and a love (*maḥabba*) arising from volition guided by virtue, utility, and pleasure.[54] To effectively hasten the bonds of the political community, political friendship is cultivated

[53] 'They will come to see in what are included in the totality constituted by the city and the nation the likenesses of what are included in the total world' (ibid., 1.20 [16.6–7], 24, tr. Mahdi, mod.). Al-Fārābī is evidently aware of Aristotle's analogy between the constitution of the animal and the well-governed city, 'For when order is once established in a city, there is no need of a special ruler with arbitrary powers to be present at every activity, but each individual performs his own task as he is ordered' (*De Motu Animalium* 703a29). Cf. *Metaphysics* 1075a19 where the same order which prevails in a household between the freeman, wives and sons, and slaves is postulated for the whole cosmos.

[54] Charles Butterworth highlights the affiliation between friendly affection or love (*maḥabba*) and justice; see al-Fārābī, *Summary of Plato's* Laws, 115n37. Cf. Porphyry's reference to Aristotle's student Theophrastus, 'But Theophrastus has made use of an argument like the following: We say that those with the same progenitors (I mean, the same father and mother) are by nature kin (*oikeious*) to one another. And for this reason we think that those who are descended from the same distant ancestors are kin to one another, as are fellow citizens since they have in common their land and mutual relations. For we do not judge such people to be kin to each other on the grounds that they are descended from the same people, unless the very founders of the clan are the first forebears. For just as we think that a Greek is kin and family to a Greek, and a barbarian to a barbarian, so we can say that every human being is kin and family to every other. We say this for one of two reasons: First, all people have the same forebears. Second, all people have in common their food, culture, and membership in the same kind' (*De Abstinentia* 3, 25, tr. Goldin and Romer). Theophrastus' reference to universal kinship may be further contrasted with Plato's distinction between Greeks and barbarians, 'So firm and sound, mark you, is the nobility and freedom of our city, and by nature barbarian-hating, because we are purely Greeks, being unmixed with barbarians' (*Menexenus* 245c–d). Cf. *Republic* 470b–c. For the role of the stranger in the *Laws*, see Derrida and Dufourmantelle, *Of Hospitality*, 5–13. Rebecca Lemoine also defends the view that Plato was a friend of cultural diversity and thereby accords a positive role to strangers and foreigners; see *Plato's Caves*, 91–132.

by a range of affective dispositions, including benevolence, generosity, and hospitality, guided by rational volition.[55] In contrast to a non-volitional love associated with familial kinship, civic love akin to benevolence and friendship binds the citizens together for the sake of attaining social harmony or concord. Benevolence and friendship as expressions of civic love are complemented by religion uniting both citizens and non-citizens in the virtuous city. By tracing the structural affinities between benevolence, friendship, and concord, we shall seek to demonstrate how the practice of these civic virtues effectively contributes to the attainment of happiness in the global community.

Chapter 4 investigates the democratic foundations of al-Fārābī's cosmopolitanism by retrieving the principles of freedom, equality, and justice contributing to the constitution of the democratic city. In contrast to Plato's critique of democracy in *Republic* XIII, al-Fārābī's *Political Regime* (*al-Siyāsa al-Madaniyya*) recasts the democratic city (*madīna jimā'iyya*) as the best alternative to the virtuous city. The democratic city as the most admirable and happy city contains more virtue than other imperfect cities since all the endeavours and purposes of the previous cities are already contained within it.[56] The cultivation of justice is paramount to ensure the relative freedom and equality afforded by the democratic city. Citizens in the democratic city are granted the freedom to either satisfy their appetites or be ruled by their rationality. If all citizens are equal and no one has a better claim than anyone else to political authority, then rule by the multitude becomes a concrete possibility. Civic love or political friendship may be expanded to the practice of equality (*musāwāt*) and justice (*'adl*) within the democratic city.[57] Since the justice arising from political friendship entails a mutual sharing of goods, al-Fārābī's *Aphorisms of the Statesman* proposes a specific kind of justice applying to citizens of respective cities and nations and a more general kind of justice applying to 'all people'.[58]

[55] Al-Fārābī recalls Aristotle's distinction between the virtuous, the useful, and the pleasant corresponding to objects of volition, 'for since there are three things that lead to choices and three that lead to avoidance, the former being what is beautiful, what is advantageous, and what is pleasant' (*Nicomachean Ethics* 1104b30–1).

[56] al-Fārābī, *Political Regime*, 115. [100.20], 87, tr. Butterworth.

[57] Cf. Aristotle's account of equality pertaining to distributive and corrective justice, 'Since the unjust person is unequal and what is unjust in unequal, it is clear that there is also a certain middle term associated with what is unequal. And this is the equal, for in whatever sort of action in which there are degrees, the more and the less, there is also the equal. If then, the unjust is unequal, the just is equal, which is in fact what is held to by the case by everyone, even without argument' (*Nicomachean Ethics* 1131a10–15).

[58] 'When that is set down as a right of the inhabitants of the city or of *all* people, no account is taken of excusing by the one to whom the injustice has occurred' (al-Fārābī, *Selected Aphorisms*, 63. [74.15], 42, tr. Butterworth). Cf. al-Fārābī, *Aphorisms of the Statesman*, 59., 55,

This more general kind of justice assesses the merits and demerits of citizens beyond the geographical and regional limits of cities and nations. The practice of equality and justice subsequently extends to the existence of those virtuous communities composed of free associations between citizens throughout the entire inhabited world.[59]

Chapter 5 introduces the ethico-political valence of generosity (*jūd*), hospitality (*ḍiyāfa*), and solidarity (*'aṣabiyya*) as cosmopolitan virtues. Al-Fārābī's *Political Regime* invokes Aristotle's biological and zoological tropes of civic association to explicitly focus upon how the individual parts of each respective political community mutually cooperate with one another to perform their respective functions. With the advent of mutual cooperation (*mu'āwana*), a certain solidarity begins to arise at the level of cities before expanding to nations and the entire global community. Despite the Neoplatonic schema of emanation, which attributes a hierarchy to cosmic and political order, the virtues of generosity, hospitality, and solidarity come to be promoted among all citizens for the sake of attaining happiness. Happiness is ultimately predicated upon the internal and external struggle (*jihād*) of individuals working to collectively achieve this end. By examining the prominence of solidarity to the political philosophies of al-Fārābī and Ibn Khaldūn, all the various parts and relations of the political community, including the relation of rulers to ruled, are to be harmonised if global happiness is to be achieved.

Finally, Chapter 6 illuminates the decisive contributions of the imagination to the creation of al-Fārābī's global community. Here we shall return to Aristotle's *De Anima* and *Rhetoric* to illustrate how the power of the imagination remains the most promising avenue for conceiving al-Fārābī's cosmopolitanism. Both the *Virtuous City* and *Political Regime* address the pivotal role accorded to the imagination for the sake of developing a regimen of civic education oriented by rhetoric and persuasion. By promulgating a diversity of opinions inherent to political affairs, the expansive power of the imagination exercised by the philosopher-ruler-*imām* produces images and symbols which

143–4, tr. Dunlop. This specification of justice is to be exercised without regard to the individual parts of the city according to rank or even if they are kin to us; see Goldin, 'Conflict and Cosmopolitanism in Plato and the Stoics', 270.

59 Al-Fārābī identifies a kind of political justice 'of which one exploits the acts of the virtues possessed by all others, whether they are nations, cities within a nation, groups within a city, or parts within each group' (*Attainment of Happiness*, 2.30 [24.18–19], 31, tr. Mahdi). Following Aristotle, political justice assumes that citizens of the polity are to be equal, free, and pursuing a self-sufficient life, 'For these are in accordance with law, and among people for whom it is natural for there to be law, and these are people among whom there is an equality of ruling and being ruled' (*Nicomachean Ethics* 1134 b15–16).

are in turn communicated to the citizens of the political community. The political community is constituted by the work of the imagination beginning with the acquisition and cultivation of civic and cosmopolitan virtues. With the valorisation of the unity between metaphysics and ethics and the affinity between theoretical and practical knowledge, the innate potential of all citizens to attain happiness is affirmed. Hence, the theory of cosmopolitanism cannot be distinguished from the practice of cosmopolitanism as a way of life.

The Revival of Platonism

The scholarship of Leo Strauss marks the inception of a radically new approach to interpreting Islamic political philosophy.[60] As the most revered and reviled proponent of al-Fārābī's Platonism, Strauss inaugurates an immensely influential commentary tradition informing the contemporary reception of al-Fārābī as a political philosopher *par excellence*. In his celebrated essay, 'Farabi's Plato', Strauss invokes Maimonides's letter to Samuel ibn Tibbon which proclaims that al-Fārābī is the greatest authority in philosophy apart from Aristotle.[61] Since one cannot wholly comprehend Maimonides's *Guide of the Perplexed* without recourse to al-Fārābī, Strauss highlights the critical importance of al-Fārābī's *Political Regime* and surmises that to genuinely understand the *Political Regime* first presupposes an intimate knowledge of the *Virtuous City*, *Book of Religion*, and the *Harmonisation of the Two Opinions of the Two Sages, Plato the Divine and Aristotle*.[62] Moreover, Strauss

[60] 'Der sog. Platonism is nur ein Flucht vor Platos Problem.' See Baracchi, *Of Myth, Life, and War in Plato's* Republic, 1, with reference to the letter composed by Leo Strauss to Karl Löwith. Among those contemporary scholars of al-Fārābī influenced by Strauss, see especially Mahdi, *Alfarabi and the Foundations of Islamic Political Philosophy*; Butterworth, 'What Might We Learn from al-Fārābī about Plato and Aristotle with respect to Lawgiving?'; Galston, *Politics and Excellence*; Parens, 'Escaping the Scholastic Paradigm'; Harvey, 'Leo Strauss's Developing Interest in Alfarabi and Its Reverberations in the Study of Medieval Islamic Philosophy'; Colmo, *Breaking with Athens*; and Orwin, *Redefining the Muslim Community*. For a critique of the Straussian reception of al-Fārābī's political philosophy, see Tamer, *Islamische Philosophie und Die Krise der Moderne*, 207–62; Gutas, 'The Study of Arabic Philosophy in the Twentieth Century', 19–25; Reisman, 'Al-Fārābī and the Philosophical Curriculum', 68; and Walbridge, 'God and Logic in Islam', 69–70. Cf. Namazi, *Leo Strauss and Islamic Political Thought*, 118–204.

[61] Strauss, 'Farabi's Plato', 357.

[62] 'the book treats the whole of philosophy proper (i.e. with the omission of logic and mathematic) within a political framework. In this respect, Fārābī takes as his model, not any of the Aristotelian writings known to him or to us, but Plato's *Republic*, and to a lesser extent, Plato's *Laws*, which also present the whole of philosophy within a political framework'

contends that the *Harmonisation* is an *exoteric* treatise with an explicit pedagogical purpose and therefore lacks the genuine *esoteric* meaning discovered in his other political treatises. Hence, the most promising approach to the reconciliation of Plato and Aristotle may be found in the *Philosophy of Plato and Aristotle*, which conceives the aims of Plato and Aristotle as identical to one another. Although one may question the validity of Strauss's exoteric-esoteric distinction, we shall instead turn our attention to the harmonisation of the *Nicomachean Ethics* with the *Republic*, *Timaeus*, and *Laws* to demonstrate how al-Fārābī's political philosophy is 'guided by the question of the perfection of man, or of happiness'.[63] If philosophy is broadly construed by Strauss as a theoretical science, then the royal art of politics personified by the figure of the philosopher-king presents the way of life needed to attain happiness.[64] Strauss concludes that al-Fārābī 'uses the identification of philosophy with the royal art as a pedagogic device for leading the reader toward the view that theoretical philosophy by itself, and nothing else, produces true happiness in this life, i.e., the only happiness which is possible'.[65] Given the privilege afforded to theoretical philosophy in the pursuit of happiness, Strauss regretfully elides the pervasive influence of the Mu'tazila upon al-Fārābī beginning with the seminal importance accorded to the principle of divine unity (*tawḥīd*).[66] The precedent afforded to theoretical philosophy had already been established with the composition of al-Kindī's *On First Philosophy* (*Kitāb fī al-Falsafa al-Ūla*), which was purportedly dedicated to

(ibid., 358). The *Harmonisation of the Opinions of the Two Sages, Plato the Divine and Aristotle* bears the influence of the *Theology of Aristotle*, a pseudo-Aristotelian text paraphrasing the last three of Plotinus's *Enneads*. The question of the authorship of the *Harmonisation of Plato and Aristotle* is addressed by Adamson, '*Plotinus Arabus* and *Proclus Arabus* in the *Harmony of the Two Philosophers* Ascribed to al-Fārābī'.

63 'After having realized that man's perfection or his happiness is identical with, or at least inseparable from "a certain science (*epistēmē*) and a certain way of life (*bios*)"' (Strauss, 'Farabi's Plato', 361).

64 'What Fārābī says is, first of all, that, according to Plato, the *homo philosophus* and the *homo rex*, are the same thing. This by itself does not mean more than that a human being cannot acquire the specific art of the philosopher without at the same time acquiring the specific art of the king and *vice versa*: it does not necessarily mean that these two arts themselves are identical' (ibid., 367).

65 Ibid., 370.

66 Strauss generally elides al-Fārābī's Neoplatonism and instead affirms the pervasive presence of Platonism throughout his political philosophy. The ethical and political context of Plato's cosmology is further investigated by Carone, *Plato's Cosmology and Its Ethical Dimensions*; O'Meara, *Platonopolis*, and *Cosmology and Politics in Plato's Later Works*; and Brisson, 'Polis as *Kosmos* in Plato's *Laws*'.

investigating 'what is beyond natural matters and the oneness of God'.[67] The Mu'tazila rank among the foremost proponents of divine unity proclaiming the absolute transcendence of God from all creation.[68] Qāḍī 'Abd al-Jabbār, a prominent tenth-century Mu'tazilite, characterises the principle of divine unity by recourse to the oneness of God:

> the knowledge that God, being unique, has attributes that no creature shares with Him. This is explained by the fact that you know that the world has a creator (*ṣāni'*) who created it and that He existed eternally in the past and He cannot perish while we exist after being non-existent and we can perish (*fanā'*). And you know that He was and is eternally all-powerful (*qādir*) and that impotence (*al-'ajz*) is not possible for Him. And you know that He is omniscient of the past and present and that ignorance (*jahl*) is not possible for Him. And you know that He knows everything that was, everything that is, and how things that are not would be if they were. And you know that He is eternally in the past and future living, and that calamities and pain are not possible for Him. And you know that He sees visible things (*mar'iyyāt*), and perceives perceptibles, and that He

[67] Ibn al-Nadīm, *Fihrist*, vol. 1, 255.27, ed. Flügel, 615, tr. Dodge. See Endress, 'The Circle of Al-Kindī', pp. 66, and 75., 'Al-Kindī's treatise "On the First Philosophy" defends the rational sciences by demonstrating their consistency with the true creed: with the *tawḥīd* Allāh. It is a reply to the question most urgent for a Muslim who took his faith as seriously as he took his science: the question if the rational activity and research was vindicated by *sharī'a* . . . In attempting to reply to this question, the philosopher joined the rationalist theologians of his day, in defending reason against the apodictic traditionalism of the *ahl al-ḥadīth* . . . His treatise, "On First Philosophy", demonstrates in an elaborate deduction, dependent directly on the Platonic *Theology* of Proclus . . . the absolute unity of the First Cause. Philosophy is engaged to defend the *tawḥīd*, the creed of Islamic monotheism, against the temptation of dualism.' Cf. Wakelnig, 'Greek Sages on the *Tawḥīd*', especially 214–15.

[68] 'God is one. The eternal God (*ṣamad*). He begot none, nor is He begotten, none is equal to Him' (Qur'ān: 112:1–4). See especially Kars, *Unsaying God*, 9–41; and Al Qurtuby, 'The Islamic Roots of Liberation, Justice and Peace'. In *Theological Opinions of the Muslims* (*Maqālāt al-Islāmiyyīn*), al-Ash'arī, the eponymous founder of the Ash'arite school, recounts the Mu'tazilite credo of divine unity in a characteristically negative theological tone, 'God is unique, nothing is like Him; He is neither body, nor individual, nor substance, nor accident. He is beyond time. He cannot dwell in a place or within a being; He is not the object of any creatural attribute or qualification. He is neither conditioned nor determined, neither engendered nor engendering. He is beyond the perception of the senses. The eyes cannot see Him, observation cannot attain Him, the imagination cannot comprehend Him. He is a thing, but he is not like any other things, He is omniscient, all-powerful, but His omniscience and almightiness cannot be compared to anything created. He created the world without any pre-established archetype and without an auxiliary' (al-Ash'arī, *Maqālāt al-Islāmiyyīn* 1:216, tr. Corbin, *History of Islamic Philosophy*, 109–10).

> does not have need of sense organs. And you know that He is eternally past and in future sufficient (*ghanī*) and it is not possible for Him to be in need. And you know that He is not like physical bodies, and that it is not possible for Him to get up or down, move about, change, be composite, have a form, limbs, and body members. And you know that He is not like the accidents of motion, rest, colour, food, or smells. And you know that He is One throughout eternity and there is no second beside Him, and that everything other than He is contingent, made, dependent (*muḥtāj*), structured (*mudabbar*), and governed by someone or something else. Thus, if you know all of that, you know the oneness of God.[69]

'Abd al-Jabbār's *Book on the Five Principles* (*Kitāb al-Uṣūl al-Khamsa*), widely revered in Mu'tazalite circles, was explicitly defended by his celebrated Basran student and disciple Abū Rashīd al-Nīsābūrī against those who denied that God could be known.[70] Despite their rejection of divine attributes, the Mu'tazila defend the essence of God as something knowable. The knowability of God as a thing (*shay'*) crucially informs the composition of al-Fārābī's *On the One and Oneness* (*Kitāb al-Wāḥid wa-l-Waḥda*).[71] Although al-Fārābī appears to agree with the Mu'tazalite argument that a thing may be classified either as 'existent' or 'non-existent', God by virtue of His transcendence cannot be called an existent. Therefore, al-Fārābī identifies God by His quiddity (*māhiyya*).[72] The quiddity of God is absolutely separate from material existence. The principle

[69] 'Abd al-Jabbār, *Kitāb al-Uṣūl al-Khamsa*, Q. 11, 5.13–19, 6.1–19. Cf. Martin, Woodward, and Atmaja, *Defenders of Reason in Islam*, 92. For 'Abd al-Jabbār's contributions to Mu'tazilite ethics, see Vasalou, *Moral Agents and Their Deserts*, 39–57; and Hourani, *Islamic Rationalism*, 17–36.

[70] See Kars, *Unsaying God*, 11–12.

[71] Cf. Al-Kindī adopts the term in his definition of creation as 'the manifestation of the thing from non-being' (*Rasā'il al-Kindī al-Falsafiyya*, vol. 1, 165.11). See Adamson ('Al-Kindī and the Mu'tazila', 64n54), 'Here, it is not only the term "thing" (*shay'*) that suggests the parallel with the Mu'tazilite position, but the term manifestation (*iẓhār*). *Ẓahara*, "come to light", "appear" has the connotation that what was hidden has been revealed, which might suggest that "the thing" was already something, namely something hidden (in God's power) before being created.'

[72] Ian Richard Netton demonstrates the pervasive influence of Mu'tazilite theology in the age of Fārābism; see *Al-Fārābī and His School*, 18–30. Cf. Vallat, *Fārābī et l'école d'Alexandrie*, 78–80. For al-Fārābī's apparent harmonisation of *Parmenides* 129a–130a and *Metaphysics* IV.6, see Janos, 'Al-Fārābī's (d. 950) *On the One and Oneness*', 105–9 and 113: 'The one is also said of that which is set apart by its quiddity (*al-munḥāz bi-māhiyyatihi*) - whichever quiddity that may be, divisible or indivisible, conceived [in the human soul, *mutaṣawwara*] or [existing] outside the soul.' Cf. *Metaphysics* 1003a32, 1028a10; and Proclus, *Commentary on Plato's* Parmenides, book I, 40, 648.1ff., book VII, 492–580, 1134–1242.

of divine unity (*tawḥīd*) belongs to God alone as 'oneness in quiddity'. God is set apart by His quiddity (*al-munḥāz bi-māhiyyatihi*) since 'every quiddity possesses its own special and proper oneness by virtue of its very existence [and this] means that God as well possesses a special and unique kind of oneness by virtue of His special existence and quiddity'.[73] Al-Fārābī's *Harmonisation* further corroborates the quiddity of God as the *sine qua non* condition for multiplicity (*kathīr*):

> Aristotle also showed in the *Theology of Aristotle* that the One (*al-wāḥid*) exists in every multiplicity, because every multiplicity in which [the One] does not exist would be absolutely infinite . . . He then shows that everything in which the One exists in the world is both One and not One in various respects. If it is not truly One, then the One exists in it, the One is other than it, and it is other than the One.[74]

The One gives rise to multiplicity generously bestowing existence upon all things. The ascription of the 'One' or 'God' to the 'First' as 'First Being' or 'First Cause' figures prominently in Mu'tazilite arguments contesting the existence of divine attributes.[75] Abū Ya'qūb al-Sijistānī, an Ismā'īlī scholar, maintains that the Mu'tazila misconceived God by attributing substance to Him and thereby argues for the negation of all divine attributes, including the knowability of God as a thing:

> The pure He-ness (*al-huwiyya al-maḥḍiyya*) associated with the glorified Originator transcends 'He' and 'not He'. It is not that He-ness is existent and not He-ness (*lā-huwiyya*) is not existent . . . The Originator is not 'He' unlike the He-ness of the existents, and not 'not-He' unlike the not-He-ness of the non-existents. His He-ness is the manifestation of the negation of the He-ness and not He-nesses from the transcendent Originator . . . We negate all He-nesses from the real Originator because every He-ness requires a cause. We found that the most noble of those things possessing a He-ness is the intellect, and the He-ness of the intellect necessitates a cause, which is the divine command, may his glory be exalted. It is thus 'He' who is the

[73] See Janos, 'Al-Fārābī's (d. 950) *On the One and Oneness*', 119.

[74] Al-Fārābī, *Harmonisation*, 56. [16b18–24], tr. Janos, 'Al-Fārābī's (d. 950) *On the One and Oneness*', 109–10. Cf. D'Ancona, 'The *Theology* Attributed to Aristotle'; and Adamson, *The Arabic Plotinus*, 183.

[75] *On the One and Oneness* (*Kitāb al-Wāḥid wa-l-Waḥda*) presents a systematic linguistic analysis of the various senses of the One; cf. Janos, 'Al-Fārābī's (d. 950) *On the One and Oneness*'.

> true Originator without a cause – exalted is 'He' above that – and accordingly 'He' does not require a He-ness, nor the negation of it. 'He' is not the negation of He-ness either. Thus, beyond the He-nesses there is no affirmation of a thing that is 'He'.[76]

Although the relationship between the Originator (*al-mubdi'*) and the intellect invokes the *Theology of Aristotle* where the First Intelligence or Intellect is created by the One, al-Fārābī's *Virtuous City* and *Political Regime* both conjoin the One with the Intellect insofar as the power of the Intellect is ascribed to the First Intelligence as the activity of thought thinking itself.[77] The *Virtuous City* gestures to the convergence between Aristotle's Unmoved Mover and the Neoplatonic principle of the One whereby the primacy of the One is described as the First Existent and hence First Cause (*al-sabab al-awwal*) of all other existents:

> The First Existent is different in its substance from everything else, and it is impossible for anything else to have the existence it has. For between the First and whatever were to have the same existence as the First, there could be no difference and no distinction at all. Thus, there would not be two things but one essence only, because, if there were a difference between the two, that in which they differed would not be the same as that which they shared, and thus that point of difference between the two would be a part of that which sustains the existence of both, and that which they have in common the other part. Thus, each of them would be divisible in thought, and each of the two parts of the First would be a cause for the subsistence of its essence; and it would not be the First but there would be another existent prior to it and a cause for its existence – and that is impossible.[78]

[76] al-Sijistānī, *Kitāb al-Yanābī'*, 71–2. Cf. al-Sijistānī, *Wellsprings of Wisdom*, tr. Walker, 49–50; Kars, *Unsaying God*, 26–7, 34; Corbin, *Trilogie Ismaélienne*, 44; and *History of Islamic Philosophy*, 79–84.

[77] al-Fārābī, *Virtuous City*, I, 1. §1–15, 57–88; Adamson, *The Arabic Plotinus*, 128–32. Cf. Al-Fārābī, *Political Regime*, I. 20–34 [42.25–53.15], 39–47; and Walker, *Early Philosophical Shiism*, 87–94. By reference to *Metaphysics* XII, the unity and simplicity of the One may be interrogated by returning to the difference between the potentiality of the Intellect and the actuality of the One. The Unmoved Mover becomes identical to the One insofar as self-sufficient actuality comes to be identified with the activity of thinking. For the activity of thought thinking itself as retaining potentiality, see Long, *Aristotle on the Nature of Truth*, 236.

[78] al-Fārābī, *Virtuous City*, I, 1, §2, 58–61, tr. Walzer. Cf. Campanini, 'Alfarabi and the Foundation of Political Theology in Islam'; and Daiber, 'The Ismailite Background of Fārābī's Political Philosophy'.

All existents are derived from the divine essence of the First which endows them with their existence.[79] Al-Fārābī describes these existents derived from the One or First by retrieving the Neoplatonic schema of emanation, 'The genesis of that which comes into existence from it [God] takes place by way of emanation [*fayḍ*], the existence of which is due to the existence of something else, so that the existence of something different from the First emanates from the First's existence.'[80] Since all existents participate in their existence by virtue of the First Existent or First Cause, this transposition of the Neoplatonic One into the First Existent or First Cause is integral to the hierarchical constitution of the cosmos insofar as the attributes of generosity, justice, and love emanate from the First Cause. Moreover, the First Cause generates the Active Intellect, which in turn transmits intelligibles to lesser intellects, including the philosopher-ruler-*imām*.

From Divine Demiurge to Nocturnal Council

Given al-Fārābī's identification of the One with the First, the Active Intellect is accorded an explicitly demiurgic function.[81] Akin to Plato's *Timaeus*, the Active Intellect qua demiurge provides an intelligible order to the cosmos

[79] 'The First is that from which everything which exists comes into existence' (al-Fārābī, *Virtuous City*, I, 2, §1, 88–9, tr. Walzer).

[80] Ibid. I, 2, §1, 88–91.

[81] Kraemer, 'Alfarabi's *Opinions of the Virtuous City* and Maimonides' *Foundations of the Law*', 114, summarises al-Fārābī's adoption of the Neoplatonic schema of emanation: '1) the First Cause and all that by which it is characterized. 2) The things separate from matter and how each one of them is characterized by attributes specific to it; and the hierarchy of things separate from matter leading ultimately to the Active Intellect, and the activity of each. 3) The heavenly substances and how each is characterized. 4) The natural bodies below them; how they come into being and pass away; that what transpires among them does do by precision, mastery, providence, justice, and wisdom; and that there is no neglect, deficiency, or injustice in them in any way. 5) The generation or existence of the human being; how the Active Intellect causes an illumination to emanate upon them so that the primary intelligibles are attained; volition and choice. 6) The First Ruler and how revelation comes about. 7) The rulers who must succeed him if he does not exist at some time. 8) The city and its people and the happiness their souls attain; and the city opposed to it and what their souls revert to after death: some to misery and some to non-existence. 9) The virtuous nation and those that oppose it.' Kraemer remarks that this 'entire plan lays stress upon the hierarchy of existence, the great chain of Being suspended from the First, which should be represented for the people of the virtuous city by political symbols, i.e. the hierarchy of rulers and ruled; for the imitation of cosmic order is what induces political order and stability in the city' (ibid., 135). Therefore, the *Political Regime* and *Virtuous City* are designed for potential rulers to be trained in Neoplatonic metaphysics before they are educated in the practical principles of political science. Cf. Burrell, *Knowing the Unknowable God*, 10–11; and Druart, 'Al-Farabi, Emanation, and Metaphysics'.

by receiving and transmitting intelligibles (*ma'qūlāt*) from the First Cause.[82] The philosopher-ruler-*imām* is prescribed with a similar demiurgic task of translating intelligibles into images for the sake of educating the citizens of virtuous cities and nations. Al-Fārābī subsequently identifies several intellects (*thawānī*) below the Active Intellect which emanate from the First Cause and possess a wholly formal nature. However, these separate intellects are to be contrasted with the Active Intellect insofar as their essence is informed by their relation to materiality given their proximity to natural bodies and hence the generation and corruption of political communities. With the introduction of several intellects which work on behalf of the Active Intellect, the cosmology of the *Timaeus* comes to be conjoined with the second-best city of the *Laws*.[83] The generation of the political community expands like a rhizome through multiple modalities in the form of cities and nations gesturing towards the possibility of a deliberative model of collective governance akin to the Nocturnal Council of the *Laws* which exceeds and perhaps even supplants the sovereign authority of the philosopher-ruler-*imām*.[84] In the *Virtuous City*, al-Fārābī describes twelve natural qualities (*khiṣāl*) of virtuous rulers

[82] 'Now as long as the craftsman keeps looking to what's in a self-same condition, using some such thing as a model, and fashions its look and power, then of necessity, everything brought to a finish in this way is beautiful' (Plato, *Timaeus* 28A, tr. Kalkavage). Damien Janos decisively demonstrates the affinity between intellection and causation, 'It should be noted that since intellection is the only activity that characterizes the immaterial beings, it is necessarily as a result of their contemplation that they are able to produce the lower effects. In other words, intellection and causation appear to be linked in al-Fārābī's account, to the point that principle of intellection possesses an inherent demiurgic power' (*Method, Structure, and Development in al-Fārābī's Cosmology*, 298). Cf. Davidson, *Alfarabi, Avicenna, Averroes, on Intellect*, 45–73.

[83] See Plato's references to the Nocturnal Council in *Laws* 908a4, 951d–962b, 961a–c, and 968a–969c; and Morrow, *Plato's Cretan City*, 500–15. For a discussion of the notion of 'possibility' to assess the viability of the city in speech of the *Republic* and the second-best city of the *Laws*, see especially Laks, *Plato's Second Republic*, 32–52.

[84] This admission of a collective body responsible for political deliberation and governance may be historically attributed to the Shī'ite imamate. The notion of a Shī'ite utopia guided by several *imāms* departs from the sovereign authority of the philosopher-king of the *Republic*. If we are to hypothetically entertain the Shī'ite imamate model as a political paradigm, then al-Fārābī's virtuous city may be said to be guided by a deliberative body akin to the Nocturnal Council of the *Laws*, 'Then it's likely that in the present case, if our founding of the country is to have an end, there must be something in it that knows, in the first place, this goal we're speaking of (whatever our political goal might happen to be), and then in what way it ought to attain this, and who – first among the laws themselves, and then among human beings – gives it advice in a noble or ignoble way. But if some city is devoid of such a thing, it won't be surprising if, lacking intelligence and senses, it acts haphazardly each time in each of its actions' (Plato, *Laws* 962a9–c3). Cf. Bakhsh, '*The Virtuous City*'; and L'Arrivee, 'Discrimination and Violence in Alfarabi's *Virtuous City*'.

to portend twelve *imāms* presiding over the affairs of the political community.[85] This deliberative council composed exclusively of *imāms* is privileged for its pedagogical approach to collective governance:

> It is up to the legislator to teach the administrators and judges how to govern each group of people so that they follow his way and pursue the correct course in that, thereby, preventing dissension from arising as a result of governing them. He mentioned this notion and gave examples of free people and slaves and the way people interact with bees in bee hives – meaning by this only evil people and vagabonds.[86]

Akin to the demiurge who labours for the sake of ordering the sensible cosmos, the legislators labour on behalf of the citizens to inform the administrators and judges about how the city should be governed. The administrators who are literally 'friends of the city' (*aṣḥāb al-siyāsāt*) and meet to deliberate upon a future course of action bear an affinity to the philosopher-ruler-*imām* who is gifted with the visionary prophecy to transmit intelligibles and personifies the intelligibility of the Law. Just as the philosopher-ruler-*imām* receives and transmits the intelligibility of the Law via revelation, the administrators are similarly endowed with the sovereignty to transmit the law into action. In contrast to the philosopher-ruler-*imām*, who receives the Law and hence already has an implicit understanding of its *telos*, Plato describes the Nocturnal

[85] 'When one single person who fulfills all these conditions cannot be found but there are two, one of whom is a philosopher and the other fulfills the remaining conditions, the two of them will be the sovereigns of this city. But when all these six qualities exist separately in different persons, philosophy in one person and the second quality in another person and so on, and when these persons are all in agreement, they should all together be the excellent sovereigns' (al-Fārābī, *Virtuous City*, V, 15, §14, 252–3, tr. Walzer, mod.). Cf. Plato, *Republic* 498b; and al-Fārābī, *Attainment of Happiness* 60. [45.1–5], 48. Subsequently, Alireza Omid Bakhsh retrieves the twelve qualities of the philosopher-ruler-*imām* from the *Virtuous City* to entertain the existence of twelve *imāms*, 'The first is physical fitness and health; second, one must be intelligent and quick at learning and understanding; having a good memory is the third quality; the fourth one is the possession of a quick wit; fifth, one must be an eloquent orator; sixth, one should be fond of learning and acquiring knowledge; love of truth and hatred of falsity make up the seventh quality; the eighth quality defines one as a pious person with an inborn sense of self-control; ninth, one should be elevated and honorable; tenth, money, wealth, and worldly attractions should not appeal to them; eleventh, one must be fond of justice and the enemy of oppression and injustice . . . The twelfth and last quality, without which the other qualities are not worthy, recognizes the virtuous ruler as courageous, brave, and decided person' (V, 15, §12. 246–9, tr. Walzer, mod.). Cf. Bakhsh, '*The Virtuous City*', 46–7.

[86] al-Fārābī, *Summary of Plato's* Laws, 8.7 [835d–844d], 169, tr. Butterworth.

Council as composed of select intelligent individuals who are responsible for interpreting the laws for the sake of cultivating virtue among the citizens of the political community. The council members must be educated to discern both the nature of the individual virtues and their unity. Therefore, Plato appears to adopt a regimen of education for the Nocturnal Council of the *Laws* akin to the philosopher-king of the *Republic*. In *Laws* VII, Plato elucidates those requisite topics of study required to comprehend the purpose and function of the laws ranging from mathematics and astronomy to music and psychology. Mathematics and astronomy are those theoretical studies which are most necessary to understand the relationship between the parts and the whole. While mathematics may only be studied by an intellectually advanced group of individuals, astronomy is afforded an even more exclusive status to be studied by a sole individual or lawgiver.[87]

This regimen of study culminates in the study of theological arguments demonstrating the existence of the soul as a self-mover in relation to all things that the divine 'intelligence (*nous*) is the master of, having arranged the whole in an order'.[88] The purpose of the Nocturnal Council thereby becomes apparent. By virtue of their contemplation of all things divine, the members of the Nocturnal Council replicate the divine order by their judgements as true guardians of the Law. The Athenian Stranger demonstrates this conclusion by affording the Nocturnal Council the duty to '[judge] by the standard of nature what things come into being in a noble fashion and what things do not'.[89] The Nocturnal Council fulfils its theoretical function by first contemplating these noble metaphysical truths about the existence of the gods, their genuine benevolence, and the rational order accorded to the cosmos before effectively deliberating about the application of the laws. Indeed, the recognition of a rational and benevolent creator and divine omnipotence of the gods becomes an absolute prerequisite for assuming a membership role on the Nocturnal Council. In addition to their theoretical studies, members of the Nocturnal Council also engage in practical studies by comparing and contrasting the laws of their community with other communities and thereby learning about the virtue which may be contained in foreign laws. Plato's relative openness to foreign laws demonstrates a certain cosmopolitan potential inherent to his political philosophy insofar as the activities of the Nocturnal Council include sending out distinguished citizens as emissaries or diplomats to these foreign communities.

[87] Plato, *Laws* 809e.

[88] Ibid., 818c–d.

[89] Ibid., 966b–c.

Despite the relative international prominence of the Nocturnal Council, members must also engage in domestic matters pertaining to the interrogation and imprisonment of atheists. The Nocturnal Council is tasked with reforming those citizens who have committed impiety out of ignorance.[90] Plato reiterates the deliberative function of the Nocturnal Council, which literally meets before dawn to vigilantly deliberate and discuss the pending cases.[91]

Among those laws that the citizens must obey are 'Agricultural Laws', which determine the boundaries between properties, 'Everyone is to prefer to try to move the largest stone that is not a boundary-marker rather than move a small stone marking a boundary between a friend and enemy, protected by an oath sworn before the gods.'[92] Plato respectively highlights the relationship between neighbours as integral to preserving the constitution of the political community. If encroachment or damage to property has transpired, including cattle grazing on the land of a neighbour or stealing a swarm of bees, then the country wardens are beholden to inspecting the damage, reaching a judgement, and assessing a penalty.[93] Al-Fārābī draws an apparent contrast between those enemies who are only interested in pursuing their own selfish ends by engaging in criminal activity and those friends who choose to work together on behalf of the entire political community:

> Some species of animals and plants are able to gain their necessary affairs only by a group of individual members coming together with one another in association. With others, each one obtains what is necessary even if isolated from one another. But it obtains its most excellent state only by individual members coming together with one another. With others, each of the individuals has completed all of its necessary and most excellent affairs, even when isolated from one another; yet, when they do come together, one does not impede another with respect to anything belonging to the others. With others, when they come together, one impedes another with respect to the necessary and most excellent affairs. Therefore, the individuals of some species always isolate themselves from one another

[90] The Nocturnal Council preserves the laws and thereby assumes a lesser role of sovereign authority than the philosopher-king; see Bobonich, *Plato's Utopia Recast*, 399–400; and Laks, *Plato's Second Republic*, 189n63.

[91] Jacques Derrida underscores the syllogistic function of the Nocturnal Council in the first session of his Death Penalty seminar, 'A synagogue is a place where one goes together, the *syllogos* is a place where one discusses together' (*The Death Penalty*, 1:6n9).

[92] Plato, *Laws* 843a1–3.

[93] Ibid., 843d6–9. Al-Fārābī adopts Plato's reference to bees gaining pleasure from human commotion to describe evil people and vagabonds; see *Summary of Plato's* Laws 8.7 [835d–844d], 169.

> with respect to all of their affairs, even procreation, as with many of the sea animals. And some of them do not isolate themselves from one another except for procreation. Others do not isolate themselves from one another for most of what goes on – like the ant and the bee and many others besides these two, such as birds that feed and fly in flocks.[94]

This distinction between rational and non-rational animals is requisite for determining their potential to engage in mutual cooperation (*mu'āwana*). The cooperative behaviour of birds and bees is likened to the development of civic friendship within the political community. These political associations may vary in rank and perfection according to their size. Since the city is composed of smaller parts, the larger parts or the whole city always takes precedence. Smaller parts of the city do not serve the whole in the same way as a village or neighbourhood. Associations which exist at the rank of villages, quarters, streets, and houses are less perfect and defective in comparison to the city. By introducing these civic divisions, the *Political Regime* gestures towards an association larger and hence more perfect than the city, 'The civic association is part of the nation, and the nation is divided into cities. The unqualifiedly perfect human association is divided into nations.'[95] In contrast to the sovereignty of a philosopher-king as the model of governance for this perfect human association, the *Virtuous City* and *Summary* at least entertain the possibility of collective governance. Like the Nocturnal Council of the *Laws*, the active participation of administrators and judges within al-Fārābī's virtuous city inaugurates this model of collective governance by espousing the supreme importance of political deliberation.[96]

Philosopher in the Cosmopolis

With the relative prominence accorded to the Creator as demiurge, the political function of the demiurge personified as working on behalf of the people

[94] al-Fārābī, *Political Regime*, 63. [69.7–22], 60, tr. Butterworth.

[95] Ibid., 64. [70.7–8], 61.

[96] 'The fact is, there are always among the many certain divine human beings – not many – whose intercourse is altogether worthwhile, and who do not by nature grow any more frequently in cities with good laws than in cities without. These the inhabitants of cities with good laws, if he's uncorruptible, must always seek and track down, by going over sea and land, in order to place on a firmer footing those legal customs that are nobly laid down, and correct others, if they are lacking something' (Plato, *Laws* 951b4–c3). Cf. Lewis, 'The Nocturnal Council and Platonic Political Philosophy'; and Klosko, 'The Nocturnal Council in Plato's *Laws*'.

deserves our further attention.[97] Given the advent of Plato's cosmogony, which stems from the myth of a demiurge who looks to the Intelligible Form to order the cosmos, I shall aim to examine how the political function of the demiurge as a labourer who works on behalf of the people might call into question the sovereignty of the philosopher-ruler-*imām*.[98] The demiurge and the philosopher-ruler-*imām* are characterised by their innate receptivity to receive intelligibles. While the demiurge receives the Intelligible Form, the philosopher-ruler-*imām* receives intelligibles (*ma'qūlāt*) from the Active Intellect (*al-'aql al-fa''āl*). Therefore, both perform an intermediary role which may be attributed to their unique imaginative capacities to transform intelligibles into sensible images and symbols. Whereas the demiurge qua manual labourer mediates between the Intelligible Form and the pre-existing material for the sake of producing a sensible image of the cosmos, the philosopher-ruler-*imām* qua prophet mediates between the Active Intellect and sense-perception by translating intelligibles into sensibles (*maḥsūsāt*), which are in turn communicated to the political community. Al-Fārābī's *Virtuous City* distinguishes between two different cases of prophecy.[99] The highest form of prophecy is identified with waking states whereby intelligibles are transmitted to the imagination of the philosopher-ruler-*imām*. In the second case, either sensibles or intelligibles are received by the imagination of the philosopher-ruler-*imām* in nocturnal states via dreams:

> Some do not see anything in their waking life but receive some of these things during sleep, whereas others do not receive any of these things in their waking life but receive whatever they receive during sleep only, so that they receive during sleep the particulars but not the intelligibles, some receive the intelligibles without receiving the particulars, others receive

[97] 'He explains in a salutary manner [a] that they have been generated by the Creator, may He be glorified and magnified, innovating them and [b] that it is He who is the efficient cause, the true one, [and the] innovator of everything, in the same manner as Plato explains in his books on Lordship, like the *Timaeus* and the *Ablūṭīyā*, and in other statements of his' (al-Fārābī, *Harmonisation*, 57. [17a9–14], 156, tr. Butterworth).

[98] Peter Kalkavage (*Plato's Timaeus*, 16) remarks that the demiurge means the one who works for the people (*demos*);. Cf. Ilievski, 'The Demiurge and His Place in Plato's Metaphysics and Cosmology', 62; and Morrow, 'The Demiurge in Politics'.

[99] al-Fārābī, *Virtuous City*, IV, 14, §7–§11, 218–27. Maimonides explicitly replicates al-Fārābī's account of prophecy, 'Prophecy is, in truth and reality, an emanation sent forth by the Divine Being through the medium of the Active Intellect, in the first instance to man's rational faculty, and then to his imaginative faculty' (*Guide of the Perplexed* II. 36. 78a.11–14, 369, tr. Pines).

some of the one and some of the other; some receive some of the particulars only, and these are the majority.[100]

The unique productive capacity of the imagination reproduces these intelligibles as sensibles for the sake of producing images. Here the philosopher-ruler-*imām* may be said to replicate the role of the Active Intellect which transmits intelligibles so that the imagination comes to be actualised and perfected. The perfection of the imagination naturally requires a surplus of its innate imaginative capacity which may be expanded through its consistent association with the Active Intellect. Therefore, the training and development of the imagination and intellect contribute to the capacities of the philosopher-ruler-*imām* qua prophet (*nabī*).[101]

The three roles of the *imām*, prophet, and philosopher are conjoined in the figure of the ruler who does not wish to rule but is instead chosen to rule by virtue of their innate intellectual capacity. By receiving and transmitting the intelligibles from the Active Intellect, the imagination and intellect of the philosopher-ruler-*imām* is actualised.[102] If the Intelligible Form of the cosmos initiates the activity of the demiurge, then the demiurge may be said to mediate between the unity of the Intelligible Form and the multiplicity of matter thereby preserving their conjunction. Despite the secondary status accorded to the demiurge in relation to the Intelligible Form, the demiurge lacks envy and bears no grudge.[103] It is only by virtue of this nascent impulse of the One to generously bestow itself that the cosmos as such comes to be conceived. The theme of cosmic unity gradually arises by the expansion and association of cities with one another composing the entire inhabited world.[104] Al-Fārābī's

100 al-Fārābī, *Virtuous City*, IV, 14, §10, 224–6, tr. Walzer.

101 See Streetman, 'If It Were God Who Sent Them . . . Aristotle and al-Fārābī on Prophetic Vision', 229.

102 Proclus identifies the demiurge with the Divine Active Intellect; see *Commentary on Plato's* Timaeus, 96, 229.26–230.4. The Divine Active Intellect responsible for emanation thereby fulfils the role of the One synonymous with the principle of divine unity. As Anthony Shaker observes, 'To that end, the Active Intellect, which was to man as the sun to sight, guided and oversaw the actualization of mortal man's intellect from its potential state (with which he is born). So much so that felicity (*sa'ādah*) meant that the soul was in the Active Intellect that put order to things and furnished the principle for human being's path to the attainment of felicity' (*Reintroducing Philosophy*, 489).

103 Herodotus alludes to the contrast between the generosity of the demiurge and the jealousy of the gods, 'In Herodotus, the gods are, above all, grudging or jealous. In Book I of the *Inquiries*, Solon tells the tyrant Croesus that "the divine is altogether jealous and troublesome" (32)' (Kalkavage, *Plato's Timaeus*, 60n18).

104 Daniel Richter's *Cosmopolis* and James Romm's *The Edges of the Earth in Ancient Thought* document how this Hellenistic notion of the entire inhabited world (*oikoumenē*) expanded the boundaries of the human imagination.

Attainment of Happiness envisions a political association constituting the totality of this entire inhabited world, 'It will become evident to them that political association and the totality that results from the association of the cities correspond to the association of the bodies that constitute the totality of the world.'[105] The divine magnitude of the entire inhabited world which proceeds from the One to the Many invokes the *Laws* where the 'supreme divinity is the world in its totality'.[106] The superabundance and expansion of the One encompasses the entire world by emanating a series or procession of multiple parts always subordinate to the first and highest principle:

> He will come to see in what are included in the totality constituted by the city and the nation the likenesses of what are included in the total world. Just as in the world there is a first principle, then other principles subordinate to it, beings that proceed from these principles, other beings subordinate to these beings, until they terminate in the beings with the lowest rank in the order of being, the nation or city includes a supreme commander, followed by other commanders, followed by other citizens, who are in turn followed by other citizens until they terminate in the citizens with the lowest rank as citizens and as human beings. Thus, the city includes the likenesses of the things included in the total world.[107]

Both the city and the nation are included in this cosmic totality. Al-Fārābī's *Book of Letters* (*Kitāb al-Ḥurūf*) describes their integration by recourse to the advent of languages deriving from differences in geography and climate. The emergence of letters and utterances in different nations is determined by the natural inclination of the human individual towards those things which one needs for survival. The natural dispositions which develop from certain geographical regions are expressed by signs and gestures that are consonant with those requisite needs. The origin of the voice arises from distinct physiological dispositions, including the mechanical structure of the different organs and their relation to one another enabling the phenomenon of vocalisation.[108]

[105] al-Fārābī, *Attainment of Happiness*, 20. [16.7–10], 24, tr. Mahdi (mod.).

[106] Plato, *Laws* 821a2.

[107] al-Fārābī, *Attainment of Happiness*, 20. [16.11–15], 24–5, tr. Mahdi.

[108] Al-Fārābī's *Commentary and Short Treatise on Aristotle's* De Interpretatione and *Book of Letters* contribute to the development of his linguistic theory. Luis Xavier López-Farjeat describes how linguistic distinctions emerge from cultural and geographical differences, 'al-Fārābī points out that this particular organic disposition differs from region to region, and also according to the different characters and temperaments of the people dwelling in certain

The advent of language remains attentive to the unique arrangement of our physical bodies. Distinctive physical gestures and vocalisations may be attributed to the vagaries of psychological comportment as certain affections of the soul come to be materialised.[109]

With the emergence of language in its multiple semantic registers, we may begin to envision how a global community is heterogeneously composed as a multifaceted collection of nations and cultures. Al-Fārābī's *Aphorisms of the Statesman* retrieves the activity of deliberation for the sake of attaining the virtuous goal shared by all nations occupying the entire inhabited world, 'The virtue of deliberation is what enables a human being to make an excellent inference about what is more useful with respect to a virtuous goal shared by nations (*ummam*), a nation (*umma*), or a city (*madīna*), when there is a shared occurrence.'[110] The practice of deliberation is paramount to how the affairs of the political community are to be conducted. Although Plato's philosopher-king and Nocturnal Council must be properly trained for the sake of perfecting the practice of deliberation, the possibility that legislators who are trained in the theoretical sciences may choose to extend deliberation beyond the scope of the city is not explicitly discounted.[111] The attainment of happiness as the 'virtuous goal shared by nations' gestures to the possibility that deliberation may extend across the entire inhabited world. *Attainment of Happiness* similarly reaffirms the global value of deliberation as a cosmopolitan virtue,

geographical areas. This would explain the emergence of distinct languages in different nations: the primary voices that are used by different people in different regions to signify to one another what they have in mind differ according to their physiological disposition to utter specific sounds, namely alphabetical letters (*ḥurūf*)' ('The Language of Non-human Animals in al-Fārābī and Avicenna', 182–3).

109 Cf. Mian, 'Muslim Political Philosophy and the Affective Turn', 54, 'Language, Fārābī, seems to be suggesting, emerges in and through our affective, bodily existence . . . In a nutshell, al-Fārābī seems to be saying that we come to name (we step into linguistic existence) through our sense-perceptive (affective and cognitive) interaction with the world.'

110 al-Fārābī, *Selected Aphorisms*, 95. [99.3–6], 63–4, tr. Butterworth. Cf. al-Fārābī, *Aphorisms of the Statesman*, 90., 75, 68, tr. Dunlop.

111 Al-Fārābī's account of deliberation in *Aphorisms of the Statesman* and *Attainment of Happiness* mirrors the role of the administrators in his *Summary of Plato's* Laws; see 8.7 [835d–844d], 169. Although Plato measures the city and limits its size to establish a harmonious relationship between citizens, the possibility of conceiving a deliberative body akin to a Nocturnal Council contributes to the administration of the global political community. Hence, a *ma'mūra* may not appear as utopian as it may seem. In contrast, Butterworth and Parens defend the view that al-Fārābī presents a blueprint for a good regime, the second-best city, rather than the best regime, the city in speech; see al-Fārābī, *Political Regime*, 97–127; and Parens, *Metaphysics as Rhetoric*, 62–7.

'There is a certain deliberative virtue that enables one to excel in the discovery of what is most useful for a virtuous end common to many nations (*ummam*), to a whole nation (*umma*), or to a whole city (*madīna*) at a time when an event occurs that affects them in common.'[112] The relative ubiquity of deliberation expressed by its heterogeneous application to both cities and nations thereby contributes to the expansion of al-Fārābī's cosmopolitanism.

[112] al-Fārābī, *Attainment of Happiness*, 28. [21.10–13], 28–9, tr. Mahdi. With the practice of deliberation common to many nations, the *Attainment of Happiness*, *Virtuous City*, and *Political Regime* allude to the existence of political community encompassing the entire inhabited world (*oikoumenē*). Cf. Orwin, 'Can Humankind Deliberate on a Global Scale?', 831–2.

2
Aristotle, the First Teacher

Peripatetic Inheritance

The Islamic reception and interpretation of Aristotle may be characterized by recounting the dream of al-Ma'mūn, the ninth-century caliph of the 'Abbāsid dynasty, who is often cited in the early Arabic translations of Aristotle's works. Al-Ma'mūn is reputed as a giant of Arabic letters responsible for promoting the early translation movement and cultivating the arts and sciences in Baghdad.[1] Like al-Fārābī, al-Ma'mūn shares a fascination with dreams as a source of prophecy and revelation:

> Al-Ma'mūn saw in a dream the likeness of a man white in color, with a ruddy complexion, broad forehead, joined eyebrows, bald head, bloodshot eyes, and good qualities sitting on his bed. Al-Ma'mūn related, 'It was as though I was in front of him, filled with fear of him. Then I said, "Who are you?" He replied, "I am Aristotle." Then I was delighted with him and said, "Oh sage, may I ask you a question?" He said, "Ask it." Then I asked, "What is good?" He replied, "What is good in the mind." I said again, "Then what is next?" He answered, "What is good in the law." I said, "Then what more?" He answered, "More? There is no more."'[2]

This dream endures throughout the Islamic Renaissance which identifies the persona of Aristotle with the indisputable wisdom of the philosopher-ruler-*imām.*

[1] For al-Ma'mūn's cosmopolitan affiliation with al-Kindī's circle in ninth-century Baghdad, see Cooperson, *Al-Ma'mūn*, 106.

[2] See Ibn al-Nadīm, *Fibrist*, 243.1–9, ed. Flügel, 583, tr. Dodge. The dream is recounted by D'Ancona, '"Arisṭū 'inda l-'Arab", and Beyond', 17–18; and Diagne, *Open to Reason*, 14–15. Cf. van Koningsveld, 'Greek Manuscripts in the Early 'Abbāsid Empire'; and Gutas, *Greek Thought, Arabic Culture*, 95–104; 'The "Alexandria to Baghdad" Complex of Narratives'.

To invoke such a dream might appear to be merely speculative if we assume that our contemporary knowledge of Aristotle is exclusively determined by the hegemonic phantasms of the West.[3] The reception of Aristotle is undoubtedly inscribed within the Christian-Latin tradition, most notably with the influence of Thomas Aquinas and the Neoplatonism of Renaissance humanism. Although the relative parochialism of the Western lineage has ostensibly occluded the Islamic heritage, the philosophy of Aristotle is integral to the development and expansion of *falsafa* and to some extent even in other disciplines, including rational theology (*kalām*) and jurisprudence (*fiqh*). Since Aristotle was revered throughout the medieval Islamic world as the paradigmatic 'First Teacher/Philosopher' (*al-mu'allim al-awwal*) who systematically investigated logic, the natural sciences, metaphysics, and ethics, we shall aim to explicate the historical image of Aristotle throughout the formative and classical periods of Islamic philosophy.[4] One such image distilled through the lens of the imagination is the pseudo-Aristotle. In the *Letter of the Golden House* written by an anonymous author during the early 'Abbāsid age (750–900 CE), Aristotle's *De Mundo* is recast as an epistolary romance. Aristotle features prominently as writing to his student Alexander, who describes in a letter to his mentor the marvels he saw in upper India. Another perspective is evident in the pseudo-*Theology of Aristotle* which envisions the Aristotelian corpus through a resolutely Neoplatonic lens thereby following the stages of ascent from logic to physics and metaphysics before culminating in rational theology. Given the relative prominence of the *Metaphysics*, the principles of divine unity (*tawḥīd*) and the One (*al-wāḥid*) are exemplified in the concluding words of al-Ma'mūn's dream, 'I [al-Ma'mūn] said, "Give me something more!" He [Aristotle] replied, "Whosoever gives you advice

[3] See Schürmann (*Broken Hegemonies*, 10), 'The establishment of a principle is its institution at the beginning of the period for which it will serve as ultimate point of reference, of recourse, thus dominating that era. Such a first becomes thinkable only when its grip begins to loosen. The establishments bequeathed to us are talked about and questioned as they collapse, so that we know history primarily by its reversals.' Retrieving Heidegger's insistence that the history of being gathers in the 'departure' (*Abschied*), Anthony F. Shaker's *Reintroducing Philosophy* offers a bold re-reading of the dissolution of these hegemonic principles by first retrieving the 'paradigmatic' role of Islamic civilisation.

[4] The reception of the Organon is undoubtedly informed by the Neoplatonism of Ammonius, Themistius, and Olympiodorus, who attempted to rationally deduce the number and identity of the categories. Ibn Sīnā's *Book of the Cure* (*Kitāb al-Shifā'*) adopts their deduction for the sake of defending Aristotle against earlier commentators who purportedly misinterpreted him. The *Rhetoric* and the *Poetics* were also studied as disciplines belonging to the Organon. Their transmission and reception reaches its fruition with an investigation into the attendant definitions of opinion (*doxa*), persuasion (*pistis*), art (*technē*), and imitation (*mimēsis*).

about gold, let him be for you like gold; and for you is oneness [of Allāh].”’[5] Aristotle’s exposition of these first principles in the *Metaphysics* may only come to be known by acquiring and practising the intellectual virtues. Therefore, the domain of ethics extending beyond metaphysics as the most crowning achievement of human investigation brings to light the ethical quandary of the philosopher who must bear his or her own inclusive exclusivity as the paradigm of sovereign authority.[6]

The *Nicomachean Ethics* inspired a robust commentary tradition throughout the ‘Abbāsid age. The history of its transmission and reception beginning with al-Fārābī’s foremost predecessors and associates is primarily dependent upon the only extant Arabic translation discovered by Arthur Arberry (1951/2) and Douglas M. Dunlop (1959) at the Qarawīyīn Library in Fez.[7] As the founder of the Baghdad circle, al-Kindī (801–66 CE), reputed as the first philosopher of the Arabs, cites the *Nicomachean Ethics* and *Eudemian Ethics* in his *Letter on the Number of Aristotle’s Books and What Is Needed to Acquire Philosophy* (*Risāla fī Kammiyyat Kutub Arisṭūṭālīs wa-Mā Yuḥtāju ilayhi fī Taḥṣīl al-Falsafa*).[8] Al-Kindī describes the composition of Aristotle’s books on ethics as the culmination of those previous books addressing the soul (*De Anima*), and the first principles or forms of things which ‘have no need for bodies at all’ (*Metaphysics*), ‘They are his books on ethics, I mean the ethical qualities and government of the soul, that it may preserve in human virtue and be one with it, which is the aim of the man of balanced nature in his present life and his

5 See Ibn al-Nadīm, *Fihrist*, 243.1–9, ed. Flügel, 583, tr. Dodge. The version of the dream cited here and above is attributed to Yaḥyā ibn ‘Adī; see ibid., 243.3–8, 583, tr. Dodge.

6 See Harvey, ‘The Place of the Philosopher in the City according to Ibn Bājjah’; and Groff, ‘Cultivating Weeds’.

7 Anna Akasoy and Alexander Fidora present an excellent introduction to Douglas M. Dunlop’s translation of the Fez manuscript in *The Arabic Version of the* Nicomachean Ethics. The Fez manuscript appears to be known to al-Kindī, al-Fārābī, al-‘Āmirī, Miskawayh, Ibn Bājja, and Ibn Rushd. The *Nicomachean Ethics*, *Eudemian Ethics*, and *Magna Moralia* are subsequently mentioned in their respective biographies of Aristotle. However, only the *Nicomachean Ethics* is translated into Arabic, ‘And among the books of Aristotle – copied from the handwritings of Yaḥyā ibn ‘Adī from the catalogue of his books – was the *Book of Ethics* explained by Porphyry, twelve Books, translated by Ḥunayn ibn Isḥāq. And there was with Abū Zakariyah’ (s.c. Yaḥyā ibn ʿAdī) in the handwriting of Ḥunayn ibn Isḥāq a number of books with the Commentary of Themistius. They came out in Syriac’ (Ibn al-Nadīm, *Fihrist*, 252, ed. Flügel, 606, tr. Dodge).

8 Richard Walzer estimates the composition of al-Kindī’s *Letter* to be during the caliphate of al-Ma’mūn (813–33 CE); see Walzer, ‘New Studies on Al-Kindi’, 176–7; Guidi and Walzer, ‘Studi su al-Kindi’, 375; and Akasoy and Fidora, *The Arabic Version of the* Nicomachean Ethics, 9.

means of salvation in the world to come, for which there is no substitute, no equivalent for its benefit and no well-being with its loss.'[9] Ethics is rather conspicuously ranked after metaphysics to indicate the perfection of the human being in both the theoretical and practical domains.[10] Akin to the discussion of the soul in its subject-matter, ethics attains a certain degree of perfection insofar as one attains greater clarity and comprehension as one departs from those treatises concerned with the principles and the motion of bodies (*Physics* and *De Caelo*). Although the study of ethics exceeds the study of the soul, the two disciplines are conjoined in their function and purpose.[11] Hence, the study of the soul in relation to those first principles identified with metaphysics is requisite for the attainment of virtue in this world and salvation in the next.

In his *Letter on the Necessary Preliminaries before the Study of Philosophy* (*Risāla fī Mā Yanbaghī an Yuqaddam qabl Ta'allum al-Falsafa*), al-Fārābī enumerates the order of Aristotle's treatises, 'As for the books from which there are learned the things which are put into operation in philosophy, from some of them is learned the improvement of morals, from others the rule of cities, and from others the rule of the household.'[12] Given the harmonisation

[9] al-Kindī, *Rasā'il al-Kindī al-Falsafiyya*, 1:363–84, tr. Akasoy and Fidora, *The Arabic Version of the* Nicomachean Ethics, 7.

[10] Al-Kindī refers to the large book on ethics (*Nīqūmakhīyā*) written to his son, Nicomachus, containing eleven books and another without name, 'And among them is another book, less than the number of these discourses (*maqālāt*) [and] resembling the meanings of his book [written] to Nīqūmākhus. He wrote it to one of his brethren' (*Rasā'il al-Kindī al-Falsafiyya*, 1:369, tr. Akasoy and Fidora, 7). This reference may be to the *Eudemian Ethics*, dedicated to Aristotle's student Eudemus. A third treatise is indicated, most likely the *Magna Moralia*, 'Apart from these three treatises, there are many books by him on minor matters, and letters on various minor matters also' (ibid.). His *Letter* concludes with a summary of the aims of the ethical-political books (*fī kutubihi al-khulqiyya al-siyāsiyya*) and mention of a second book, 'As for the aim in his second book, and it is that which is called *Būlīṭīqī*, i.e. the *Statesman* (*al-Madanī*), which he wrote to one of his brethren, it deals with the like of what he said in the first [book]. He spoke in it more of political government. Some of its discourses are exactly the same as some of the discourses of the first book' (ibid., 384, tr. Akasoy and Fidora, 7). This reference is likely to the *Politics*. Akasoy and Fidora surmise that al-Kindī identifies the second book with the *Politicus* (*Statesman*) by identification of *Kitāb Būlīṭīqī* with *al-Madanī* (*The Arabic Version of the* Nicomachean Ethics, 8–11).

[11] Cf. Aristotle, *Nicomachean Ethics* 1102a14–26.

[12] al-Fārābī, *Alfārābīs Philosophische Abhandlungen*, 86, tr. Dieterici. A similar method of enumeration is presented in *Philosophy of Aristotle* (*Falsafat Arisṭūṭālīs*); see al-Fārābī, *Philosophy of Aristotle*, 3. [69.6–70.4], 80–1. In contrast, al-Kindī, al-Ya'qūbī, and Ibn al-Nadīm refer to the *Nicomachean Ethics* as following the *Metaphysics*. Although Ibn Abī Uṣaybi'a cites *Philosophy of Aristotle* as being incomplete, Qāḍī Ṣā'id claims that *Philosophy of Aristotle* concludes with a reference to the *Metaphysics*; see Akasoy and Fidora, *The Arabic Version of the* Nicomachean

of Plato and Aristotle, the order of the treatises are oriented by the ultimate aim of human perfection, 'Aristotle sees the perfection of the human as Plato sees it and more. However, because human perfection is not self-evident or easy to explain by demonstration leading to certainty, he saw fit to start from a position anterior to that from which Plato had started.'[13] Al-Fārābī's *Philosophy of Aristotle* (*Falsafat Āristūṭālīs*) privileges this anteriority by recourse to Aristotle's method of logical demonstration beginning with the four things that everyone considers desirable and good by nature, '(1) the soundness of the human body, (2) the soundness of the senses, (3) the soundness of the capacity for knowing how to discern what leads to the soundness of the body and the senses, and (4) the soundness of the power to labour at what leads to their soundness'.[14] This ordering is by no means incidental. Both sound discernment and sound labour are instrumental to achieving the soundness of the body and the senses. With respect to the distinction between sound discernment and labour, a practical consideration is introduced, namely, that labour precedes discernment and knowing. In this sense, human nature is not exclusively defined by the capacity to know as much as the capacity to labour for the sake of what is both useful and necessary. Furthermore, labour may be contrasted with discernment and knowing, which only develops later in the order of time. The human being is first and foremost a physical organism arising from the functions of the body and the senses which are then cultivated through labour to arrive at their perfection. Therefore, labour remains the most useful, necessary, and preferred activity:

> And this is the kind of labour that is useful, necessary, and preferred to everything else, be it the labour of a person by oneself, or accompanied by the labour of others for them, or accompanied by their labour for others, and whether one performs it by deed and speech. The deed by which this labour is performed is the useful and necessary deed that has priority, and the speech by which this labour is performed is the useful and necessary

Ethics, 17. In *Philosophy of Aristotle*, theoretical philosophy, including logic and metaphysics, is distinct from ethics. It is plausible that al-Fārābī was not yet acquainted with Aristotle's ethical writings. Al-Fārābī purportedly wrote either a complete or partial commentary on the *Nicomachean Ethics*; see Neria, 'Al-Fārābī's Lost Commentary on the Ethics'.

[13] al-Fārābī, *Philosophy of Aristotle*, 1. [59.5–8], 71, tr. Mahdi (mod.). The abbreviated title, *Philosophy of Aristotle*, omits the scope of the complete title, *The Philosophy of Aristotle, the Parts of His Philosophy, the Ranks of Order of Its Parts, the Position from Which He Started and the One He Reached.*

[14] Ibid., 1. [59.10–12], 71, tr. Mahdi (mod.).

> speech. Beyond this, one may prefer also that these four things exist in the most excellent state of their soundness.[15]

The intellect (*'aql*) is paired with discernment (*tamyīz*) for the sake of determining that which is to be pursued and avoided and is thereby exclusively oriented to a singular item of practical attainment. Their conjunction informs those pursuits related to the soundness of the body and the senses, and ultimately, the power to labour, by determining their respective ends, 'He [Aristotle] explained that one cannot find the useful things, nor how to labour, nor with what to labour, without knowing the end for the sake of which one should labour and without having that end defined and present before them.'[16] Therefore, the apprehension of the respective ends in the practical sciences cannot be separated from discernment.

Discernment is attributed not merely to the human species but ultimately to other animals. This identification of discernment as a power that humans share with other animals remains innovative for his time, 'For every animal has a body and senses and a power to discern somehow that by means of which it labors toward the soundness of its body and senses. But it does not have a desire to understand the causes of what it sees in the heaven and on earth, let alone having a sense of wonder about things whose causes it desires to understand.'[17] The attribution of discernment to animal nature effectively interrogates the intellectual superiority accorded to human nature. This departure from the Platonic division between body and soul confirms the relative unity between the human and animal faculties and even gestures to a desire for knowledge which exceeds the limits of the human, 'Is then the soul's desire for these things an overreaching by a person, an intemperate appetite, and an infirmity attached to one by nature which must be removed and suppressed, or ought it to reach its completion? There is thus in all these questions room for perplexity and diversity of opinion, and topics for consideration.'[18] The definition of the human ever so gradually begins to unfold by interrogating the distinction between the human and other animals. Although the enterprise of philosophy is not discounted as utterly useless, al-Fārābī entertains those opinions which may call it into question and requests convincing evidence to support the contention that the proper human activity should be identified with the practice of philosophy *tout court*. If the knowledge of first principles

[15] Ibid., 1. [59.13–18], 71–2, tr. Madhi (mod.).
[16] Ibid., 3. [63.12–14], 75, tr. Mahdi (mod.).
[17] Ibid., 3. [65.16–19], 77, tr. Mahdi.
[18] Ibid., 3. [66.11–15], 77, tr. Mahdi (mod.).

is rather fleeting this is due to the immense human labour required to comprehend them. By contrasting labour with leisure, we are compelled to seek out and define the substance and hence final perfection of the human essence:

> Therefore the human is forced to consider what their substance is, what is their final perfection, and what is the act the performance of which leads to the final perfection of their substance. But this implies knowing *what, by what,* and *how* is the human, and *from what* and *for what* they exist, so that when they labour, their labour will be directed toward reaching this end. For if they do not, of their own accord, learn what this perfection is, they will not know the end for which they labour.[19]

Discernment is distinguished by its capacity to formulate and resolve such perplexities and comes to be identified with the activity of the intellect connecting the parts with the whole.[20] This relationship between the parts and the whole effectively brings to light the function and purpose of the individual human essence and the entire world, 'Thus if the human is a part of the world, and if we wish to understand their purpose and activity and use and place, first we have to know the purpose of the whole world so that we may see clearly what the purpose of the human is . . . that is why we are forced to know the purpose of the totality of the world.'[21] With such a gesture, the power of the intellect qua discernment comes to be manifested for the sake of pursuing these perennial questions. The conclusion of the *Philosophy of Aristotle* only sporadically returns to the necessity of the intellect informing these theoretical activities aimed at knowing the purpose of the human and the purpose of the cosmos. However, the relevance of the intellect as a practical faculty does not disappear but rather becomes enhanced in relation to its capacity to labour on behalf of attaining human perfection insofar as it comes to be identified with human will and choice.

Al-Fārābī's *Letter on the Intellect* (*Risala fī al-'Aql*) expands upon the differences between the practical and theoretical intellect. After identifying six kinds of intellect, al-Fārābī introduces the power of the intellect to arrive at certainty about true and universal premises before describing how the intellect pertains to human volition in Aristotle's *Book of Ethics* (*Kitāb al-Akhlāq*), namely, by explicating the relationship between the intellect (*'aql*) and practical wisdom (*ta'aqqul*):

[19] Ibid., 3. [68.1–8], 79, tr. Mahdi (mod.).
[20] Aristotle, *Metaphysics* 1069a18–1072b25.
[21] al-Fārābī, *Philosophy of Aristotle*, 3. [68.19–20; 69.1–5], 79–80, tr. Mahdi (mod.).

> When Aristotle uses the term, 'intellect' in Book Six of the [*Nicomachean*] *Ethics*, he means the part of the soul in which there occurs, by the assiduous habituation to one thing after another in each genus of things and by long experience of one thing after another in each genus over a lengthy period of time, certainty about any propositions and premises concerning the things pertaining to human volition that should be preferred or avoided.[22]

Given Aristotle's exposition of the practically wise person (*phrōnimos*), al-Fārābī highlights the role of practical wisdom as a species of 'excellent deliberation in deducing what is in fact good in order to do [that good], and in deducing what is evil in order to avoid that evil'.[23] Al-Fārābī's *Harmonisation* subsequently retrieves the *Book of Ethics* to dismiss those commentators who claim that Plato and Aristotle disagree about the acquisition and cultivation of moral habits (*malakāt*):

> In truth, the matter is not as they presume because in his book known as the *Nicomachea*, Aristotle speaks only about political laws, as we have explained in several places of our commentary on that book. Even had he also discussed moral habits, as Porphyry and many commentators after him say [he did], his discussion would have been about moral laws – and a legal discussion is always universal and unconditional, and not relative to anything else.[24]

The composition of the *Harmonisation* undoubtedly reflects the influence of Porphyry who composed a treatise bearing the same title.[25] Al-Fārābī adopts Aristotle's dialectical method of sifting through received opinions (*endoxa*) to introduce the pivotal debate regarding whether the world is generated or eternal. His brief explication of the *Nicomachean Ethics* is rather conspicuously situated between chapters on vision, learning, and recollection, perhaps to

22 al-Fārābī, *Letter on the Intellect* III.7 [9.4–9], 70, tr. McGinnis and Reisman.

23 Ibid., III.2 [5.4–6], 69.

24 al-Fārābī, *Harmonisation*, 9.43 [12a15–21], 147–8, tr. Butterworth. Several commentators including Ibn al-Qifṭī, Ibn Abī Uṣaybi'a, and Ibn al-Nadīm deserve careful scrutiny. In the aforementioned passage, al-Fārābī's defence of Aristotle replicates Socrates' argument that moral virtues are produced by habituation. Hence, they are liable to change and can only be judged according to a higher standard of the law (*Republic* 518d–e).

25 With the exception of Ibn al-Qifṭī and Ibn al-Nadīm, the Arabic sources of Porphyry's commentary have received minor attention. However, al-Fārābī cites Porphyry and his predecessors; see al-Fārābī, *Alfārābīs Philosophische Abhandlungen*, 27, tr. Dieterici.

indict those commentators who neglect to observe the harmonization of Plato and Aristotle. Only the true or genuine philosopher is virtuously disposed to correctly discern the beliefs and arguments of his predecessors without falsification, prejudice, or contention:

> Aristotle does not deny that for some people and some individuals it is easier to transfer from one moral habit to another and for others it is harder, as he has explicitly declared in his book known as *Nicomachea minor*. He enumerated the reasons for the difficulty and ease of transferring from one moral habit to another – how many there are, what they are, how each of them reasons [functions], and what facilitates or impedes them.[26]

This rhetorical strategy of retrieving the habits of the soul and their acquisition is presented as a moral lesson to confront the false arguments of his detractors, 'Aristotle explicitly declares in his *Nicomachean Ethics* that all moral habits are habits, that they undergo change, that none of them is by nature, and that a human being is capable of moving from one to another by habituation.'[27] Here the intersection between ethics and politics becomes apparent for the sake of cultivating the moral habits of the legislators. The *Nicomachean Ethics* when

[26] al-Fārābī, *Harmonisation*, 9.44 [12b.16–22], 148–9, tr. Butterworth. Al-Fārābī rather curiously distinguishes between a major and minor *Nicomachean Ethics*, 'And Aristotle has mentioned in his "Book to Young Nicomachus about Politics" something similar to what Plato has explained' (*Harmonisation*, 7.33 [9a21–5], 142, tr. Butterworth), alluding to the possibility that the *Nicomachean Ethics* was divided into two treatises. Butterworth remarks that al-Fārābī's choice of language here is 'admittingly strange' (*Kitābuh ilā Nīqūmākhus al-Ṣaghīr fī al-Siyāsa*) in reference to *Nicomachean Ethics* 1131b16–17, 1132b18–19, 1136b15–29, 1137b27–30, and cites 'Abd al-Raḥmān Badawī's conclusion that *Nīqūmākhus al-Ṣaghīr* is distinct from the *Nicomachean Ethics* and the *Eudemian Ethics*; see Badawī, *Al-Akhlāq, Ta'līf Arisṭūṭālīs Tarjamat Isḥāq Ibn Ḥunayn*, 1:22–5; and al-Fārābī, *Harmonisation*, 142n43. The identity of the minor *Nicomachean Ethics* with the *Magna Moralia* is defended by Smith, *Dictionary of Greek and Roman Biography and Mythology*, 330; Mansfeld, *Prolegomena*, 18n54, 20, 124–5n67; Akasoy and Fidora, *The Arabic Version of the* Nicomachean Ethics, 14n60. Akasoy and Fidora subsequently conclude that 'the *Magna Moralia* is less than half the length of the *Nicomachean Ethics*, each of the two books of the *Magna Moralia* is considerably larger than any of the ten books of the *Nicomachean Ethics* and assuming that in both works each book formed a single roll, the two rolls would evidently have been the larger, whence the name. We thus have good grounds to identify the "little *Nīqūmākhiyā*" with the *Nicomachean Ethics*' (ibid., 15n61). This conclusion is corroborated in the *Harmonisation*, 9.44 [12b.16–22], 148–9; and *Guide of the Perplexed* (III. 43, 96a–96b, 571–2), which cites a similar passage from al-Fārābī's lost commentary on the *Nicomachean Ethics*.

[27] al-Fārābī, *Harmonisation*, 9.42 [12a.1–4], 147, tr. Butterworth.

conjoined with the *Republic* and *Laws* fulfils a pedagogical function for the sake of training future founders and rulers of political regimes.

Al-Fārābī's Circle

Al-Fārābī's Peripatetic influence extends to his most immediate associates, namely, Yaḥyā ibn ʿAdī (893–974 CE), Abū Sulaymān al-Sijistānī (913–87 CE), Abū al-Ḥasan al-ʿĀmirī (913–92 CE), and Abū Ḥayyān al-Tawḥīdī (922–1023 CE). Among his most notable students, Yaḥyā ibn ʿAdī, a Monophysite Jacobite Christian of Baghdad, is revered as a great copyist and translator who supported himself by collecting, copying, editing, and translating books from Plato and Aristotle. Ibn ʿAdī's apologetics are aptly portrayed in a famous rebuttal to an anti-Trinitarian polemic composed by al-Kindī. His *Reformation of Morals* (*Tahdhīb al-Akhlāq*) demonstrates a fidelity to both Christian Neoplatonism and Stoicism. Beginning with the Platonic tripartition of the soul into the appetitive, irascible, and rational parts, Ibn ʿAdī presents twenty virtues and vices to be commended or abhorred by reference to the social status of the persons who practise them:

> One who loves perfection must also make it a habit to love (*maḥabba*) people generally, to treat them with affection, to act sympathetically toward them, and to be gentle and compassionate with them. Humans are a single tribe (*qabīl*), related to one another, joined together by their humanity (*insāniyya*). The adornment of the divine power is in all of them and in each one of them, and it is the rational soul. By means of this soul, one becomes human. It is the nobler of the two parts of the human, which are the soul and the body. So the human, in reality, is the rational soul, and it is one substance in all humans. All humans are a single thing (*shay' wāḥid*), but they are many individuals. Since their souls are one, and love is only in the soul, all of them must show affection for one another and love one another.[28]

Alongside Ibn ʿAdī, al-Sijistānī is a remarkably eclectic figure bringing together an intimate circle of students dedicated to philosophical dialogue. His *Cupboard of Wisdom* (*Ṣiwān al-Ḥikma*) consists of spoken opinions and quotations from Thales, Pythagoras, Socrates, Plato, Aristotle, Homer, Euclid, Hippocrates, Ptolemy, Euripides, Thucydides, Sophocles, Plotinus, Philo, Porphyry, and Galen.

[28] Ibn ʿAdī, *Reformation of Morals*, 5.14, 106–7, tr. Griffith (mod.).

Al-Sijistānī's extensive survey of the historical transmission of knowledge from antiquity to his own age conjoins the vegetative, animal, and rational parts of the Aristotelian soul with the Neoplatonic principle of the soul as 'a divine force which mediates between Nature (*al-Ṭabī'a*) and the Intellect (*al-'Aql*)'.[29] Despite this divine force attributed to the human intellect, the essence of the soul remains obstructed by its attachment to the physical body. Hence, the individual soul remains a mere microcosm of the Neoplatonic World Soul.[30]

Al-'Āmirī, a younger contemporary of al-Fārābī (and perhaps his student), develops an account of happiness (*sa'āda*) in accordance with divine law (*sharī'a*).[31] His *Book of Happiness and Making Happy* (*Kitāb al-Sa'āda wa-l-Is'ād*) explicitly refers to Porphyry's commentary on the *Nicomachean Ethics* by presenting a definition of happiness as informed by Neoplatonic angelology, 'Porphyry said: Happiness is simply a man's perfecting his form, and man's perfection, in so far as he is a man, is in voluntary actions, and his perfection, in so far as he is an angel (*malak*) and an intelligence, is in speculation, and each of the two perfections is complete in each of the two subjects, and if one be compared with the other, it is the human perfection which is defective.'[32] Al-'Āmirī's allegiance to Ṣūfism comes to be expressed by his creative integration of the Aristotelian corpus with the *Epistles* (*Rasā'il*) of the Ikhwān al-Ṣafā' to effectively distinguish between the divine and material worlds for the sake of proposing a fundamental epistemology of salvation. One may come to know the divine intellect only by activating the human intellect which serves as an intermediary between both worlds:

[29] See Kraemer, *Philosophy in the Renaissance of Islam*, 119–35; al-Sijistānī, *Muntakhab Ṣiwān al-Ḥikma wa-Thalāth Rasā'il*, 25–6, tr. Netton, *Al-Fārābī and His School*, 64.

[30] Joel Kraemer attends to the relation between microcosm and macrocosm inherent to al-Sijistānī's Neoplatonism, 'The notion that the human soul is a small part of the universal soul – the doctrine of monopsychism – is affiliated with the idea that man is a microcosmic replica of the cosmic hierarchy in the sense that he is endowed with nature, soul, and intellect. He does not contain the one in the same way but has cognition of it. It is implied that the One is glimpsed by means of contemplation of the great chain of being' (*Philosophy in the Renaissance of Islam*, 227).

[31] Cf. Akasoy, 'The Arabic and Islamic Reception of the *Nicomachean Ethics*', 101. Al-'Āmirī appears to be conversant enough with al-Fārābī's writings to refer to him as a 'recent' philosopher, 'one of the recent philosophers says' (*qāla ba'ḍ al-ḥuddāth min al-mutafalsifīn*) (*Kitāb al-Sa'āda wa-l-Is'ād*, 211, tr. Akasoy and Fidora, *The Arabic Reception of the* Nicomachean Ethics, 19).

[32] al-'Āmirī, *Kitāb al-Sa'āda wa-l-Is'ād*, 5–6, tr. Akasoy and Fidora, *The Arabic Reception of the* Nicomachean Ethics, 19–24. Al-'Āmirī was evidently aware of Porphyry's commentary on the *Nicomachean Ethics*; see Porphyry, *Porphyrii philosophi fragmenta*, 165.

> The eternal truths (*al-'ulūm al-ḥaqīqiyya*) which are known with certainty – such as our belief that things equal to one thing are equal to each other, and that the whole is greater than its part – these are not established by bodily sense, *which is liable to error and inadvertence.* Rather, they are acquired by the innate (*gharīzī*) intellect, which is a divine proof, having the same relationship to the soul as the visual power has to the corporeal eye.[33]

Al-Tawḥīdī, the author of the *Book of Pleasure and Conviviality* (*Kitāb al-Imtā' wa-l-Mu'ānasa*), also contributed extensively to the philosophy of the Būyid age as a student and disciple of al-Sijistānī. Akin to Plato's relationship to Socrates, al-Tawḥīdī assiduously documented the activities of al-Sijistānī's circle as their primary scribe. His *Book of Pleasure and Conviviality* demonstrates an encyclopaedic knowledge of Aristotle ranging from his definition of knowledge (*al-'ilm*) as 'the perception by the Rational Soul of things as they really are' to his definition of wisdom (*ḥikma*) as 'the essence of knowledge about eternal things'.[34] Al-Tawḥīdī explores various topics ranging from jurisprudence (*fiqh*), theology (*kalām*), grammar, language, and logic, to medicine, astronomy, astrology, arithmetic, geometry, rhetoric, and mysticism (*taṣawwuf*). In contrast to the *Epistles* of the Ikhwān al-Ṣafā', his *Book of Pleasure and Conviviality* has been compared to *One Thousand and One Arabian Nights* and remains an exemplary form of *adab* literature.[35] Like al-'Āmirī, al-Tawḥīdī also studied with Ṣūfī masters, including Abū Ḥayyān. The cosmopolitan character of al-Tawḥīdī's writings is portrayed in his own biography serving different careers as a secretary-courtier to the wazīr al-Ṣāhib ibn 'Abbād, before fully dedicating himself to Ṣūfism.[36]

The eclectic intellectual inclinations of al-Fārābī's associates epitomize his Peripatetic influence. The apparent harmonization of Plato and Aristotle remains decisive to the proliferation of his cosmopolitan paradigm and assists us with comprehending the aims of his political philosophy. Rather than simply defending al-Fārābī as exclusively affiliated with one school of ancient philosophy, we shall instead strive to comprehend the ambitious degree of harmonization between these respective schools as made evident by his influence upon his immediate students and more distant disciples. Here we cannot

[33] al-'Āmirī, *Kitāb al-Amad 'alā al-Abad*, 95, tr. Rowson.

[34] al-Tawḥīdī, *al-Muqābasāt*, 362, tr. Netton, *Al-Fārābī and His School*, 79.

[35] See Fakhry, *A History of Islamic Philosophy*, 183. A comprehensive presentation of the dialogue between al-Tawḥīdī and Miskawayh about topics pertaining to the *Book of Pleasure and Conviviality* is found in al-Tawḥīdī and Miskawayh, *The Philosopher Responds*, vols. 1 and 2.

[36] See Netton, *Al-Fārābī and His School*, 80–3; and Alshaar, *Ethics in Islam*, 60–2.

discount how the expansion of this cosmopolitan paradigm extending from the 'Abbāsid to the Būyid ages actively contributed to the convivial atmosphere of royal court culture patronizing the arts and letters and thereby promoting the study of philosophy, music, theology, and poetry.[37]

In what follows, I shall concentrically expand al-Fārābī's circle from his immediate associates and successors to his more distant disciples, namely, Miskawyah, al-Ghazālī, Ibn Rushd, and al-Ṭūsī, who prominently express their own inclinations towards cosmopolitanism. To begin to imagine how happiness may be attained on a global scale, I shall begin with the seminal contributions of Abū 'Alī Aḥmad Miskawayh (932–1030 CE), a tenth-century historian and philosopher. In contrast to al-ʿĀmirī, Miskawayh was actively engaged in political life serving as a diplomat to the Būyid dynasty. His contributions as a scholar and translator influenced the composition of the *Summa Alexandrinorum*, the Latin summary of the *Nicomachean Ethics.*[38] As a patron of the Būyid caliphs of tenth- and eleventh-century Baghdad, Miskawayh's philosophical circle contributed widely to the expansion of cosmopolitanism.[39] Miskawayh is attributed as a formative influence upon Maimonides's *Guide of the Perplexed* (*Dalālat al-Hā'irīn*). However, Maimonides does not espouse Miskawayh but instead retrieves al-Fārābī's lost commentary on the *Nicomachean Ethics* which was

[37] See Kraemer, *Philosophy in the Renaissance of Islam*, 24–30. Ian Richard Netton presents four prominent cultural paradigms beginning with *exotic paradigm* which mythologises historical events akin to *One Thousand and One Arabian Nights.* In contrast to the fanciful portrayal of the relationship between artists and court-patrons, for example, the 'Abbāsid caliph Hārūn al-Rashīd summoning his wazīr to his bedside to tell him a story as a result of his insomnia, the dominant paradigm was much more likely the *paradigm of patronage* where an uneasy relationship existed between the artist and court-patron who often made personal sacrifices to appease the will of the patron. The relationship between artists and patrons often degenerated into the *paradigm of the sycophant* whereby the artist would often explicitly cater his own art to the will of the patron for the sake of pleasing him or her. We can imagine that even al-Fārābī with his own philosophical renown was called to the court of the Ḥamdānid prince Sayf al-Dawla to provide entertainment, receiving a stipend of four dirhams a day. In the *ideal paradigm*, Netton recounts a series of literary salons (*majālis*) hosted by a Barmakid wazīr for Hārūn al-Rashīd dedicated to the theme of passionate love (*'ishq*). The participants included two Shī'ites, a Khārijite, and two Mu'tazalites, in a scene reminiscent of Plato's *Symposium* (*Al-Fārābī and His School*, 18–30). Cf. Sweeney, 'Greek Essence and Islamic Tolerance'.

[38] The *Summa Alexandrinorum* translated from Arabic by Hermannus Alemannus (Hermann the German) was completed in 1243–4 CE; see Woerther, 'Al-Fārābī and the Didascalia'.

[39] See Wakelnig, *A Philosophy Reader from the Circle of Miskawayh,* §200–22; and Goodman, 'Friendship in Aristotle, Miskawayh, and al-Ghāzalī'.

[40] Anna Akasoy remarks 'that the Jewish philosopher may not have been so convinced of it as to recommend it to his students ... Miskawayh's text may have struck Maimonides as too eclectic' ('The Arabic and Islamic Reception of the *Nicomachean Ethics*', 103n19).

widely disseminated among his successors.[40] By conjoining Aristotle's ethics with divine law (*sharī'a*) and invoking Ibn al-Khammār, a disciple of Yaḥyā ibn 'Adī, the noted translator and commentator of Plato and Aristotle, and student of al-Fārābī, Miskawayh's *Refinement of Character* (*Tahdhīb al-Akhlāq*) echoes Yaḥyā ibn 'Adī's claim that 'humans are a single tribe (*qabīl*), related to one another, joined together by their humanity (*insāniyya*). The adornment of the divine power is in all of them and in each one of them, and it is the rational soul.'[41] Miskawayh's assessment that the unity of humanity expressed in a natural sociability (*uns*) extends even to strangers corresponds to those Arab grammarians who claim that the word for 'human' (*insān*) is derived from the same stem *a-n-s* ('to be sociable').[42] Thus, Miskawayh aspires to the realization of a great society in order to attain common happiness:

> Since these human goods and the corresponding aptitudes in the soul are many in number, and since it is not within the power of one to achieve them all, it is necessary that a large group associate in this total achievement. This is why the number of individual human beings should be large, and they should get together at the same time for the achievement of these common kinds of happiness, so that each one among them may attain this perfection through the cooperation of the others.[43]

Like al-Fārābī, Miskawayh highlights the virtue of benevolence (*tafaḍḍul*) aimed at ensuring that justice is equally distributed throughout society. The benevolent person exercises circumspection to discern justice as a virtue, 'Benevolence, then, does not violate the conditions of justice, but is rather circumspect in it. For this reason, it has been said that the benevolent man is

Cf. Maimonides' *Guide of the Perplexed*, 'i.e. Abū Naṣr [al-Fārābī] said in the first part of his *Commentary on the Nicomachean Ethics*: As regards those who have the power to make their souls pass from ethical quality to ethical quality, they are those of whom Plato said that God's care for them is greater' (III. 18, 37b.25–7, 18, tr. Pines). For further evidence defending the authenticity of the lost commentary, see Neria, 'Al-Fārābī's Lost Commentary on the Ethics', 77–80. Al-'Āmirī's and Miskawayh's summaries of the *Nicomachean Ethics* appear to be derived from Porphyry's commentary. For the influence of Porphyry, see Miskawayh, *Refinement of Character*, 3. [76.16–18], 70. Cf. Akasoy and Fidora, *The Arabic Version of the* Nicomachean Ethics, 28–9.

41 Ibn 'Adī, *Reformation of Morals*, 5.14, 106–7, tr. Griffith (mod.).

42 Kraemer, *Humanism in the Renaissance of Islam*, 233; Goodman, *Islamic Humanism*, 82–121.

43 Miskawayh, *Refinement of Character*, 1. [14.18–15.2], 14, tr. Zurayk.

44 Ibid., 4. [130.12], 115. Cf. Seyyed Mohsen Eslami and Alfred Archer, who claim that Miskawayh is among the first philosophers to explicitly propose benevolence as a supererogatory principle ('The Cautionary Account of Supererogation', 21).

nobler than the just.'[44] Here benevolence is defined as an excessive attention to the singular individual beyond the universal law 'exercised in the kind of justice which pertains to the human'.[45] Miskawayh introduces love (*maḥabba*) as an expression of benevolence aimed at the attainment of individual perfection, 'To this end, people must love one another, for each finds their own perfection in someone else, and the latter's happiness is incomplete without the former. Each one thus becomes like an organ of the same body; and the human constitution depends upon the totality of organs forming his body.'[46] Benevolence extends to the love of humanity as a guiding source for both ethical and political perfection.

Abū Ḥāmid al-Ghazālī (1058–1111 CE) presents another promising avenue for exploring the expansion of cosmopolitanism through the practice of hospitality towards guests (*ādāb al-ḍiyāfa*). His *Revival of the Religious Sciences* (*Iḥyā' 'Ulūm al-Dīn*) expounds upon the theme of manners related to everyday habits, particularly the ritual of eating with guests in his eleventh book, *On the Manners relating to Eating* (*Kitāb Ādāb al-Akl*), 'The Emissary of God (may God bless him and grant him peace) said, "Do not so go out of your way for a guest that you will come to dislike him, for he who dislikes a guest dislikes God, and he who has disliked God, God has disliked him." He said, "There is no good in someone who is not hospitable."'[47] Al-Ghazālī's practice of hospitality is concretely informed by his allegiance to Ṣūfism. In *Disciplining the Soul* (*Kitāb Riyāḍat al-Nafs*) al-Ghazālī describes how hospitality arises from the practice of disciplining one's soul so as to become closer to God, 'The Emissary of God (may God bless him and grant him peace) said, "The believer is beset with five afflictions: a believer who envies him, a hypocrite who hates him, an unbeliever who makes war on him, a devil who misguides him, and a soul which struggles against him."'[48] Hospitality stems from the virtue of temperance or self-control insofar as appetites, passions, and desires are to be moderated if one is to give freely and liberally to another. Hospitality may be conditionally understood as a prudent calculation towards one's neighbour. One must first and foremost be rightly oriented towards an absolute sense of hospitality, namely, one's relation to God if one is to give of oneself in the most generous and charitable way.[49] Therefore, hospitality is enacted through

45 Miskawayh, *Refinement of Character*, 4. [131.21–2], 116.
46 Aristotle, *Nicomachean Ethics* 1167a4; Miskawayh, *Refinement of Character*, 1. [15.6–9], 14, tr. Zurayk.
47 al-Ghazālī, *On the Manners relating to Eating*, 4., 29, tr. Johnson-Davies.
48 al-Ghazālī, *On Disciplining the Soul*, 22.8, 56, tr. Winter.
49 See Zargar, *The Polished Mirror*, 91–101.

a series of practices oriented by bodily renunciation and abstention from dawn until dusk. These practices are aimed to prepare oneself for meeting with God in the guise of the stranger or neighbour. In conjunction with the practices of renunciation, the activities of eating and sharing a meal epitomize companionship and friendship. Al-Ghazālī's *Manners relating to Eating* identifies the guest as an angel sent by the Prophet Muḥammad by an act of divine intercession, 'A house which is not entered by guests is not entered by angels.'[50] This decree to practise hospitality did not after all fall upon deaf ears.

Beginning with *The Incoherence of the Incoherence* (*Tahāfut al-Tahāfut*), Abū al-Walīd Muḥammad ibn Aḥmad Ibn Rushd (1126–98 CE) defends the cosmopolitanism of al-Fārābī and Miskawayh. Ibn Rushd contributed extensively to the interpretation of Aristotle's corpus ranging from short epitomes to great commentaries. His propensity towards jurisprudence (*fiqh*) privileges the conjunction of political association with reverence for divine law (*sharī'a*).[51] Despite the lack of access to the *Politics*, his *Commentary on Plato's* Republic, lost in Arabic but preserved in Hebrew, bears the influence of both Aristotle and al-Fārābī.[52] However, Ibn Rushd importantly departs from Aristotle by claiming that both men and women possess a common nature, 'This being so – and it is clear from the case of the females that they are to share with the males in war and the rest – it is fitting that in choosing them, we seek for those very natures that we sought for in the men and that they should be trained in the same way through music and gymnastic.'[53] This belief that women ought to share in the same end as men attests to the equality attributed to al-Fārābī's democratic city where 'no human being is superior to another in anything at all'.[54] Ibn Rushd affirms the lack of virtue and honour present in the citizens of the democratic city. If not strengthened by virtue and honour, the democratic city risks its own demise. Therefore, the wise leaders of the democratic

[50] al-Ghazālī, *On the Manners relating to Eating*, 4., 30, tr. Johnson-Davies. The philosopher-ruler-*imām* is visited by angels in his or her dreams which itself would involve the same kind of hospitality in such an openness to the divine Other as a guest.

[51] E. I. J. Rosenthal contends that 'Ibn Rushd was a Muslim philosopher first and a disciple of Plato, Aristotle, and their commentators second' (*Political Thought in Medieval Islam*, 177).

[52] Ibn Rushd describes Aristotle's *Politics* as 'the book in which (is contained the perfection of wisdom)' since 'that which is (contained in Plato's *Politea* is not complete)'. Near the beginning of his commentary on the *Republic*, Ibn Rushd states, 'The first part of this art is in Aristotle's book known as the *Nicomachea*, and the second in his book known as the Governance [*Politics*] and also in the book of Plato's that we intend to explain since Aristotle's book on governance has not yet fallen into our hands' (*Averroes on Plato's Republic*, 1. [22.3–6], 4, tr. Lerner).

[53] Ibid., 1. [54.14–18], 59.

[54] al-Fārābī, *Political Regime*, 113. [99.13–14], 86, tr. Butterworth.

city bear the responsibility of ensuring that the citizens become virtuous and honourable. Like al-Fārābī, Ibn Rushd defends the view that the democratic city may become a global community (*ma'mūra*), 'Out of this city will come forth the virtuous city and the other kinds of these cities, because they exist in it potentially since all the states of the soul exist in this city.'[55] Despite the desirability of geographical location, Ibn Rushd acknowledges the possibility of cities which are large enough to be coterminous with entire climate zones if not the entire inhabited world:

> Yet if these communities be of a determined number intended to limit them, then the truth of this ought to be shown by the conformity of this opinion to the natural climates or all the natural people. This is alluded to in the saying of the Lawgiver: 'I have been sent to the Red and the Black.' If this be the [correct] opinion, Plato does not favor it; but it is Aristotle's opinion, and it is the indubitable truth.[56]

In an admission to the realization of this global community, Ibn Rushd's *Decisive Treatise* (*Kitāb Faṣl al-Maqāl*) cites the Prophet Muḥammad if only to valorize the ecumenical mission to promote the expansion of Islam via the practice of philosophy.[57] Assent to the divine law by demonstration, dialectic, and rhetoric is available to all human beings, 'That is because, when this Divine Law of ours called to people by means of these three methods, assent to it was extended to every human being . . . Therefore, he [that is, the Prophet] (peace upon him) was selected to be sent to "the red and black".'[58] His allusion

[55] Ibn Rushd, *Averroes on Plato's Republic*, 3. [93.20–2], 127–8, tr. Lerner.

[56] Ibid., 1. [46.17–19], 46.

[57] 'The process by which philosophy is carried out is ... the concern of humanity as a whole. Both are eternal, and philosophy must always be being enacted in one part of the world or another' (Urvoy, *Ibn Rushd (Averroes)*, 110).

[58] Ibn Rushd, *Decisive Treatise*, 13. [7.2–3], 128, tr. Butterworth.

[59] Ibn Rushd's reference to pursuing the universal mission of Islam, the 'red and the black', even extends to his discussion of the afterlife: 'It seems that the learned person who commits an error with respect to the question is to be excused and the one who hits the mark is to be thanked or rewarded – that is if he acknowledges the existence [of the next life] and gives a manner of interpretation of it not leading to a disavowal of its existence. With respect to this [question], denying its *existence* is what is unbelief, because it is one of the roots of the Law and something to which assent comes about by the three methods shared by the red and black' (ibid., 33. [17.11–19], 134, tr. Butterworth).

to the 'red and black' extends the ecumenical mission of Islam to all human beings and thus decisively expands al-Fārābī's own cosmopolitan vision.[59]

Ibn Rushd's *Middle Commentary on the Nicomachean Ethics* is lost in Arabic but survives in both Hebrew and Latin translations.[60] The completion of the *Middle Commentary* is primarily indebted to Abū 'Amr, who supplied Ibn Rushd with al-Fārābī's commentary on the *Nicomachean Ethics* in ten books.[61] However, the *Middle Commentary*, disseminated to his successors Ibn Bājja, Ibn Ṭufayl, and Maimonides, is eleven books.[62] The additional book, a commentary on *Nicomachean Ethics* VII, may be attributed to Porphyry who cites his animus against Christian scholars (*al-Masīḥiyya*) in a defence of philosophy. Porphyry's authorship is attributed to an alleged distinction drawn between the esoteric and exoteric works of Aristotle:

> i.e. as to the rest of the virtues, we have already spoken of them in the exoteric discourses, where sufficient has been said. For these being common doctrines applying to ethics in general, there are contained in them many excellent doctrines. But perhaps we seek special things more than

[60] See especially Woerther, 'Averroes' Goals in the Paraphrase (Middle Commentary) of Aristotle's *Nicomachean Ethics*'.

[61] Ibn Rushd remarks that he had only four books but later received the complete work from Abū 'Amr; see Berman, 'Ibn Rushd's *Middle Commentary* on the *Nicomachean Ethics* in Medieval Hebrew Literature', 291; 'The Revised Hebrew Translation of Averroes' *Middle Commentary on the Nicomachean Ethics*'; and Harvey and Woerther, 'Averroes' *Middle Commentary* on Book I of the *Nicomachean Ethics*'.

[62] al-Sijistānī, *Muntakhab Ṣiwān al-Ḥikma wa-Thalāth Rasā'il*, 20, §24; Akasoy and Fidora, *The Arabic Version of the* Nicomachean Ethics, 57n228. Akasoy and Fidora conclude that 'it is al-Fārābī who has written the preamble to the *Middle Commentary* on the EN, and he there explains that the number of the Books is shown to be 10 by the fact that each Book ends with the beginning of the next Book ... It was apparently the absence of such connecting words at the beginning and end of the "Seventh Book" and the presence of words connecting Book VI and Book VII (Book VIII of the Arabic) which suggested to al-Fārābī that the "Seventh Book" belonged elsewhere and was not a part of the *Nicomachean Ethics*' (ibid., 54–5). For the controversy regarding the inclusion of the seventh book into the Arabic version, see Gauthier and Jolif, *Aristote. L'èthique à Nicomaque*. Cf. Jaeger, *Aristotle*; and Berti, *La philosophia del 'primo' Aristotele*. For confirmation of the Peripatetic character of the seventh book, see Akasoy and Fidora, *The Arabic Version of the* Nicomachean Ethics, 57.

[63] Akasoy and Fidora, *The Arabic Version of the* Nicomachean Ethics, 57, tr. Dunlop, 8, 3., 58, tr. Dunlop, 8, 4–5: 'i.e. the legislator in all this wished to rectify and to equalize between the person who falls short and the person who has an excess by what the one exceeds and is defective [respectively]. It seems that the Christians in this do not do well and that is ludicrous, for they assert that the person who is beaten with whips has more good. It does not appear so to the legislator, because the person has more evil, which means that they have less [good].'

> concealed things. Someone may say that the reason for that is that we are loved because of honor more than because of philosophy.[63]

Although we cannot confirm the presence of exoteric and esoteric works in the *Corpus Aristotelicum*, Porphyry's reference to seeking 'special things more than concealed things' for 'we are loved because of honor more than because of philosophy' invokes Aristotle, who cites his love of truth more than his love of friends in homage to his teacher, Plato.[64] Given al-Fārābī's purported influence upon Ibn Rushd's composition of the *Middle Commentary on the Rhetoric* (*Talkhīṣ Kitāb al-Khaṭāba*), perhaps Ibn Rushd rather elliptically affirms his debt to Porphyry rather than to his predecessor, al-Fārābī, when addressing Aristotle's distinction between theoretical and practical wisdom.[65] Here we should not discount Ibn Rushd's appropriation of a rhetorical strategy which privileges the necessary correspondence between the practical sciences of ethics, rhetoric, and politics, namely, the opinions of the citizens and the actions of the philosopher-king-*imām*, and the theoretical science of metaphysics. Ibn Rushd explicitly interrogates this distinction between theory and practice insofar as the kinds of speech encountered in both domains come to be conjoined. This paradigm of the political as infused by both rhetoric and philosophy is already at least adumbrated by the Platonic philosopher-king who inhabits both the metaphysical and ethico-political domains. With the figure of the philosopher-king-*imām*, we are confronted with the apparent erasure of the distinction between metaphysics and ethics and hence a reminder of their irreducible unity.[66]

Naṣīr al-Dīn al-Ṭūsī (1201–74 CE), the Persian author of the *Nasirean Ethics* (*Akhlāq-i Nāṣirī*), also develops an account of moral virtue akin to Ibn Rushd's reverence for divine law (*sharī'a*): 'The determiner in every case of the middle point in every case, so that by knowledge thereof the repulsion of (other) things may be effected in equilibrium, is the Divine Law. Thus, in reality, the positor of equality and justice is the Divine Law, for God (exalted

[64] Aristotle, *Nicomachean Ethics* 1096a15–16.

[65] Despite Ibn Rushd's reluctance to acknowledge al-Fārābī as the first philosopher to defend the *kallipolis*, his *Middle Commentary on the Rhetoric* may be said to serve as a substitute for the absence of the *Politics* in the Islamic world. Cf. Ibn Rushd, *Commentaire moyen à la Rhétorique d'Aristote*; and Vagelpohl, 'The *Rhetoric* and *Poetics* in the Islamic World'.

[66] See Baracchi, 'The Shining and the Hidden', 219–20.

[67] al-Ṭūsī, *Nasirean Ethics*, I.2.7, 97, tr. Wickens; Akasoy, 'The Arabic and Islamic Reception of the *Nicomachean Ethics*', 103. Majid Khadduri boldly claims that the *Nasirean Ethics* is widely considered to be the 'best known ethical digest to be composed in medieval Persia, if not all of Islam' (*The Islamic Conception of Justice*, 122).

be mention of Him!) is the source of unity.'[67] Rivalling Miskawayh's *Refinement of Character*, the *Nasirean Ethics* was widely revered throughout medieval Persia. Following in the footsteps of al-Fārābī and Miskawayh, al-Ṭūsī's cosmopolitanism is attributed to his professional acumen as a counsellor to the Mongol conqueror Hūlāgū Khān (1218–65 CE) and the Ismā'īlī governor of Quhistān during the demise of the 'Abbāsid Caliphate. Al-Ṭūsī introduces the principle of equality (*musāwāt*) alongside his definition of justice (*'adālat*), which evidently reflects his Peripatetic inheritance, 'none is more perfect than the virtue of justice, as is obvious in the discipline of ethics (*ṣinā'at-i akhlāq*) for the true midpoint is justice, all else being peripheral to it and taking its reference therefrom.'[68] His ethical writings engaging the *ḥadīth* commentary tradition beginning with what the believer owes to Allāh are expressed primarily by the virtues of justice and generosity, 'It is for this reason, that people love the liberal man more than the just, notwithstanding the fact that the order of the universe depends more on justice than liberality.'[69] Justice is the mean between favour and disdain, 'favour is praiseworthy, but it has no part in justice, for justice is equivalence, while favour is augmentation.'[70] By rejecting the conclusion that favour is blameworthy, al-Ṭūsī contends that favour performs the same role as circumspection (*iḥtiyāṭ*). Whereas Miskawayh distinguishes benevolence as a condition for justice, al-Ṭūsī argues that 'favour cannot be realized without prior observance of the conditions for justice, which first fulfils the obligation of merit (*istiḥqāq*) and then, out of circumspection (*iḥtiyāṭ*), adjoins an augmentation thereto.'[71] Although circumspection enables one to discern the given circumstances of a situation prior to the application of justice and is requisite for attaining order within the city, circumspection may be superseded by love (*maḥabba*) in its comprehensive attention to nobility, virtue, and perfection.

In his third discourse from the *Nasirean Ethics*, al-Ṭūsī further develops the themes of love and friendship. The generality of love is contrasted with the singularity of friendship, 'love is more general than friendship (*az ṣadāqat 'āmm-tar*) for love is conceivable amid a swarming throng, but friendship does not reach this degree of comprehensiveness.'[72] Given his attention to

68 al-Ṭūsī, *Nasirean Ethics*, I.2.7, 95, tr. Wickens. Cf. Aristotle, 'the best man is not he who exercises his virtue toward himself but he who exercises its towards another' (*Nicomachean Ethics* 1130a6).

69 al-Ṭūsī, *Nasirean Ethics*, I.2.7, 105, tr. Wickens.

70 Ibid., I.2.7, 106.

71 Ibid.

72 Ibid., III.2, 197.

the dialectic of unity and multiplicity, the Neoplatonic commentary tradition attributed to Plato's *Symposium* becomes apparent, 'but division into halves is one of the consequences of multiplicity, whereas love is one of the causes of union.'[73] The perfection of both civic and global political association is attained by a synthesis congruent with the organs of the body cooperating with one another. Love is the expression of this natural yearning for synthesis and perfection.[74] The striving for the consummation between love and its object may be applied to society in the case of divine love guided by divine law. The possessor of divine law is granted the duty of 'performing his observance and ceremonies [to] impose respect and veneration for the Religious Law in one's heart producing a speedy response and obedience to the calls of goodness'.[75] Divine law works to ensure happiness within the city by promoting the social bond through devotion to the divine good. This act of religious devotion is perhaps most concretely realized in the pilgrimage (*ḥajj*) to Mecca:

> all the inhabitants of the world have been put under the obligation of combining together, once in a life-time, in one location . . . the intention was, rather, that by making matters easy the inhabitants of distant lands might come together, acquiring some share of that felicity to which the inhabitants of cities and localities have been made receptive, and making a display of that natural fellowship (*uns-i ṭabī'ī*) to be found in their innate disposition (*fiṭrat*).[76]

The pilgrimage sustains a cosmopolitan vision capable of bringing citizens together in global fellowship. Rather than merely rehearsing Aristotelian arguments, al-Fārābī's immediate associates and distant disciples are inspired by a uniquely Peripatetic form of inquiry which calls into question received opinions about the distinction between theory and practice and the relationship between ruler and ruled. In contrast to Platonism and Neoplatonism, which explicitly promote a hierarchical conception of the cosmos and ultimately privilege the rulership of the philosopher-king, the Peripatetic paradigm of human nature presents the possibility that human achievement and

73 Ibid., III.2, 196.

74 'For no individual can reach perfection in isolation, as has been explained. This being so, there is an inescapable need for a synthesis, which will render all individuals, cooperating together, comparable to the organs of one individual. Again, since the human has been created with a natural direction towards perfection, he has a natural yearning for the synthesis in question. This yearning for the synthesis is called Love' (ibid., III.2, 195).

75 Ibid., III.2, 200–1.

76 Ibid., III.2, 200.

excellence are possible not merely for those select individuals who occupy a position of political power but ultimately for all citizens within the political community.

Prophecy and Egalitarianism

Aristotle's eudaimonism is prominent throughout al-Fārābī's *Attainment of Happiness* and contributes extensively to both the formation and development of his cosmopolitan paradigm.[77] Moreover, eudaimonism as an ethical and political principle presupposes an equality among all peoples which is potentially more inclusive than the conception of political community proposed by Platonism and Neoplatonism. In contrast to Plato's city in speech which is exclusively determined by the education of the philosopher-king as the sovereign political authority, Aristotle's eudaimonism demonstrates an inherent egalitarian character by privileging the development of the rational capacities and dispositions of individual citizens. Here the philosopher-ruler-*imām* aims to enquire into different classes of society for the sake of developing a regimen of common education which applies to every group within every nation:

> Then one [the supreme ruler] should inquire next into the different classes of nations by inquiring into every nation and into the human states of character and the acts for which all nations are equipped by that nature which is common to them, until one comes to inquire into all or most nations. One should inquire into that in which all nations share – that is, the *human nature* common to them – and then into all the things that pertain specifically to every group within every nation. One should discern all of these, draw up an actual – if approximate – list of the acts

[77] For a discussion of the ethical perfection of the citizen in al-Fārābī's political community, see Daiber, *Islamic Thought in the Dialogue of Cultures*, 73–5.

[78] al-Fārābī, *Attainment of Happiness*, 45. [34.12–15], 39, tr. Mahdi (mod.). The distinctive emphasis upon human nature common to all citizens of nations is to be contrasted with the innate disposition of the philosopher-ruler-*imām*: 'Moreover, one should be brought up according to the laws and habits that resemble their innate disposition. One should have sound conviction about the opinions of the religion in which one is reared, hold fast to the virtuous acts in his religion, and not forsake all or most of them. Furthermore, one should hold fast to the generally accepted virtues and not forsake the generally accepted noble acts. For if a youth is such, and then sets out to study philosophy and learns it, it is possible that they will not become a counterfeit or a vain or a false philosopher' (ibid., 60. [45.5–45.11], 48, tr. Mahdi, mod.).

> and the states of character with which every nation can be set aright and guided toward happiness and specify the classes of persuasive arguments (regarding both the theoretical and practical virtues) that ought to be employed among them.[78]

Since ethical principles are oriented towards the cultivation of virtues for every individual citizen who strives to attain them, the primary condition for the cultivation of virtues is the exercise of rationality among the individual citizens of the political community. In contrast to this egalitarian eudaimonism, Neoplatonism promotes a hierarchical conception of political community exemplified by the Active Intellect which interacts with the philosopher-ruler-*imām* in both waking and dream states for the sake of discerning present and future events portending benefits or harms to the citizens of a given political community.

Prophetism is identified with a strong aversion to egalitarianism promoting any kind of common human nature.[79] Among al-Fārābī's predecessors, Abū Bakr al-Rāzī (Rhazes) in his *Proofs of Prophecy* (*A'lām al-Nubuwwa*) stridently argues that all persons are equal in intellect, will, and natural talent against the Ismā'īlī scholar Abū Ḥātim al-Rāzī, who defends the primacy of the prophet:

> I said: People are equal in intellect, will, and natural talent, or are they not?
>
> He said: (Rhazes): If they study and keep themselves active, then yes, they are equal in will and intellect.
>
> I said: To say this is to deny the evidence. On the contrary, we see and find every day that people are divided into categories. . . . No one can learn without a master, everyone needs a leader. No can deny this without denying the evidence. Thus it is necessary that there is a hierarchy (*tafāḍul*) among people . . . If therefore, it is so, there is nothing strange about the fact that God chose one people, choosing His prophets from among them, ennobling them with His revelation, in order that they should teach to other people that which they could not otherwise know, that which will lead them to what is best for them in matters of religion and in the world, giving apposite laws.[80]

[79] See Daiber, 'The Ismailite Background of Fārābī's Political Philosophy'.

[80] al-Rāzī, *A'lām al-Nubūwwa (The Proofs of Prophecy)*, tr. Khalidi (mod.), 3.11–13. Cf. Bausani, *Un filosofo laico del Medioevo musulmano*, 47–9; and Campanini, *An Introduction to Islamic Philosophy*, 55.

Despite the innate aptitude of certain individuals to become philosopher-kings, all individual citizens are born with the aptitude to learn and thereby exercise their power of imagination. Therefore, one must determine to what extent the cultivation of the imagination contributes to the development of intellectual and moral virtues. The imagination as an intermediary between sense-perception and intellect is a powerful tool of persuasion producing images for the sake of common assent. The imagination unites the ruler as philosopher and *imām* with the citizens through the common bond of religion, 'They are the person who knows every action by which felicity can be reached. This is the first condition for being a ruler. Moreover, they should be a good orator and able to rouse [other people's] imagination by well-chosen words. They should be able to lead people well along the right path to felicity and to the actions by which felicity is reached.'[81] Religion communicates images and symbols for the sake of preserving unity within the political community. Therefore, religion serves a distinctive political purpose when conjoined with speech and rhetoric.

Al-Fārābī endorses civic religion for the sake of attaining virtue in the political community. His *Book of Letters* defines religion as that which 'aims simply to instruct the multitude in theoretical and practical matters . . . by persuasion or imaginative representation'.[82] Given his recourse to harmonizing Plato and Aristotle, it is not surprising that religion serves an explicit pedagogical purpose to instruct the citizens of the political community. In contrast to the philosophical arts of logic and dialectic which aim at certainty and therefore perform a unitary function by placing all singularities under the hegemonic principle of the One, religion is an act of dissemination whereby the One becomes the multiple by its transmission into various images and symbols to the multitude. Through the mediation of demonstrative truths, the role of the philosopher is inseparable from the dissemination of *logos* into the world.

If philosophy is universal and hence concerned with absolute and global truths, then religion is particular in its various iterations by appealing to the individual or the multitude within a prescribed community. Only specific images and symbols will accommodate the multitude in the quest to understand the truth. The multitude are to be taught and trained with images and

[81] al-Fārābī, *On the Perfect State*, V, 15, §9, 246–7, tr. Walzer (mod.).

[82] al-Fārābī, *Book of Letters*, 108., 1, tr. Khalidi. Cf. Mian, 'Muslim Political Philosophy and the Affective Turn'.

[83] For the pedagogical power of music to transmit images and symbols, see Druart, 'What Does Music Have to Do with Language, Logic and Rulership?'.

symbols before preceding to concepts and ideas. The transmission and hence expression of images and symbols are communicated by the arts of rhetoric, poetry, music, memorization, linguistics, and writing.[83] However, the source of such unity remains the power of religion which provokes the multitude to attain happiness, 'Through religion, the multitude are taught, educated, and given all that is needed to attain happiness.'[84] Religion requires the existence of a lawgiver or prophet and hence only becomes an expression of philosophical truth insofar as the prophet is able to successfully safeguard and disseminate that truth. In contrast to religion, which arises wholly out of convention for the sake of the city, philosophy arises by nature and requires the influence of a transcendent authority, namely, the Active Intellect, to instantiate its presence in the individual person. One must already be innately predisposed to receive philosophical truths by having trained their intellect and imagination in anticipation of such a revelation. Revelation is thereby to be situated on the side of philosophy and the philosopher who only assumes a religious role by the transmission of revelation to the multitude.[85] Therefore, the validity of religion is wholly dependent upon the rational perfection of the philosopher to receive divine messages from the Active Intellect.

Given Aristotle's omission of any kind of revealed religion which would purportedly transcend the territorial and geographical limits of the city, we shall instead shift our attention to the ethical comportment of the philosopher-ruler-*imām* who promotes the attainment of virtue by communicating these intelligibles as images and symbols to the citizens of the political community.[86] The ethical comportment of the philosopher-ruler-*imām* 'investigates these intellectual principles and the acts and states of character with which the human being labours toward this perfection. From this in turn emerges, the science of the human being and political science.'[87] Despite the lack of availability of Aristotle's *Politics*, al-Fārābī's harmonisation of the *Republic* and *Laws* with the *Nicomachean Ethics* adopts a uniquely Peripatetic rhetorical strategy which stridently promotes the

[84] al-Fārābī, *Book of Letters*, 144., 19, tr. Khalidi.

[85] Aristotle's *On Sleep and Dreams* (*De Somnis*) is especially pertinent to the convergence between Aristotle's psychology and Shī'ite theology. At the level of dreams, al-Fārābī retrieves the conjunction between the intellect and the imagination from *De Anima* and *Rhetoric* which shall be explored in my concluding chapter.

[86] See Mor Segev, *Aristotle on Religion*, 49–85.

[87] al-Fārābī, *Attainment of Happiness*, 18. [14.15–17], 23, tr. Mahdi.

eudaimonism of a global community. Here the possibility is broached that those virtues which originate from the philosopher-ruler-*imām* may transcend their relative locality to be practised by citizens of various cities on a global scale, 'It consists of knowing the things by which the citizens of cities attain happiness through political association in the measure that innate disposition equips each of them for it.'[88] As the 'Second Teacher' (*al-mu'allim al-thānī*), al-Fārābī's Aristotelianism marks a decisive turning point for the inception of cosmopolitanism and its subsequent reception among his immediate successors and distant disciples.[89]

[88] Ibid., 20. [16.4–6], 24, tr. Mahdi (mod.).

[89] Al-Fārābī's *Letter* enumerating Aristotle's treatises is cited by Qāḍī Ṣā'id, *Book of the Categories of the Nations* (*Kitāb Ṭabaqāt al-Umam*), 25–6, tr. Blachère, 66. Al-Fārābī and Qāḍī Ṣā'id present their accounts of the seven ancient schools of philosophy according to one of the most important Nestorian Christian translators, Ḥunayn ibn Isḥāq. See Akasoy and Fidora, *The Arabic Version of the* Nicomachean Ethics, 34n140. Cf. Westerink, *Anonymous Prolegomena to Platonic Philosophy*, xxv; and Ibn Bājja, *Rasā'il Ibn Bājja al-Ilāhiyya*, 41–2. Multiple excerpts from Ibn Bājja confirm the influence of *Eudemian Ethics*. The *Eudemian Ethics* and the *Magna Moralia* came to be known through al-Fārābī's lost commentary on the *Nicomachean Ethics* as cited by Ibn Bājja in *Rasā'il Ibn Bājja al-Ilāhiyya* and Ibn Ṭufayl in *Ḥayy ibn Yaqẓān*; see Akasoy, 'The Arabic and Islamic Reception of the *Nicomachean Ethics*', 103.

3
Civic Virtues

Friendship in Plato and Aristotle

Beginning with the *Timaeus*, lost in Greek but preserved in Arabic translation, the conception of the cosmos as a self-governing unity is integral to the cosmopolitan heritage of Islam. The fertile integration of Platonic cosmology with Aristotelian metaphysics and Islamic theology culminating in the *Theology of Aristotle* is indebted to a re-ordering of the traditional relationship between the ethical and metaphysical domains. The *Nicomachean Ethics* was subsequently interpreted as a culmination of the *Metaphysics* insofar as the moral virtues orient the investigation into first principles. Ethical comportment thus serves as a *sine qua non* condition for metaphysical inquiry. This alleged unity between ethics and metaphysics is accompanied by a reconceptualisation of the cosmos which makes possible the attainment of virtue on a global scale. Both the Platonic and Aristotelian traditions illuminate the interdependence between ethics and politics by situating the human being in a cosmos in which they are neither central nor prominent.[1] It is precisely the intersection between ethics and politics which shall be explored as we reflect upon the nature of the relationship between cosmopolitanism and friendship.

[1] Al-Fārābī's *Harmonisation* is remarkable for the degree of syncretism established between the Platonic and Aristotelian corpus, especially the common and controversial account of divine causation, 'He has also explained there the issue of causes - how many they are - and affirmed the efficient cause. And he has also explained there the issue of the bringer into being and the mover, and that it is other than the brought into being and the moved. And just as Plato, in his book known as *Timaeus*, has explained that whatever is brought into being is brought into being only by a cause necessarily bringing into being and that what is brought into being is not a cause of its own being, so has Aristotle explained in the *Theology* that the one exists in every multiplicity, because any multiplicity in which the one does not exist would never end' (*Harmonisation*, 56. [16b11-16], 155-6, tr. Butterworth).

We shall retrieve the *Timaeus* creation myth to envision this unity between ethics and politics. This myth is conspicuously situated within another myth recounted in the narrative context of the four speakers: Socrates, Hermocrates, Critias, and Timaeus. Plato sets the scene at the onset of the dialogue as a meeting between friends. However, the circumstance of their friendship is circumscribed by trepidation, especially if we are to recall that Hermocrates was a Syracusan general who vanquished the Athenians when they ventured into Sicily and was effectively a *persona non grata*. The practice of friendship between the four speakers mirrors the *ēthos* of hospitality whereby even a public enemy is welcomed as a friend. Both cosmos and friendship come to be conjoined in the bond of hospitality.

It is not surprising that the Indo-European linguist Émile Benveniste comments on the archaic language of friendship as designated by a complexity of habits and behaviours related to welcoming the stranger and thereby informed by an implicit political dimension.[2] Political friendship or 'civic friendship' resonates quite peculiarly with Plato where the question of the cosmos and the place of the city within the cosmos, namely, a political community held together by friendship, is raised anew. These incipient gestures towards hospitality and friendship only further prepare the ground for Aristotle's introduction of civic friendship which 'seems to hold together a polis, and legislators seem to pay more attention to friendship than to justice'.[3] Such a gesture beyond justice rather curiously invokes a community of friends constituted not by intimacy and familiarity, but literally by the nascent friendship which arises between the meeting of those unfamiliar to us. The friendship conceived in both the Platonic and Aristotelian heritage is a friendship among strangers to recall Socrates' recounting of the Myth of Er, 'I am an erring star, a star with unpredictable movements, and wander in the company of men like me.'[4] Our understanding of cosmopolitanism as hospitality and hence the welcoming of the other as a stranger is itself sustained by the mutual recognition of this errancy. We find ourselves wandering and inhabiting this planetary life together. Friendship is thus sparked by an errant meeting, accident, collision, contingency, and unpredictability, to recount the remarkable convergence of the four speakers. With a view to such strangeness, we might begin to glimpse

2 Benveniste, *Dictionary of Indo-European Concepts and Society*, 273–88.

3 Aristotle, *Nicomachean Ethics* 1155a22. This holding together of the political community is characterised by a dynamic elasticity synonymous with the practice of friendship.

4 Plato, *Republic* 614b–c. Socrates, who ventures outside the city walls in the *Phaedrus*, a dialogue pre-eminently concerned with friendship, portends Aristotle's remarks about travel, 'Even in travels one can see the extent to which every human is near and dear to one another' (Aristotle, *Nicomachean Ethics* 1155a21–2).

how the virtue of friendship gradually extends beyond the boundaries of relative intimacy and familiarity to the composition of the political community.

Beginning with those virtues identified with civic friendship, we shall now turn to al-Fārābī's *Aphorisms of the Statesman* to investigate the prospective contributions of benevolence and concord to the flourishing of the political community.[5] The structure of *Aphorisms of the Statesman* diverges from the *Political Regime* and *Virtuous City* by eliding the traditional Neoplatonic scheme of emanation for the sake of introducing a series of analogies between soul and body attributed to Plato and Aristotle. The physician must know how to attain excellence for the body just as the statesman must know to attain excellence for the soul:

> Just as the health of the body is an equilibrium of its temperament and its sickness is a deviation from equilibrium, so, too, are the health of the city and its uprightness an equilibrium of the moral habits of its inhabitants and its sickness a disparity found in their moral habits. When the body deviates from equilibrium in its temperament, the one who brings it back to equilibrium and preserves it there is the physician. So, too, when the city deviates from the equilibrium with respect to the moral habits of the inhabitants, the one who brings it back to uprightness and preserves it there is the statesman.[6]

[5] Here we shall retain the convenient title suggested by Douglas M. Dunlop as *Aphorisms of the Statesman* (*Fuṣūl al-Madanī*), to highlight the role of the central figure of the political community. The title 'Statesman' should not be confused with Plato's dialogue of the same name and does not bear any discernible influence upon its composition; see al-Fārābī, *Fuṣūl al-Madanī*, 9. Dunlop subsequently observes that *Aphorisms of the Statesman* is purportedly divided into ninety-five sections (*fuṣūl*) in the present Arabic text (11). I shall cite the editions edited by Dunlop and Butterworth with modifications to both translations.

[6] al-Fārābī, *Selected Aphorisms*, 3. [24.9–17], 12, tr. Butterworth. Cf. al-Fārābī, *Aphorisms of the Statesman*, 4., 28, 105, tr. Dunlop. The opening of the treatise explicitly invokes the excellence of the soul in *Nicomachean Ethics* I.13 where Aristotle encourages the statesman to study the soul for the sake of attaining virtue. Just as the physician cures the body, the statesman restores the health of the political community, 'Clearly, it is human virtue that we should be examining, for what we are seeking, too, was the good and happiness for man; and by 'human virtue', we mean not that of the body but that of the soul, for it is of the soul too, that happiness is stated by us to be an activity. If such be the case, it is clear that the statesman should understand in some way the attributes of the soul, like the doctor who attends to the eyes or the whole body, and to the degree that the politics is more honorable and better than medical science. Now the cultivated among the doctors take the trouble to learn many things about the body. So the statesman, too, should be investigating attributes of the soul, both for the sake of these and as much as is adequate to what is sought, for greater precision is perhaps rather burdensome in view of what he is aiming at' (*Nicomachean Ethics* 1102a14–26).

The statesman is responsible for restoring the health of the political body. The restorative function of the statesman implies that most cities are generally in a state of disrepair and demise and have fallen away from any healthy state of equilibrium. By retrieving *Nicomachean Ethics* 1102a14–26 where the art of medicine and art of politics perform a therapeutic function, al-Fārābī similarly concludes that politics is more honourable than medicine because it concerns the study of the soul which contributes directly to the flourishing of the political community. However, the degree of precision and refinement attained by medicine with regard to the knowledge of the body cannot be reached with the study of the soul since the latter like politics admits of a certain imprecision. The imprecise nature of the study of the soul and the art of politics may be attributed to the variation which exists among individuals and between cities. Therefore, an intermediate or mean is subsequently introduced to account for these relevant differences:

> The one who extrapolates and infers what is intermediate and equilibrated with respect to nutriments and medicaments, however it occurs, is the physician. The art by which one extrapolates that is medicine. The one who infers what is intermediate and equilibrated with respect to moral habits and actions is the governor of cities and the king. The art by which one extrapolates that is the political art and the kingly craft.[7]

The extrapolation and inference from the intermediate is determined according to what is best for those from a certain region and at a specific time. Al-Fārābī distinguishes between households and cities as units of economic and political order and geographical dwellings which vary according to region for the sake of investigating how different kinds of dwellings cultivate divergent moral habits contributing to either virtue or vice, 'Dwellings may engender different morals in their inhabitants. For example, dwellings of hair and leather in the desert engender in their inhabitants the states of character of alertness and resoluteness. Sometimes the matter intensifies to the point that courage and boldness are engendered.'[8] Since different kinds of dwellings avail themselves to a range of virtues, some dwellings may influence the origin and cultivation of various kinds of friendship. Friendship first arises between members of the household, namely, the husband and the wife, the father and the child, the lord and the slave:

[7] al-Fārābī, *Selected Aphorisms*, 21. [39.15–20], 22, tr. Butterworth. Cf. al-Fārābī, *Aphorisms of the Statesman*, 19., 36, 116, tr. Dunlop.

[8] al-Fārābī, *Selected Aphorisms*, 23. [40.6–10], 23, tr. Butterworth. Cf. al-Fārābī, *Aphorisms of the Statesman*, 21., 36–7, 116–17, tr. Dunlop.

> The one who governs these parts and partnerships, brings some into concord with others, and ties each to the other so that from all of them there is a partnership with respect to actions and a mutual assistance in perfecting a single purpose and in completing the prosperity of the household through good things and preserving them for the members is the lord of the household and its governor.[9]

Friendship cannot come into existence in the household without the presence of a lord or governor who initiates these partnerships. Whereas the rational faculty presides over the non-rational faculties, and the soul presides over the body, the lord or governor presides over the household. A series of analogies are developed beginning with the relationship between the various parts of the body.[10] The different parts of the body and their capacity to work in unison are compared to the members of the city who come together to perfect the purpose of the city. In both cases, a partnership between the various parts is required for the parts to work on behalf of the whole.[11] This relationship is expanded to include how the parts of the city interact with one another by contrasting the necessary city with the virtuous city:

> The city may be necessary and may be virtuous. The necessary city is the one whose parts mutually assist one another in obtaining only what is necessary for a human being's constitution, subsistence, and preservation of life. The virtuous city is the one whose inhabitants mutually assist one another in obtaining the best things for a human being's existence, constitution, subsistence, and preservation of life.[12]

[9] al-Fārābī, *Selected Aphorisms*, 24. [40.19–20–41.1–5], 23, tr. Butterworth (mod.). Cf. al-Fārābī, *Aphorisms of the Statesman*, 21., 36–7, 116–17, tr. Dunlop.

[10] 'Both the city and household have an analogy with the body of the human being. The body is composed of different parts of a definite number, some better and some baser, adjacent to one another in rank, each doing a certain action, so that from all their actions they come together in mutual assistance to perfect the purpose of the human being's body' (al-Fārābī, *Selected Aphorisms*, 24. [41.6–10], 23, tr. Butterworth. Cf. al-Fārābī, *Aphorisms of the Statesman*, 21., 36–7, 116–17, tr. Dunlop).

[11] Cf. *Nicomachean Ethics* 1102a5–1103a4 where Aristotle gestures to the relationship between the rational part and the non-rational parts of the soul as a kind of partnership which is dependent upon their collaboration for the sake of a common purpose.

[12] al-Fārābī, *Selected Aphorisms*, 28. [45.1–5], 25, tr. Butterworth. Cf. al-Fārābī, *Aphorisms of the Statesman*, 25., 39, 120, tr. Dunlop.

Here the contrast between the necessary city and the virtuous city echoes the distinction between the city of necessity and city in speech in *Republic* II.[13] Such a contrast is important for the formation of friendship. The necessary city is where all the basic requisites of the citizens are met. However, the necessary city crucially omits a concern for what is best for the existence of the citizens. This mutual cooperation of the citizens to obtain the best possible existence in relation to the composition of the virtuous city requires the introduction of philosophy and hence the rule of a philosopher-king. Although the role of the Platonic philosopher-king is not explicitly addressed, the king or governor of the city is akin to the lord of the household insofar as the intention of the king is to rule in the most benevolent manner to effect flourishing and happiness in the city:

> The king in truth is the one whose purpose and intention concerning the art by which they govern cities are to provide themselves and the rest of the inhabitants of the city true happiness. This is the goal and the purpose of the kingly craft. It necessarily follows that the king of the virtuous city be the most perfect among the inhabitants of the city in happiness since he is the reason for their being happy.[14]

The king of the city is compared to a physician who must bring his patients to health. Since the health of the city is tied to the happiness of the city, the physician must exercise his craft regardless of whether or not they are recognised by the city, 'So, too, the physician is a physician by means of the medical craft – whether they are recognized (*'arafa*) by the people for it or not.'[15] Despite the service of the king to the political community, the king may not be recognised by the citizens if he lacks honour and hence proper dominion. The authority of the king is not derived from an innate sovereignty as much as an ability to use the kingly craft in such a way which benefits the citizens. Like the demiurge who literally labours on behalf of the people by exercising his craft to bring the cosmos into order, the sovereignty of the king is dependent upon a certain relationship to his citizens which hinges upon earned recognition. Al-Fārābī's *Attainment of Happiness* also broaches this question of recognising the sovereignty of the philosopher-ruler-*imām*:

[13] Plato, *Republic* 369c.

[14] al-Fārābī, *Selected Aphorisms*, 30. [47.11–15], 27, tr. Butterworth (mod.). Cf. al-Fārābī, *Aphorisms of the Statesman*, 27., 40, 122, tr. Dunlop.

[15] al-Fārābī, *Selected Aphorisms*, 32. [49.8–9], 28, tr. Butterworth (mod.). Cf. al-Fārābī, *Aphorisms of the Statesman*, 29., 41–2, 123–4, tr. Dunlop.

> Therefore, the prince or the *imām* is the prince or *imām* by virtue of their skill and art, regardless of whether or not anyone acknowledges them, whether or not they are obeyed, whether or not they are supported in their purpose by any group . . . [N]either the imamate of the *imām*, the philosophy of the philosopher, nor the princeship of the prince is done away with by their not having tools to use in their activities or others to employ in reaching their purpose.[16]

The relative utility of the king, prince, or *imām* as civil servants supersedes the possibility of civic recognition insofar as all the attributes of leadership are embodied and hence oriented to fulfilling the happiness of the citizens. In *Aphorisms of the Statesman*, al-Fārābī concedes to the relative difficulty, if not impossibility, of such a task. The kingship in truth or the perfect king thus seems to exist only as a theoretical paradigm to be emulated rather than as a concrete model to be implemented. The qualities of the perfect king or perfect ruler are presented in six stipulations which may come together in one person or be dispersed among multiple persons, 'wisdom, complete prudence, excellent persuasion, excellent imaginative evocation, bodily capacity for struggle, and having nothing in their body that prevents them from carrying out the things pertaining to struggle'.[17] Perhaps this shift from a traditional kingship to collective governance alludes to the Nocturnal Council of the *Laws*:

> But they do exist dispersed among a group, so that one of them gives the goal, the second gives what leads to the goal, the third has excellent persuasion and excellent imaginative evocation, and another the capability for struggle. So this group all together takes the place of the king, and they are called superior rulers and the possessors of virtues (*al-faḍā'il*). Their rulership is called the rulership of the virtuous.[18]

16 al-Fārābī, *Attainment of Happiness*, 62. [46.15-20-47.1-4], 49, tr. Mahdi (mod.). Cf. Baracchi ('The Shining and the Hidden', 232), 'Just as philosophy may be experienced in this distorted and diminished way, so, conversely, it may happen that a most evolved member of the communal organism remain unacknowledged - and even be ostracized. He might be a prince, could wisely lead others in the ways of happiness, and yet it may be said that "no use is made of him". The city bears its own *arkhe*, its own ruling principle in its midst, yet cannot recognize it.'

17 al-Fārābī, *Selected Aphorisms*, 58. [66.3-5], 37, tr. Butterworth (mod.). Cf. al-Fārābī, *Aphorisms of the Statesman*, 54., 50, 134, tr. Dunlop.

18 al-Fārābī, *Selected Aphorisms*, 58. [66.15-20-67.1], 37-8, tr. Butterworth. Cf. al-Fārābī, *Aphorisms of the Statesman*, 54., 50, 134, tr. Dunlop. Cf. Strauss, 'Some Remarks on the Political Science of Maimonides and Farabi'.

Such a rulership of the virtuous arises when the rulers work in concert with one another to promote the happiness of the political community. Their concord (*i'tilāf*) presupposes that they are bound together by love not merely because they partake in virtue but for the sake of what brings the most utility and pleasure to the citizens. Following Aristotle's definition of the human qua political animal as innately disposed to seek shelter and to dwell in the neighbourhood of others, *Aphorisms of the Statesman* distinguishes between different kinds of civic dispositions, including a kind of love (*maḥabba*) directed towards the good of fellow citizens.[19] In contrast to a non-volitional kind of love associated with familial kinship, civic love as an expression of benevolence (*tafaḍḍul)* unites the citizens of the virtuous city so they are in concord with one another. Benevolence is a prerequisite for the cultivation of friendship and concord within the virtuous city. By tracing the structural affinities between benevolence, friendship, and concord in relation to the *Nicomachean Ethics*, *Eudemian Ethics*, and *Magna Moralia*, the civic virtues effectively contribute to the attainment of happiness in the political community. This aspiration for human perfection first originates at the level of intimate relationships through shared doctrines and rituals via religion before extending to the political community writ large.

Benevolence and Civic Friendship

Aristotle describes benevolence as the condition for both friendship and concord to most fully manifest themselves.[20] Benevolence may arise by nature, like the love of parents for a child, but may also arise by volition. In this sense, the constitution of benevolence is aporetic insofar as it cannot exclusively be identified with either nature or choice.[21] If benevolence arises by nature, then this inherent tendency towards generation and corruption only serves to expose its fragile and tenuous nature as the origin of friendship and political community. Hence, benevolence may either remain latent as 'inoperative friendship' where friendship fails to arise or fully mature into 'operative

[19] Aristotle, *Politics* 1253a15.

[20] Moral accounts of benevolence range from Mill's utilitarian requirement to be strictly impartial as a disinterested spectator to the sentimentalism of Hume, who claims that benevolence is most worthy of all social virtues, and Kant, who identifies benevolence with the rationality of the good will. Likewise, Emmanuel Levinas identifies benevolence as the foundation for justice; see Poirié, *Emmanuel Levinas (Qui êtes-vous?)*, 103; and Llewelyn, *The Middle Voice of Ecological Conscience*, 280n23.

[21] Aristotle, *Nicomachean Ethics* 1106a15–24. Virtue is always inflected by a given disposition and hence how one finds oneself always already situated by the presence of certain emotions.

friendship'. Aristotle necessarily admits that benevolence is capable of suffering from a certain kind of alteration in the retention of this ambivalence between inoperative and operative friendship. Since benevolence contributes to the development of moral character, benevolence becomes most pronounced as the origin of a specific kind of friendship, namely political friendship, identified with the constitution of the political community.[22]

In *Aphorisms of the Statesman*, al-Fārābī identifies benevolence as a disposition which preserves the political community by making possible the application of justice, 'justice follows upon love'.[23] The mutual reciprocity between benevolence and concord gestures to the expansion of friendship into the political domain.[24] Despite the supreme importance accorded to benevolence for the generation of political friendship and the cultivation of concord among the citizens of political community, benevolence always retains the possibility of its own in-operativity insofar as it is conditioned by shared virtues, opinions, and actions. The cultivation of benevolence within any given political community hinges upon the enactment of shared opinions, 'When the opinions of the inhabitants of the city are in agreement with these things and that then is perfected actions through which happiness is gained for some with others, that is necessarily followed by the love of some for others.'[25] The fickle nature of benevolence effectively leads to a secondary question regarding whether benevolence can be expanded beyond mere neighbours. If we are to imagine the possibility of a cosmopolitanism arising from benevolence, then any differences of opinion which reside within a political community are effectively elided for the sake of sharing a common agreement about the divine source of sovereignty. Whereas Aristotle establishes the Unmoved Mover as the first principle of his natural teleology, al-Fārābī demonstrates that any agreement of opinion must initially proceed from a prior agreement regarding divine providence:

> Agreement of opinion about the beginning is agreement of their opinions about God, may he be exalted, about the spiritual beings, and about the

[22] Hence, benevolence may develop into civic or political friendship rather than proper friendship identified as a friendship between intimates.

[23] al-Fārābī, *Selected Aphorisms*, 61. [70.12], 40, tr. Butterworth. Cf. al-Fārābī, *Aphorisms of the Statesman*, 57., 53, 140–1, tr. Dunlop.

[24] 'With inoperative friendship, benevolence becomes reciprocal to concord by planning for the common good, concord (*homonoia*) operates not in what we think and believe, but in what we plan to do' (Aristotle, *Magna Moralia* 1212a18–19). Cf. *Nicomachean Ethics* 1167b2; *Eudemian Ethics* 1241a33.

[25] al-Fārābī, *Selected Aphorisms*, 61. [71.4–7], 40, tr. Butterworth. Cf. al-Fārābī, *Aphorisms of the Statesman*, 57., 53, 140–1, tr. Dunlop.

> devout who are the standard; how the world and its parts began, how human began to come about; then the ranks of the parts of the world, the link of some to others, and their level with respect to God - may he be exalted - and to the spiritual beings; then the level of human beings with respect to God and to the spiritual beings. So this is the beginning. The end is happiness. What is between the two is the actions through which happiness is gained.[26]

Divine providence obliges common obedience among all citizens. However, a certain incommensurable difference is necessarily retained between agreements of opinion about a past good derived from theological and metaphysical speculation and agreements of opinion about a future good derived from practical action.[27] This exposition of the relative conditions of benevolence is undoubtedly informed by Aristotle's own admission that friendship requires (1) feeling benevolence for each other, that is, wishing each other's good, (2) mutual recognition whereby each feels benevolence for the other, and (3) the cause of benevolence must be the reason why people are friends; for example, for the sake of goodness or pleasure or usefulness.[28] Benevolence as the origin of friendship is the limit from which friendship begins to unfold.[29] Friendship implies a continuous negotiation of benevolence and thus never remains concretely settled. Therefore, friendship cannot be strictly comprehended as complete activity insofar as it always remains in excess of itself. This intimate experience of friendship remains an altogether finite and rare phenomenon.

Both Aristotle and al-Fārābī mutually recognise the liminal status of friendship by first turning to the irreplaceable singularity of perfect friendship as

[26] al-Fārābī, *Selected Aphorisms*, 61. [70.15–25], 40, tr. Butterworth. Cf. al-Fārābī, *Aphorisms of the Statesman*, 57., 53, 140–1, tr. Dunlop.

[27] See Pogge, 'Cosmopolitanism and Sovereignty', 48–9. This provisional turn to deliberate about a future good is reminiscent of Aristotle's definition of the human being as a political animal aiming to make clear 'what is advantageous and disadvantageous' (*Politics* 1253a15).

[28] Aristotle, *Nicomachean Ethics* 1156a3–5. Peter Hadreas argues that benevolence should be understood in cognitive rather than volitional terms, 'Taking the lead from the etymology, let us assume an understanding of εὔνοια that is not volition-based, but rather cognition-based. It follows from the cognition model of εὔνοια that is allogenic, i.e., arises from a cognition or judgment made of another, whereas on the volition model, εὔνοια would be autogenic, i.e., deriving from our own choices or dispositions' ('εὔνοια: Aristotle on the Beginning of Friendship', 397). Contra Hadreas, I shall argue for the retention of the volitional and cognitive models of benevolence as constituting the activities of wishing and thinking well of another person.

[29] See Aristotle, *Physics* 212a7.

sharing in virtue or goodness against the generic utility of political friendship. Benevolence may either come to be enacted or remain latent at this pivotal juncture between the singularity of perfect friendship and the universality of political friendship. Al-Fārābī aptly characterises all natural dispositions as constituted by a natural ambivalence to either develop or not develop into a requisite virtue, 'But when there is a natural disposition for virtuous actions and those actions are repeated, a trait is established in the soul, and those very actions issue forth from it, then the trait established by custom is what is said to be a virtue.'[30] If the manifestation of benevolence is an expression of the lived experience of friendship as a virtue, what is withheld in its in-operativity if benevolence as Aristotle states is 'nothing other than inoperative friendship'?[31] This admission of the transition from inoperative to operative friendship demonstrates how benevolence is capable of being altered and hence changed to generate friendship.[32] Since benevolence is identified as a natural and hence affective disposition, benevolence may potentially constitute the beginning of friendship as its primary cause.[33] Therefore, benevolence is wholly dependent upon how it suddenly becomes enacted in this initial experience which may lead either to its preservation or destruction.[34] Benevolence is marked by a sudden change or transformation between spectators who see excellence displayed in an athletic contest and then momentarily wish that the competitors are successful, 'moreover, while loving requires familiarity, benevolence can also arise

[30] al-Fārābī, *Selected Aphorisms*, 10. [31.12–15], 17, tr. Butterworth. Cf. al-Fārābī, *Aphorisms of the Statesman*, 9., 31–2, 109–10, tr. Dunlop.

[31] Aristotle, *Nicomachean Ethics* 1167a12. Benevolence is always inscribed by the generation and of corruption of friendship.

[32] See Aristotle, *Metaphysics* 1046a10–11.

[33] The inception of benevolence may be attributed to Aristotle's definition of affection, 'Affection means in one sense a quality in virtue of which a thing can be altered, such as white and black, or sweet and bitter, or heaviness and lightness, or whatever else is of this sort. And in another sense, it means the actualizations and the alterations of these. Of the latter, it implies especially harmful alterations and motions, and of these most of all those which are painful. Also, misfortunes and pains of considerable magnitude are called affects' (*Metaphysics* 1022b15–22). The disposition of benevolence which affects the spectator is accompanied by a superficial and momentary pleasure. Arguably, benevolence in a general sense could be coextensive with those affects accompanied by pleasure in *Rhetoric* II.2 where Aristotle remarks that 'benevolence and friendship need to be spoken about in the discussion of the affects' (1378a18–19). In a narrow sense, we might also draw a possible parallel between benevolence and charity. Aristotle describes charity as a favor between one person and another (1381b5). Beyond reciprocity, charity implies a certain kind of solidarity that might not necessarily imply direct or intimate involvement with the other person (1133a3–6).

[34] See Aristotle, *Physics* 201b32–4.

in a moment, as it arises i.e., in spectators for contestants.'[35] When benevolence is momentarily generated among the spectators, we may compare its temporal character with how images are evoked among the citizens of the virtuous city:

> What is intended by excellence in imaginative evocation is that a human being be moved to accept something and be inspired toward it, even if what he knows about the thing requires the converse of what is imaginatively evoked. Many people love or detest something, or prefer or avoid it, only due to the imaginative evocation, to the exclusion of deliberation, either because they naturally have no deliberation or because they have rejected it in their affairs.[36]

Akin to the feeling of love as a positive affection which prompts one to pursue that thing, the spectators momentarily experience benevolence for the contestants before its spontaneous intensity dissipates. Therefore, the generation of benevolence and hence its operativity as an affective disposition always presents the possibility of its sudden passing away or in-operativity. Here Aristotle subsequently remarks that 'benevolence would seem to be a feature of friendship, but it is still not friendship'.[37] Despite the excellence of the contestants which inspire the spectators to be overcome by benevolence, the spectators are physically separated from the contestants making any relative friendship with them an impossibility. The contestants ultimately remain unfamiliar or unknown to the spectators insofar as they do not directly participate in the same activities.[38] The benevolence of the spectators may be compared to a sudden pleasure which overcomes them. Aristotle identifies this pleasure with sight as a perfect or complete activity, 'Now seeing is thought to be complete at any interval of time, for it needs nothing, which when it comes into being later, will complete the form of seeing. Pleasure resembles a thing such as seeing, for it is a whole.'[39] Benevolence as a momentary pleasure first requires the experience of seeing and cognising the contestants in action for the spectators to be overcome by the feeling of wishing for their success.

35 Aristotle, *Nicomachean Ethics* 1166b35–1167a4. This spontaneous wish overcoming the spectators may be naturally described as a change from one state of events to another. For example, the disposition of the spectators withdraws and leaves behind a past disposition to become the present disposition that it is.

36 al-Fārābī, *Selected Aphorisms*, 55. [63.19–20–64.1–5], 36, tr. Butterworth. Cf. al-Fārābī, *Aphorisms of the Statesman*, 51., 48–9, 134–5, tr. Dunlop.

37 Aristotle, *Nicomachean Ethics* 1166b30–1.

38 Ibid., 1166b31, 1167a10.

39 Ibid., 1174a15–19.

In relation to the activity of the intellect, benevolence evokes a kind of thinking stretched beyond itself and directed towards the good of the contestants.[40] Although one does not fall in love with the contestants or even necessarily develop a liking for them, the spectators may nevertheless be overcome by benevolence for them, 'just like the pleasure of being in love with another by sight. For no one is in love if he or she has not first been pleased by the look of the beloved.'[41] Benevolence as the origin of friendship thus betrays its own ambivalence insofar as it is directed to both thinking and wishing good things for the sake of another. If one wishes or thinks good things for someone simply because it is useful or pleasurable to oneself, then this wishing or thinking is not directed towards the other and thereby cannot be identified with benevolence.[42] Therefore, benevolence always harbours within itself the possibility to remain latent as inoperative friendship or active as operative friendship.

[40] Here we may identify an etymological affinity between benevolence (*eunoia*) and love (*maḥabba*). If *eunoia* is determined as an intention which aims beyond itself at the good, then *maḥabba* may be said to connote two principal lexical meanings, namely, as *ḥubb* (love) and as *ḥabba* (grain or seed). The latter lexical meaning of love as a grain or seed may be accentuated to indicate the ripening of the seed whereby the seed becomes actualised. The emanation of the First may serve as the foremost expression of this love (*maḥabba*), 'The First's substance is also such that the existents, when they have issued from it in their ranks, are necessarily united and connected with one another and arranged in a way that they become one whole and are established like one thing. Some of them are connected and united by something within their substance, so that their substances to which they owe their existence produce their connection and their union; others by modes which accompany their substances, such as love by which human beings are connected, for love is a mode in them and not the substance to which they owe their existence. These modes of theirs are also derived from the First, because its substance is such that many existents receive from it together with their substances the modes by which they are connected with each other and united and arranged' (al-Fārābī, *Virtuous City*, I, 2, §3, 96–7, tr. Walzer).

[41] Aristotle, *Nicomachean Ethics* 1167a5–7. However, such a pleasure may be compared to Aristotle's definition of motion, especially since 'the one who enjoys the form of a person is not by this alone in love, unless he or she also longs for that person when absent and desires that person's presence' (*Nicomachean Ethics* 1167a7–9). Aristotle contrasts liking (*philēsis*) with benevolence (*eunoia*) claiming that benevolence may arise towards those whom one has not yet met but appear to be either useful or pleasurable as long as they resemble that which is good (1155b35–6). Likewise, those who express benevolence may approve of one another but do not live together (1157b18); benevolence may arise from only seeing someone or hearing some good of that person from another (1212a4). Aristotle rather comically compares benevolence to those older people of a sour disposition who wish for good things and help each other on occasions of need but do not spend time together or seek out the company of each other (1158a7–11).

[42] Aristotle, *Eudemian Ethics* 1241a6–7; *Nicomachean Ethics* 1167a13–14.

Concord and the Politics of Friendship

In *Nicomachean Ethics* IX, Aristotle compares concord to the bond of friendship which holds cities together, 'And friendship seems to hold cities together, and lawmakers seem to take it more seriously than justice for concord seems to be something similar to friendship.'[43] Moreover, Aristotle surmises that the kinship between concord and friendship may even be a substitution for justice in the political community. Concord and friendship appear to be more natural than justice by holding the city together as complete in itself for the sake of pleasure, utility, and happiness. In a similar manner, al-Fārābī's *Aphorisms of the Statesman* presents concord (*i'tilāf*) as following from friendship:

> When the opinions of the inhabitants of the virtuous city are in agreement about these things and that is then perfected by the actions through which happiness is gained for some with others, that is necessarily followed by the love of some for others. Because they are neighbors of one another in one dwelling and some of them need others while some of the are useful to others, that is also followed by the love that comes about for the sake of the useful. Then, due to their sharing in the virtues and because some of them are useful to others, some take pleasure in others. So that is also followed by the love that comes about for the sake of pleasure. So by this they are in concord and bound.[44]

Both concord and friendship achieve a certain degree of self-sufficiency by inclining those citizens to act in the most just manner, 'among [those] things that are just, what inclines toward friendship seems to be most just of all'.[45] This inclination towards friendship mutually constitutes benevolence and concord. Benevolence and concord are compared to equity (*isotēs*) as requisite conditions for the application of justice. Equity always entails a sense of what is appropriate and enables the recognition of specific circumstances which may call for a departure from strict justice. In his exposition of equity, Aristotle elevates equity over that justice insofar as 'the equitable thing is better than a certain kind of just thing'.[46] The superior value of equity may lead us to wonder whether the analogy between equity and justice may be extended

[43] Aristotle, *Nicomachean Ethics* 1155a22–6.

[44] al-Fārābī, *Selected Aphorisms*, 61. [71.4–13], 40, tr. Butterworth. Cf. al-Fārābī, *Aphorisms of the Statesman*, 57., 53, 140–1, tr. Dunlop.

[45] Aristotle, *Nicomachean Ethics* 1155a28–9.

[46] Here we shall distinguish equity from prudence which also discerns the right means to the right ends in particular circumstances. Cf. Aristotle, *Nicomachean Ethics* 1137b8.

to benevolence and concord as conditions for friendship. In *Aphorisms of the Statesman*, the relationship between concord (*i'tilāf*) and equity (*i'tidāl*) reappears as the renumeration of what has been lost or stolen by robbery or usurpation:

> what is returned is either returned to them personally or to the city. To whichever of the two the equivalent is returned, justice is that the divided goods remain preserved for the inhabitants of the city. And injustice is for someone's portion of the goods to go out of their hand without its equivalent being returned to them or to the inhabitants of the city. Further, what is returned to them personally ought either to be useful to the city or not harmful to it.[47]

This insistence upon the preservation of those things that the citizens or inhabitants hold in person or in common contributes to the difference between justice and injustice in the city. Without such a preservation of both personal and common goods, neither concord nor equity can be attained. If we are to heed Aristotle's remark that concord is always present among equitable people, 'since they are of like mind both with themselves and with one another, being on the same terms, so to speak . . . and they want things that are just and advantageous, and aim at these in common', then equity is the condition for justice as a habit which enables justice to be applied to a particular situation.[48] Since benevolence contributes to the cultivation of friendship, we might assume that the bond which unites benevolence and friendship is nothing other than concord. Although benevolence remains inoperative friendship and hence friendship only in principle without the presence of concord, concord cannot by itself facilitate the enactment of friendship. The intimacy required by proper friendship conditioned by spatial and temporal proximity is surpassed by civic or political friendship, 'concord seems to be friendship in a political sense, just as people mean it, for it has to do with what is advantageous and relates to life.'[49] The object of concord is what is advantageous and most practical to life, namely, the common good of the political community. Therefore, concord requires constant deliberation about those things which citizens can choose and put into action.

47 al-Fārābī, *Selected Aphorisms*, 62. [72.20–73.1–5], 41, tr. Butterworth. Cf. al-Fārābī, *Aphorisms of the Statesman*, 58., 53–4, 142–3, tr. Dunlop.

48 Aristotle, *Nicomachean Ethics* 1167b6–10.

49 Ibid., 1167b2.

Aristotle cites numerous practical examples of concord which appear to promote the harmony and stability of the political community beginning with the claim that all citizens think that offices ought to be elective.[50] His account of civic friendship thus reflects a shared concern for both ruling and being ruled which would indeed allow for the democratic practice of ruling in turns, 'not each deciding on himself but both each deciding on the same one'.[51] With the admission that civic friendship is a species of friendship defined by utility, concord indicates the existence of an original political bond between citizens who are mutually concerned with pursuing the common good. Benevolence makes possible this political bond insofar as this inclination to be well-disposed towards one another by wishing one well is transferred from the private sphere of relative intimates or friends to the public sphere of citizens. Hence, concord promotes the universalisation of friendship. This universalisation comes to be concretely enacted as citizens collectively deliberate and vote upon a single individual to rule. The mutual deliberation and agreement achieved by concord also accords a certain degree of respect to individuals by virtue of their goodness and integrity.[52] Because concord 'cannot be said simply', concord requires that 'the primary and natural manifestation of it is good'.[53]

In *Aphorisms of the Statesman*, al-Fārābī similarly describes how individuals contribute to the common good of the virtuous city insofar as those traits are born by individual bodies possessing different temperaments. Akin to the various metals constituting the various classes in *Republic* III, natural temperaments condition the composition of the political regime:

> That is because the condition of regimes and their link to souls is like the condition of the seasons and their link to bodies possessing different temperaments. Just as some of the bodies are improved in temperament and condition in the fall and some improved in the summer, while some find the winter season to be most beneficial and most agreeable for them, and some are greatly improved in the spring, such is the condition of souls and their link to regimes.[54]

This retrieval of these natural bodies possessing different seasonal temperaments explicitly calls into question any facile distinction between the natural

[50] Ibid., 1166a31–3, 1167a24–6; *Magna Moralia* 1212a15–18.

[51] Aristotle, *Eudemian Ethics* 1241a33; *Magna Moralia* 1212a25–6.

[52] 'Concord occurs in the case of good human beings' (Aristotle, *Eudemian Ethics* 1241a22).

[53] Ibid., 1241a23–6.

[54] al-Fārābī, *Selected Aphorisms*, 92. [93.15–20], 58–9, tr. Butterworth. Cf. al-Fārābī, *Aphorisms of the Statesman*, 87., 70–1, 162, tr. Dunlop.

and the voluntary. The analogy between the temperaments of the bodies and those of the soul is tenuous insofar as certain traits and ways of life are combined from both natural and voluntary things. In this sense, the combination of the natural and the voluntary only further contributes to a rather fortuitous and circumstantial composition of the city originating from benevolence.

The civic friendship concomitant with concord cannot arise without benevolence as the initial inclination to friendship as both a well-wishing and good-thinking for the sake of another. Benevolence makes possible the existence of concord since only good persons 'are of one mind with themselves and with others, as they always more or less stand on the same ground'.[55] Therefore, the original political bond of concord is always inscribed by a certain respect for the goodness and integrity of individual persons. Aristotle's examples of concord are primarily retrieved from oligarchic constitutions where respect for individuals might be limited to a powerful few. With the case of whether Pittacus should or should not rule Mytilene as an elective dictator, the constitution of the political community does not preclude the possibility that all citizens be accorded the same degree of respect.[56] In *Politics* VII, Aristotle subsequently proposes that property division in the best constitution (according to which citizens would own property both in the city and in the country) is conducive to establishing concord among all citizens for the sake of protecting the political community with respect to border wars.[57] Like Aristotle, al-Fārābī is vitally concerned that the prospect of war may potentially harm or even destroy the health of the city if undertaken with an unjust motive. Therefore, only just wars mutually benefit both the ruler and the citizens insofar as they entail 'carrying or forcing a certain group to what is best and most fortunate for them in themselves . . . or warring against those who do not submit to slavery and servitude . . . And this is something shared with two [of the preceding] concerns: [one is] earning a good for the city and the other is that they be carried to give justice and equity.'[58] In the case of war, both benevolence and concord assist in promoting a conception of political community which indicates a respect for preserving the goodness and integrity of every citizen. The individual warrior who puts himself at risk of death does not do so for personal honour or gain but rather for the sake of preserving the happiness of the entire city.

[55] Aristotle, *Nicomachean Ethics* 1167b6–7; *Eudemian Ethics* 1241a23–8.

[56] Aristotle, *Nicomachean Ethics* 1166a31–3.

[57] Aristotle, *Politics* 1330a18.

[58] al-Fārābī, *Selected Aphorisms*, 67. [76.17–20–77.1–5], 43–4, tr. Butterworth. Cf. al-Fārābī, *Aphorisms of the Statesman*, 63., 56–7, 146–7, tr. Dunlop.

If we are to develop these respective accounts of benevolence and concord in an explicitly cosmopolitan direction, we shall return to Aristotle's account of civic friendship which may be cultivated for the sake of composing a community characterised by both commonality and difference.[59] Benevolence as the incipient inclination towards friendship is always directed towards the individual and hence 'is a feeling of character for character'.[60] While benevolence may be cultivated through the experience of seeing someone engaged in action, such as the spectator observing the contestants and thereby wishing that the contestants be successful, benevolence extends most prominently to parental affection. In *Magna Moralia*, Aristotle asks, 'Why is it that the father loves the son more than the son the father?'[61] Although benevolence may appear to be merely a natural expression of biological paternity, Aristotle quite explicitly contrasts the friendship between a father and son with those activities whereby the activity and its end are one and the same.[62] Therefore, benevolence cannot be the same as its end. Benevolence is oriented by the existence of another person as an object of perception or thought which constitutes the formal cause of wishing and thinking goodness towards that person. Hence, Aristotle concludes that the activity of the father 'is always of a fuller kind than this, because the son is his own creation'.[63] The father naturally feels benevolence for his son because the son naturally participates in the form of the father as his product or creation. Nevertheless, benevolence should not be taken to mean that father derives any utility or pleasure from his relation to his son. Rather, benevolence is always a species of wishing and thinking for the sake of another.[64]

Benevolence is exclusively directed towards the irreplaceable singularity of an individual in contrast to its generic understanding as a species of universal

[59] 'It could be seen that the Aristotelian reflection provides resources for the systematic overcoming of the opposition between public and private, universality and singularity; that indeed, far from such a dichotomy, from the hierarchy it entails, and from its mere inversion, this reflection allows us to think universality together with singularity' (Baracchi, *Friendship*, 115).

[60] Aristotle, *Magna Moralia* 1212a12–13.

[61] Ibid., 1211b21-2.

[62] 'the flute player's activity and aim, are, for instance, identical; to him, his playing is end and activity at once' (Aristotle, *Magna Moralia* 1211b29–31). In contrast to the activity of thinking, where thinking and the object are one and the same, benevolence (*eunoia*) demonstrates an ecstatic intensification of thinking and wishing.

[63] Aristotle, *Magna Moralia* 1211b34.

[64] Like the activity of building or the father engendering the son, 'in one way or another, they are all favorably disposed to what they themselves have made' (ibid., 1211b37). Cf. Aristotle, *Nicomachean Ethics*, where benevolence is defined as 'wishing good things for the sake of another' (1156a32–3).

love. With the case of the spectators observing an athletic contest, benevolence is inscribed by a specific temporal dimension by its inception and dissipation. With the relationship between father and son, the ecstatic dimension of benevolence is constituted equally by memory and anticipation which indicates a certain favour towards what has been generated insofar as the son is the fruit of the labour of the father and the hope that the son shall become like the father. A temporal identity between benevolence and concord is thereby established by their shared concern for the future.[65] Like benevolence, concord presupposes a certain kind of respect for the individual integrity of another person insofar as both foretell future prosperity. This turn to deliberation for the sake of choosing a future good is reminiscent of the essential activity of political discourse which concerns that which is advantageous or disadvantageous.[66] Since the future is not apparent to us, the activity of deliberating and choosing for the sake of some good is only made possible by the work of benevolence and concord which promotes a respect for individuality and hence the integrity of each person.

The work of benevolence and concord may also be said to promote the equality of all persons.[67] Instead of addressing the relative similarity or even homogeneity of political community, concord affords the possibility of envisioning a community irreducible to any kind of political identification with the introduction of a human being so unique as to be 'of all tribes'.[68] Here Aristotle remarks that such lovers of humankind are potentially all human beings insofar as the friendship which seems to be present in a parent for a child expands to relationships between fellow travellers.[69] This kinship reflects the

[65] 'concord operates not in what we think and believe, but in what we plan to do' (Aristotle, *Magna Moralia* 1212a18–19).

[66] Aristotle, *Politics* 1253a15.

[67] For a further examination of the cosmopolitan principle of universality, namely, that persons are ultimate units of concern for everyone and should be treated equally, see especially Pogge, 'Cosmopolitanism and Sovereignty'.

[68] Perhaps Aristotle's account of political friendship finds precedent in the *Republic*, 'The community in which one belongs becomes increasingly inclusive. The broadening of the political organism culminates in the "cosmopolitan dream" of the ending myth: the figure of Er points to a human being so unique as to be *pamphulos* "of all tribes", irreducible to any political, tribal, territorial identification (614b)' (Baracchi, *Aristotle's Ethics as First Philosophy*, 285n14). Here we may begin to approximate a uniquely Platonic and Aristotelian account of cosmopolitanism. We cannot neglect the figure of Socrates who echoes Diogenes's refrain, 'When Socrates was asked to which [country] he belonged, he would say, "To the world," for he thought that he was an inhabitant and citizen of the whole world' (Cicero, *Tusculan Disputations*, 108, tr. King).

[69] 'which is why we praise people who are "lovers of humankind" (*philanthrōpous*). One might see in one's travels too that every human being is akin (*oikeiōs*) to every other human being and a friend to him' (Aristotle, *Nicomachean Ethics* 1155a19–22).

disposition of concord if we are to conclude that possessing like-mindedness (*homonoia*) first and foremost implies the sharing of a common intellect among all human beings.

We shall only briefly gesture towards another such historical example of cosmopolitanism which exceeds our relative familiarity with the ancient Greek heritage by illustrating how this discourse was adopted and assimilated into al-Kindī's circle in Baghdad. It is not surprising that the possibility of a global community could be imagined. The philosophers in his circle travelled widely from one court to another thereby establishing a cosmopolitan network of hospitality, friendship, and solidarity. By way of conclusion, we shall return to *Aphorisms of the Statesman* to further elucidate how this cosmopolitan paradigm came to be enacted through a distinctly Aristotelian and Peripatetic lens. As we have demonstrated above, al-Fārābī explicitly refers to a love (*maḥabba*) which is strangely akin to Aristotle's own description of benevolence (*eunoia*), a love which binds the parts of the city together so they are in concord (*i'tilāf*) and hence mutual cooperation (*mu'āwana*) with one another. This love marks the incipience of a benevolence (*tafaḍḍul*) which silently bears the fate of the political within itself:

> They are bound by love, and they hold together and stay preserved through justice and actions of justice. Love may come about by nature, like the love of parents for the child. And it may come about by *volition* in that its starting point is voluntary things followed by love. That which is by *volition* is threefold: one is by sharing in virtue, the second is for the sake of the useful; and the third is for the sake of pleasure.[70]

Among those things which remain useful for citizens in attaining happiness in the civic and cosmic order is friendship. Al-Fārābī distinguishes between different kinds of volition, including benevolence directed towards the good of another. In contrast to a non-volitional kind of love associated with familial kinship, benevolence is defined by the relationship between the host to the stranger and hence an expression of hospitality which may involve either acceptance or rejection. The inception of friendship demands an exorbitant responsibility to the undecidable and hence to an extraneity which remains undetermined insofar as the stranger could be an enemy. It is such an undecidability which constitutes benevolence as the extension of a friendly feeling without expectation of reciprocity. In such a moment of exposure and

[70] al-Fārābī, *Selected Aphorisms*, 61. [70.3–5], 40, tr. Butterworth. Cf. al-Fārābī, *Aphorisms of the Statesman*, 57., 53, 140–1, tr. Dunlop.

vulnerability, whereby the host is betrothed to the guest in submission and trust as hostage, benevolence becomes the possibility upon which friendship so decisively depends. Friendship thus always emerges with respect to a certain foreignness, strangeness, and unknowability. Hence, benevolence may even be said to supersede justice by originating from an unlimited generosity towards the stranger.[71] Without animosity and admission of the categorial distinction between the friend and enemy, we are left with an unconditional hospitality towards all human beings as friends to cite the words of 'Alī ibn Abī Ṭālib, 'You should take friends. They will be counted in this world and the next.'[72] With the absence of animosity, benevolence expresses the unlimited generosity of the divine and thus assumes an extra-political and extra-judicial register which may be applied beyond the relative geographical constraints of the ancient Greek political community to the future global community.

By allusion to Aristotle's claim that 'friendship seems to be innate in a parent for offspring and in an offspring for a parent . . . it is innate too in those that are alike in kind to one another', familial love which arises from a spontaneous innate disposition is contrasted with friendship which arises from a volition guided by virtue, utility, and pleasure.[73] This account of a friendship guided by utility comes to be identified with civic friendship or concord aimed at ensuring that the political community remains intact. The bond of civic friendship brings the citizens together in unison and solidarity with one another.[74] Civic friendship is needed to hold the political community together in contrast to familial love which arises naturally and spontaneously. Therefore, civic friendship is a matter of choice determined by a range of dispositions to be cultivated. Civic friendship extends to equality (*musāwāt*) and justice (*'adl*) within the political community. Equality or fairness is a mode of justice responsible for assessing individual citizens depending upon merit or what is deserved. Both equality and justice arise from a love which involves

[71] Benevolence denotes a wide range of meanings in Arabic. For a discussion of benevolence in the Qur'ān, see Ashfaq, 'Islamic Philosophy of Benevolence (*Al-Iḥsān*) and Aesthetic Reflection'; and Izutzu, *Ethico-religious Concepts in the Qur'ān*, 75–80. The identification of benevolence with generosity also effectively calls into question Émile Benveniste's friend–enemy distinction. Despite numerous Arabic synonyms for friendship, no antonym to friendship exists in Arabic. For an Arabic etymology of friendship, see Al Jallad, 'A Lexicological Study of Friendship in Arabic'; and Obiedat, 'Friendship in Arabic'.

[72] al-Ghazālī, *Revival of the Religious Sciences*, 92.

[73] Aristotle, *Nicomachean Ethics* 1155a18–19.

[74] al-Fārābī, *Selected Aphorisms*, 61. [70.3–5], 40, tr. Butterworth. Cf. al-Fārābī, *Aphorisms of the Statesman*, 57., 53, 140–1, tr. Dunlop.

the mutual sharing and dividing of goods among all inhabitants of the city.[75] Moreover, a specific kind of legal justice applies to the inhabitants of the city and a general kind of political justice to 'all people' as if to discern the equal status of all persons beyond civic and national boundaries.[76] This assessment of the value of equality and justice is reflected in the composition of the democratic city where equality is to be measured at the level of human character between free associations of individuals. This multifarious community of free individuals mutually cooperating in the pursuit of happiness may therefore be imagined on a global and cosmic scale. The cosmic community is neither homogeneous nor uniform, but plural in the varieties of cities and nations.

This association between community and cosmos invokes a broadly Platonic and Neoplatonic vision of cosmopolitanism. The individual human being is in fact homologous with the political organism itself in all its excellence mirroring the sublime perfection of the cosmos. This insistence upon the cosmic significance of the city is itself a re-inscription of the divine paradigm of antiquity whereby the creative activity of the demiurge ordering the cosmos is analogously mirrored in the philosopher-ruler-*imām* who orders the community. The radical ambition of envisioning and imagining a cosmic community is strikingly reminiscent of the Platonic gesture of the city in speech. The attainment of happiness and human perfection is to be arrived at only through the mutual belonging of cosmos and community. The enactment of the city in speech is not so much an endeavour of the intellect as much as an expression of the imagination of the philosopher-ruler-*imām* who guides the citizens to such a realisation.[77] If the perfection of the imagination signifies the perfection of the human being, then this correspondence may be attributed to a cosmic image presented by the Ikhwān al-Ṣafā' of tenth-century Baghdad who composed highly eclectic *Epistles* (*Rasā'il*) syncretising major figures throughout antiquity ranging from Pythagoras, Plato, and Aristotle, to the Neoplatonists:

> Know, O Brother, that by the universe (*'ālam*) the sages (*ḥukamā'*) mean the seven heavens and the earths and what is between them of all creatures. They also call it the great person (*al-insān al-kabīr*) because it is seen that the world has one body in all its spheres, gradations of heavens, its generating elements (*arkān*), and their productions. It is also seen that it has one Soul

[75] al-Fārābī, *Selected Aphorisms*, 62. [71.14–15], 40, tr. Butterworth. Cf. al-Fārābī, *Aphorisms of the Statesman*, 58., 53–44, 141–3, tr. Dunlop.

[76] al-Fārābī, *Selected Aphorisms*, 63. [74.13–15], 42, tr. Butterworth. Cf. al-Fārābī, *Aphorisms of the Statesman*, 59., 55, 143–4, tr. Dunlop.

[77] See al-Fārābī, *Virtuous City*, V, 17, §2, 279–81, tr. Walzer.

> (*nafs*) whose powers run in all organs of its body, just like the person who has one soul which runs into all of its organs. We desire to mention in this treatise the form of the world and describe the composition of its body as the body of the person is described in the book of anatomy.[78]

Here the Neoplatonic schema of emanation may be transposed into an all-embracing vision bringing together the principle of divine unity with the one body of the world. The intimate bond between the One and all Creation presupposes that the human aspires in their worldly existence to perfection to approximate the unity of the divine. It should be consistently underscored that such perfection is attributed to the power of the imagination as the bridge between sense-perception and intellect enabling those intelligibles (*ma'qūlāt*) transmitted by the Active Intellect (*al-'aql al-fa''āl*) to the philosopher-ruler-*imām* to be symbolised into images (*mithālāt*), which can in turn be communicated to the citizens for the sake of attaining happiness within the political community. It should suffice to only mention the degree of similarity established between the acquired intellect (*al-'aql al-mustafād*) synonymous with the highest stage of human intellectual development and the power of the imagination, particularly the primacy of the productive imagination (*al-quwwa al-mutakhayyila*), most active in its prophetic state when the intelligibles are transmitted to the philosopher-ruler-*imām* in waking states and dreams.[79] By interrogating this distinction between the power of the intellect to comprehend these intelligibles as universals and the power of sense to receive singular perceptions, the imagination as a source of mediation (*tawassaṭa*) conjoins the theoretical and practical intellect to the concrete materiality of sense-perception through the production and reproduction of images.

It may even be said that the power of the imagination inspired the composition of Dante's *Purgatorio* XVII, which is itself conceived as a canticle to the divine mystery, 'And your imagination (*tua imagine*) will quickly / Come to see how, at first, I saw the sun / again which was now setting / So matching mine to the trusty steps /of my master (*mio maestro*), I came forth from such a fog / to the rays which were already dead on low shores.'[80] In *Purgatorio* XVII.17, the apotheosis of the imagination comes to be disclosed by 'a light formed in

[78] See *Rasā'il Ikhwān al-Ṣafā'*, II, 20, in Nasr, *An Introduction to Islamic Cosmological Doctrines*, 67–8. For an excellent discussion of the role of slavery in al-Fārābī and the Ikhwān al-Ṣafā', see Loevy, 'Literary Resistance to the Philosophy of Slavery'. Cf. Netton, *Muslim Neoplatonists*, 95–105.

[79] See al-Fārābī, *Political Regime*, 80. [79.19–80.8], 69.

[80] Alighieri, *Purgatorio*, Canto XVII. 7–12; Stone, 'Dante and the *Falasifa*', 148.

Heaven (*moveti lume che nel ciel s'informa*)'. The source of this divine illumination is described as inhabiting the form of an angel who has literally touched Dante's own imagination. Here such a divine visitation clearly replicates the role of the Active Intellect responsible for transmitting the divine intelligibles to the philosopher-ruler-*imām*. Since the faculty of the imagination is the vehicle of prophetic revelation and the primary conduit for the reception of the Active Intellect, we cannot easily discount its utterly transcendent power within the human soul in relation to the intellect.[81] The narrative of the *Purgatorio* describing Dante's ascent of Mount Purgatory recognises the practical efficacy of the imagination for the sake of translating and transmitting the divine intelligibles into popular images. The concrete materiality of such an image unmistakably bears al-Fārābī's imprint and reflects the intimate degree of their philosophical kinship. With Dante's harmonisation of the ancient Greek and Islamic heritage, the privilege afforded to the imagination in its traversal of cultural and geographical boundaries remains an enduring contribution to the topography of the cosmopolitan paradigm. Despite the historical prominence accorded to the Italian Renaissance, the Aristotelian commentaries of Thomas Aquinas remain indebted to Ibn Rushd as a primary interlocutor and perhaps Dante could not have completed his *Purgatorio* without the inspiration of al-Fārābī. In conclusion, we may only surmise that Dante's global political community conjoining the universality of the common law with the local laws of nations is indebted to the prophetic imagination of the philosopher-ruler-*imām* who makes this shared cosmopolitan vision possible.[82]

[81] Stephen Ogden's *Averroes on the Intellect* convincingly argues that the intellect which 'becomes all things' in *De Anima* II.4 and the intellect which 'makes all things' in *De Anima* III.5 share the same ontological status.

[82] For the application of the imagination of the philosopher-ruler-*imām* to the composition of the virtuous city, see al-Fārābī, *Virtuous City*, V, 17, §2, 279–81. For the ecumenical intersection between al-Fārābī and Dante, see especially Stone, *Dante's Pluralism and the Islamic Philosophy of Religion.*

4
The Democratic City

The Political Animal

Al-Fārābī's *Political Regime* and *Virtuous City* notably depart from *Republic* VIII by casting the democratic city (*madīna jimā'iyya*) in a relatively positive light as the most viable alternative to the virtuous city. Since the democratic city contains more virtue than the other imperfect cities, we shall aim to compare the cultivation of justice among citizens within the virtuous city in relation to the relative freedom and equality afforded by the democratic city. Citizens in the democratic city are granted the freedom of individuality and may choose to either satisfy their appetites or be ruled by reason. The equality of all citizens presupposes no one has a better claim than anyone else to political authority. Therefore, collective rule becomes a concrete possibility in accordance with the constitution of the democratic city. To illustrate the cosmopolitan character of the democratic city, we shall begin by calling attention to the translation of *madanī* as 'a person or thing that belongs or pertains to a city'.[1] In his *Enumeration of the Sciences*, al-Fārābī defines *madanī* according to the science which 'investigates (a) the various kinds of voluntary actions and ways of life (*al-siyar*) [and] (b) the acquired habits (*malakāt*), the mores (*akhlāq*), the natural characteristics, and the inborn traits from which these actions and ways of life arise'.[2] Dimitri Gutas has conclusively argued that al-Fārābī's commentators and translators have too narrowly rendered *madanī* as pertaining exclusively to the political domain.[3] However, al-Fārābī is not defining the 'political' per se, but 'ways of life', including habits, mores, and character traits which ought to be comprehended in a more ethical context.

[1] Gutas, 'The Meaning of *Madanī* in al-Fārābī's "Political Philosophy"', 261.
[2] al-Fārābī, *Iḥṣā' al-'Ulūm* (*Enumeration of the Sciences*), 1. [102.1–3], 19, tr. Butterworth (mod.).
[3] Gutas, 'The Meaning of *Madanī* in al-Fārābī's "Political Philosophy"', 261.

The interpretive problem of attributing a narrow political objective to a 'way of life' (*sīra*) is already outlined by Aristotle who ascribes such a way of life (*bios*) quite broadly to all living beings who seek to assure their endurance in a particular place (*topos*).[4] Therefore, Gutas retrieves al-Fārābī's *Prolegomena to the Study of Aristotle's Philosophy* (*Risāla fī Mā Yanbaghī an Yuqaddam qabl Ta'allum Falsafat Arisṭūṭalīs*) to demonstrate that his account of 'political science' remains inseparable from 'ethics'.[5] Here al-Fārābī cites Aristotle's student Theophrastus, who 'allegedly maintained that the starting point of philosophical studies is ethics or the improvement of one's character'.[6] Despite the conclusion of Strauss and his disciples that al-Fārābī's philosophy bears an exclusive political focus, Gutas contends that al-Fārābī's ethical inquiry aimed at 'ways of life' oriented by civic organisation is the most favourable means to attain human perfection, 'The human, in other words, is a city animal, and not a political animal.'[7]

Al-Fārābī's *Attainment of Happiness* presents a pedagogical regimen beginning with training in the theoretical sciences as a prerequisite for participation in civic life:

> For one who sets out to inquire ought to be innately equipped for the theoretical sciences – that is fulfill the conditions prescribed by Plato in his *Republic.* One should excel in comprehending and conceiving that which is essential. Moreover, one should have good memory and be able to endure the toil of study. One should love truthfulness and truthful people, and justice and just people; and not be headstrong or a wrangler about what he desires. One should not be gluttonous for food and drink, and should by natural disposition disdain the appetites, the *dirhem*, the *dinar*, and the like. One should be high-minded and avoid what is disgraceful in people. One should be pious, yield easily to goodness and justice, and be stubborn in yielding to evil and injustice. And one should be strongly determined in favor of the right thing.[8]

The pronounced philosophical labour as an exercise in self-cultivation is wholly informed by ways of life disposed to engaging in community with

[4] Brill, *Aristotle on the Concept of Shared Life*, 11.
[5] Gutas, 'The Starting Point of Philosophical Studies in Alexandrian and Arabic Aristotelianism', 115.
[6] Ibid.
[7] Gutas, 'The Meaning of *Madanī* in al-Fārābī's "Political Philosophy"', 266.
[8] al-Fārābī, *Attainment of Happiness*, 60. [44.17–45.5], 48, tr. Mahdi (mod.).

others. Following Aristotle, *bios* comes to include the study of first philosophy. This cultivation of *bios* by practising the virtues of truthfulness, justice, piety, and prudence in a certain sense even subtends or supervenes upon what we might come to identify as the metaphysical domain, 'they arrive at the ultimate perfection (whereby they attain that which renders them truly substantial) only when they labour with those principles towards achieving this perfection.'[9] This 'way of life' enacted as philosophical labour requires both deliberation and solicitude. Since these intellectual or rational principles naturally inhere within us, the work of human perfection requires a labour supplemental to our own natural determination.

By virtue of investigating this commitment to explicating *bios* as a social phenomenon, we should not underestimate the communal bond which makes human perfection possible. The individual is oriented to being with others in their multiplicity and difference as both a structural and anthropological condition. To heed Aristotle's claim that political inquiry regards 'beautiful and just things which have many differences and fluctuations', the striving of the individual to attain perfection is always conditioned by the relationship with other individuals in the learning and cultivation of habits.[10] Individuality and community designate the twofold condition of the political animal. It is only in this light that human perfection may be achieved. Therefore, *bios* informs the essence of this interdependent community of individuals which extends beyond itself and thereby encompasses ever-increasing spheres of multiplicity in its manifold parts. If we are to gesture to what kind of community this interdependent unity might entail, then we may presuppose a vision of political association exhibiting a natural order emerging and perhaps akin to the cosmos itself, 'It will become evident . . . that political association and the totality that results from the association of citizens in cities corresponds to the associations of the bodies that constitute the totality of the world. They will come to see in what are included in the totality constituted by the city and the nation the likenesses of what are in the total world.'[11] The cosmic community is neither homogeneous nor uniform but variegated at the level of cities and nations. Cosmopolitanism is rooted in a concrete time and place composed of multiple mutually interdependent communities as we move from the association of citizens in cities, to the association of cities in the world, to the cosmos writ large. The inclusion of the democratic city within those cities at least approximates the best and most perfect city. In what follows, we shall aim

[9] Ibid., 18. [14.1–3], 22–3, tr. Mahdi (mod.).
[10] Aristotle, *Nicomachean Ethics* 1094b14–16.
[11] al-Fārābī, *Attainment of Happiness*, 20. [16.7–8], 24, tr. Mahdi (mod.).

to retrieve the role of an unruly element within the composition of the city which ultimately contributes to its either its growth or demise, namely, the presence of oppositionists or weeds (*nawābit*).[12]

Weeds, Vipers, and Beasts

Among those philosophers who have retrieved the liminality of plant life, al-Fārābī introduces the weeds as a segment of society in those imperfect cities which remain resistant to change. The weeds are defined by their opposition to the status quo and hence an unwillingness to conform to civic norms and therefore present both a potential threat to the general stability of the city and an opportunity for the city to grow in a new direction. This vision of the city wholly depends on the ancient metaphor of the city as an organism. The resistance or opposition of the weeds enables the city to flourish and grow and may even strengthen its commitment to the democratic principles of justice, freedom, and equality. The weeds retain a certain potential to lead the city since they are raised and trained in such a way which reflects their spirit of fierce resistance to accepted norms.

The *Political Regime* describes how the weeds develop in conjunction with the composition of the city, 'These, then, are the sorts [of weeds] growing among the inhabitants of the city. From their opinions, no city at all is attained, nor a large association from the multitude. But they are embedded among the inhabitants of the city as a whole.'[13] Some weeds appear to possess a certain degree of discernment (*tamyīz*) akin to the philosopher-ruler-*imām* which enables them to distinguish between true and false images. The philosophical training of the weeds is specifically designed to practise dialectical techniques for the sake of arriving at the truth. This designation of a segment of society as weeds may also serve to disclose the rather vexed relationship between those two forms of life identified with the animal (*zōē*) and the human (*bios*). The weeds have a disturbing effect on the city by disrupting the growth of other citizen-plants but also contributing to their flourishing. If the weeds prevail, then the city will be harmed by them. Only with the existence of a few weeds may we envision a city creating opposition to promote positive change. Most importantly, the weeds possess the potential to become philosophers and hence potential rulers. Although the weeds are construed as initially unruly, if they are trained properly and receive guidance in dialectic, then their critical and interrogative character may be utilised for the sake of

[12] See Alon, 'Fārābī's Funny Flora'; and Kochin, 'Weeds'.

[13] al-Fārābī, *Political Regime*, 126. [107.30–5], 94, tr. Butterworth.

attaining happiness in the city. Therefore, the weeds demonstrate an uncanny ability to engage in the activity of opposition and hence disruption. Some may be deemed simply ineducable and are therefore unable to be trained in dialectic while others have the capacity to discern images and to identify the truth which resides in those images. By allusion to the tenuous distinction between sophistry and philosophy, the ambivalence of the weeds presents a dilemma by their potential to either improve or harm the city.[14] Here al-Fārābī remains readily aware of those individuals populating imperfect cities. Cities as living organisms, which are generated and cultivated, are liable to corruption and decline.[15] This metaphor of the city as a living organism replicates this cycle of growth (*phuō*) and decay. The city is related to nature (*phūsis*) as a whole and to light (*phōs*) synonymous with generation, growth, and cultivation.[16] Such activities are integral to the formation and ordering of the city. Beginning with the composition of the individual souls of the citizens, the presence of the appetitive soul distinguishes plants from animals and humans, 'This soul . . . shares not at all in opinions and reasoning and mind but in sensation, pleasant and painful, together with desires.'[17] Given Plato's identification of the plant with appetites and desires, the civic organism literally gives birth to the weeds who appear to be ruled by their appetites and passions. Plato contrasts those domestic plants capable of cultivation with those uncultivated plants or weeds which grow in the wild and thus introduces a hierarchical distinction between them.[18] Following *Republic* VIII where each of the imperfect cities is constituted by a specific principle identified with the pursuit of appetites or desires which leads to its dissolution, the *Political Regime* replicates these imperfect cities beginning with timocracy identified with the desire for honour attained partially if not wholly by the pursuit of wealth, leisure, and domination. Timocracy is defined by the accumulation of merit arising from a relentless desire to attain honour by distinguishing oneself over and against others:

14 See McCoy, *Plato on the Rhetoric of Philosophers and Sophists*, 11–22, 111–37.

15 Cf. Crone, 'Al-Fārābī's Imperfect Constitutions'.

16 See Marder, *The Philosopher's Plant*, 11.

17 Plato, *Timaeus* 77b.

18 Plotinus appropriates this distinction in his description of the world-plant resistant to pruning and cultivation. The universal tree synonymous with the world-soul grows in such a way that it does admit any empty spaces to grow between branches instead filling them 'with shoots which also grow from the root, those, too, in a different way' (*Ennead* III.3.7, 22). This different way is the way of evil insofar as the formative principle succumbs to the material principle. These shoots are like weeds that spread rampantly alluding to the increase of evil in the world-plant, 'unboundedness in relation to limit, and formlessness in relation to the formative principle', and are 'always undefined, nowhere stable, subject to every sort of influence, instantiate complete poverty' (*Ennead* I.8.2.10–20).

> for according to them, the most exalted thing a human being is to be honored for is being well-known for domination over one, two, or many things; not being dominated either due to himself, because his supporters are many or powerful, or both of these, and not being subjected to what is loathsome, while subjecting someone else to what is loathsome when he wills.[19]

A certain violence resides in the heart of a timocracy wholly concerned with the pursuit of honour insofar as the appetites of the citizens are exclusively aimed at elevating their own social status through the domination and subjection of others.[20] Since war is the foremost expression of conquest and domination, the pursuit of honour may potentially obstruct the pursuit of virtue. In a timocracy, the desire for power elevating the rank and status of individual citizens ultimately harms the general health of the city.

Another operative metaphor appearing in a timocracy is that of opportunists or hunters (*mutaqanniṣūn*) who are always seeking power and glory. The dangers and attendant harms associated with the pursuit of power are inherent to the composition of a timocracy. The citizens may be obedient but incapable of properly discerning between healthy and unhealthy forms of authority and therefore liable to being seduced by the deception of sophistry. The problem of sophistry associated with the weeds becomes visibly apparent as a vice, 'for the status of weeds in cities is that of darnel in wheat, the thorns of plants within the crop, or the rest of the grasses that are useless or harmful to the crops or seedlings.'[21] Certain weeds are classified as opportunists or hunters who live according to the actions by which virtue and happiness are gained although they relentlessly pursue honour and wealth.[22] Here we might identify an affinity with Plato's luxurious city where nothing stands in the way of their appetites. In contrast to the city of necessity or the city of pigs, an unsatiable appetite (*pleonexia*) overcomes the luxurious city, 'For these things, as it seems, won't satisfy some, or this way of life, but couches, tables, and other furniture will be added, and, of course, relishes, perfume, incense, courtesans, and cakes – all sorts of all of them.'[23] With the accumulation of things contributing to the city

[19] al-Fārābī, *Political Regime*, 98. [90.22–6], 77–8, tr. Butterworth.

[20] Whereas Plotinus warns against the prevalence of the material principle to overcome the formative principle, those citizens residing in a timocracy are ruled by material appetites for honour which can only come about through physical conquest and hence brute force; see *Ennead* II.4.12.

[21] al-Fārābī, *Political Regime*, 92. [87.10–12], 76, tr. Butterworth.

[22] Ibid., 122. [104.11–15], 90.

[23] Plato, *Republic* 373a.

in its engorgement, Plato includes individuals and social classes responsible for producing and pursuing these appetites and desires, 'all the hunters and imitators, many concerned with figures and colors, many with music; and poets and their helpers, rhapsodes, actors, choral dancers, contractors, and craftsmen of all sorts of equipment, for feminine adornment, as well as other things'.[24] The weeds manipulate the means to happiness to attain their own ends as individualists intent upon only improving themselves. Although some weeds are not exclusively oriented by the pursuit of honour and wealth, their designation as hunters also corresponds to those citizens affiliated with oligarchies. The feverish city composed of hunters constantly seeking out their elusive prey reflects the appetites and desires of those citizens in the city of pigs who are never satiated, 'And once more, we are going to need swineherds. This animal was not in our earlier city - there was no need - but in this one there will be need of it in addition. And there will also be need of very many other fatted beasts if someone will eat them, won't there?'[25] Given this tendency to oligarchy, al-Fārābī proceeds to describe an even more derogatory group of weeds who are exclusively identified with the ignorant or defective city:

> And among them are those who have a passion for one of the ends of the inhabitants of the ignorant cities, but the Laws of the city and its religion prevent them from it. So they apply themselves to the utterances and statements of the lawgiver for his precepts and interpret them so as to agree with their passion, thereby embellishing that thing by their interpretation. These [people] are called distorters (*muḥarrifa*).[26]

These weeds are akin to sophists who distort (*zayyafa*) the laws of the city and harm the constitution. They ultimately aim to mislead the citizens in their quest to distortingly (*ḥarrafū*) interpret (*ta'wīl*) the utterances of the lawgiver. They possess a requisite intelligence to interpret the law only to suit their own selfish ends by engaging in the art of embellishment. Since their training embellishes precepts for the sake of pursuing their own passions, they intentionally mislead the citizens and therefore circumvent them from receiving a correct interpretation of the laws. This distortion of the judicial and religious laws indicates their profound opposition to the attainment of happiness as the ultimate end of the virtuous city. However, the laws of the city and religion prevent them from explicitly pursuing their appetites and passions.

[24] Ibid., 373b.
[25] Ibid., 373c.
[26] al-Fārābī, *Political Regime*, 122. [104.16–21], 91, tr. Butterworth.

Therefore, they must appeal to the divine lawgiver, in this case, the Prophet Muḥammad, who sets down the laws. The distorters are contrasted with other weeds, namely schismatics (*māriqa*), who misunderstand the precepts of the lawgiver due to a lack of intelligence and a defective grasp of his statements:

> And among them are those who are not intent on distortion. But due to their poor understanding of the lawgiver's intention and their defective grasp (*nuqṣān taṣawwurih*) of his statements, they understand the Laws of the city differently from the way the lawgiver intended. So their actions fall outside the intention of the first ruler and they err without being conscious of it. These people are called schismatics.[27]

The schismatics fail to comprehend the precepts of the lawgiver and therefore have a poor understanding of his intentions. Their defective comprehension of the precepts implies that they simply lack the intellectual ability to understand the law. Moreover, the schismatics error without being conscious of the error they have committed. Since their ignorance presents the opportunity to learn from their errors, they should not be accorded the same degree of guilt as the distorters who intentionally misconstrue the aims of the law. Although the schismatics are unable to initially distinguish between true and false images, they present a similar emancipatory potential to the prisoners of Plato's Allegory. The schismatics may be identified with those citizens ruled by their appetites in the city of pigs. They are unwilfully ignorant and thus possess the potential to be properly educated. In contrast to the distorters who intentionally misuse their knowledge to harm the city, the schismatics may be properly steered to contribute to the good of the city. Therefore, philosophers are especially needed to guide the city out of ignorance and defection.

Al-Fārābī subsequently supplants the schismatics with another group of weeds identified as sceptics (*mustarshidūn*) who seek the right path and are capable of discerning between truth and false images by engaging in dialectical inquiry, 'Another sort has already imagined things we have mentioned, except that they are not persuaded by what they have imagined. So, for themselves and for others, they show those things to be false by arguments. In doing so, they are not contending against the virtuous city. Rather, they are asking for guidance and seeking the truth.'[28] By detecting false images, the sceptics are not persuaded by what they have imagined. With their dialectical demonstration of the difference between truth and falsity, the sceptics do not oppose the

[27] Ibid., 122. [104.22–7], 91.
[28] Ibid., 123. [104.28–105.2], 91.

aims of the virtuous city but rather contribute to its ultimate aim. The sceptics require further education to refine their own intellects to identify the correspondence between the image and the thing. If the correspondence between the image and the thing is proven to be true, then the dialectic continues to a higher stage. However, if there is a lack of correspondence, then one proceeds to another level of imagination which only approximates the truth, 'Whoever is like this has their level of imagination elevated to things that the arguments they bring forth do not show to be false. If they are persuaded in thus being elevated, they are left there. But if they are not persuaded by that either and fall upon topics they can contend against, they are elevated to another level.'[29] The role of images in relation to the exercise of the imagination is ambivalent for the sceptics. Images may contain truth and thus serve as a vehicle for promoting the attainment of happiness in the virtuous city. If the imagination is subsumed at a higher level of the dialectic with the intellect, then one must resist being persuaded by those images associated with a lower level of the dialectic in order to be elevated to a higher level of truth. Despite the liberatory potential of the sceptics who seek the truth, the problem of sophistry persistently threatens the welfare of the city with those weeds who revel in dissimulation and falsity:

> Among them, another sort presents as false what they imagine. Whenever, they are elevated in rank, they present it as false – even when they attain the ranking of truth. They do this all in seeking domination alone or in seeking to embellish one of the purposes of the inhabitants of the ignorant cities to which they are inclined. So they present as false [what they imagine] in every way they can. They do not like to hear anything that strengthens happiness and truth in the soul nor any argument that embellishes them and prescribes them for the soul, but meet them with sham arguments that they presume will discredit happiness. In doing so, many of them are intent on appearing to be excused for inclining to one of the purposes of the inhabitants of the ignorant cities.[30]

Since these weeds deliberately present true images to deceive and hence mislead the citizens, they appear to have some training in dialectic to discern between true and false images. Nevertheless, they knowingly betray their own knowledge of the truth only to further their own craving for power. In the *Political Regime*, this kind of sophistry that reappears in the necessary city,

[29] Ibid., 123. [105.3–10], 91, tr. Butterworth (mod.).
[30] Ibid., 124. [105.11–21], 91–2.

the plutocratic city, the hedonistic city, the timocratic city, and the democratic city culminates in the city of domination which indicates a city ruled by absolute force, 'Their love and their purpose in all of that are domination, conquest, humiliation, and that the conquered possesses neither himself nor any other thing for the sake of which he has been dominated but is subject to obeying the conqueror in whatever passion he has.'[31] The one who loves to dominate subsumes the interests of all the others under their own selfish interests. Although the timocratic city feigns virtue in the pursuit of honour and thus is accorded a slightly higher status, the city of domination clearly ranks among the worst of the defective cities. In a city obsessed with conquest and domination, the ruler who subverts the citizens into believing in false images to limit their own innate intellectual potential and blindly obey authority becomes identical to the sophist who wilfully betrays the citizens to preserve their own power.

Al-Fārābī concludes his presentation of the weeds with those who imagine happiness and moreover the first principles of philosophy but lack the power to understand (*taṣawwur*) concepts and therefore cannot distinguish between truth and falsity. In opposition to the sophists who clearly possess this capacity and misuse it for their own ends, these weeds by virtue of their defective imagination are unable to comprehend truth (*ṣādiq*):

> Among them is a sort that imagines happiness and principles [of the existents] but it is not within the power of their minds to form a concept of them at all. Or it is not within the power of their understanding to form a sufficient concept of them. So they present as false what they imagine and seize on the topics of contention in them. Whenever they are elevated to a level of imagination that is closer to the truth, they present it as false. It is not possible for them to be elevated to the level of truth, because it is not within the power of their minds to understand it. It may chance that many of these people present as false much of what they imagine, not because there are truly topics of contention in what they imagine, but because their imagination is defective. So, due to their poor understanding, they present that as false – not because there is a topic of contention in it.[32]

In contrast to Plato's Allegory, which presents an account of prisoners who are liberated from their ignorance, these radically ignorant weeds are incapable of even perceiving the difference between true and false images. Hence, we may

[31] Ibid., 104. [94.21–4], 82.
[32] Ibid., 125. [105.22–35], 92.

begin to envision how those who have an innate disposition to be liberated and become philosopher-ruler-*imāms* are also effectively constrained and persecuted by those segments of society associated with the most derogatory weeds. The existence of such weeds ultimately calls into question any purported teleology which would culminate in the concrete manifestation of the virtuous city. Here al-Fārābī's presentation of the weeds is compounded by an even more sinister form of natural identification with the introduction of vipers (*afāʿī*):

> For example, poisonous animals naturally hostile to the rest of the species of animals that act hostilely to the rest of the species of animals: vipers, for example, serve the elements by means of their poison by dissolving the species of animals into them. The poisons in plants are like that, yet these are sometimes poisons relatively. For that species serves two things. It ought to be known that predatory animals are not like vipers. Vipers do not have poison in order to improve their nutrition by means of the rest of animals. Rather, they act hostilely by nature toward all species of animals and are intent on nullifying them.[33]

The correspondence between the vipers and weeds highlights how the vipers subvert any rational cosmic order which would accord with a benevolent ruler aimed at the common good. The malevolence of the vipers and weeds gestures to the overturning of Platonism. The vipers upset any natural teleology and do not aspire to the Good. If we are to discount the utopian tendencies portending the existence of a unified global political community, then the introduction of the vipers and weeds is presented as a rhetorical device to interrogate the rational foundations of the virtuous city and thereby affirms a certain materiality whereby the distinction between the sensible and the intelligible domains comes to be inverted.[34] The vipers and weeds exemplify a recalcitrant materiality which effectively disrupts those assumptions privileging the hegemony of form. The vipers merely eradicate or nullify that which stands in their way by exercising a violence towards every other species of creatures.[35]

[33] Ibid., 62. [68.22-7], 59.

[34] Here we may anticipate a similar gesture in Aristotle's psychology and epistemology beginning with the role of the imagination in induction. The primacy of formal knowledge may be called into question by further highlighting the materiality of the imagination, 'there is no thinking without a phantasm' (Aristotle, *De Anima* 431a16–17).

[35] The vipers exhibit an errancy reminiscent of the receptacle (*khōra*) (Plato, *Timaeus* 51a2–52d). Given the harmonisation of Plato and Aristotle within Neoplatonism, Plotinus introduces a rather prescriptive account of errancy whereby materiality comes to be explicitly identified with evil by its resistance to form; see *Ennead* I.6.6, I.7.3.

Although the weeds possess an oppositional nature tending towards resistance and disruption which may serve the good of the city, the vipers remain absolutely hostile to all order.

Al-Fārābī's distinction between various species of animals which come together to either benefit or harm one another demonstrates an intimate familiarity with Aristotle's classificatory scheme in his *History of Animals*.[36] Among those species which obtain what is necessary despite being isolated from or at war with one another are wild elephants who 'fight fiercely against each other' and enslave the defeated elephant, who 'does not stand against the victor's voice'.[37] Additionally, certain species of fish may fiercely fight against one another in competition for food or mates but may all come together under certain conditions favourable to their collective survival, 'among the fishes some form shoals with each other and are friends, while those that do not shoal are at war.'[38] Cattle, goats, and sheep may tend to mindlessly and independently wander for the sake of obtaining their own sustenance yet when they do reunite they do not impede one another, 'the cattle too graze with their companions in habitual groups, and if one strays, the others follow; hence if the cowherds fail to find a particular one, they immediately look for them as well.'[39] In contrast, certain species of animals are constantly at war with one another, to include the eagle and the snake, the owl and the crow, the turtle dove and the pyralis, 'for they have the same feeding place and livelihood . . . so that their food makes enemies of these too.'[40] Those species of animals which are not engaged in constant war may nevertheless isolate themselves from members of the same species for the sake of procreation, 'Over the feeding of the young both birds carry out the work; they give to each, watching habitually the one that has already had it, so that it should not get it twice.'[41] Many birds also exhibit behaviour akin to prudence, 'Many instances of intelligence seem to occur among the cranes too. For they migrate a long way, and fly to a great height in order to survey the distance . . . And when they settle, while the others sleep with their head under their wing, standing on one foot and then the other, the leader with his head uncovered keeps a lookout.'[42] Likewise, the

[36] See al-Fārābī, *Political Regime*, 63. [69.6–21], 60, tr. Butterworth; and Aristotle, *History of Animals* 488a2–4.

[37] Aristotle, *History of Animals* 610a15–17.

[38] Ibid., 610b1–3.

[39] Ibid., 611a1–9.

[40] Ibid., 609a20–4.

[41] Ibid., 612b26–8.

[42] Ibid., 614b18–27.

industriousness of ants cooperate in the pursuit of a common cause, 'Now the working of the ants is on the surface for all to see, and how they all go on one path and put aside and store their food; for they work at night too when there is a full moon.'[43] Those birds and insects which are more likely to engage in mutual cooperation (*mu'āwana*) with each other and other animals for the sake of living well present a compelling alternative to the hierarchically organised political community.[44]

With the primacy afforded to the power of the imagination, we might entertain the possibility of a more inclusive account of animal nature intent on remedying the defects identified with natural teleology. The radical resistance granted to materiality struggling against the hegemony of form becomes apparent. We shall not exclusively pursue the political implications of such a materialism at this stage. However, this interrogation of the form-matter distinction informs the emergence of a cosmopolitan paradigm which recognises the anarchic multiplicity of materiality in contrast to the hegemony of form. The *Political Regime* concludes with an empirical account of the material conditions of the political community. The perfect or virtuous community does not exist in a vacuum but is only determined in and by relation to those imperfect communities. This ambivalent relation between perfection and imperfection demonstrates a remarkable reluctance to strictly demarcate between the intelligible and the sensible domains. If *Attainment of Happiness* is to be received as a cautionary tale about the dangers of utopian and proto-utopian tendencies of communities leading to their absolute homogenisation and totalisation, then heterogeneity and multiplicity are validated insofar as religions coexist with one another alongside the practice of philosophy. Rather

[43] Ibid., 610a22b14–18.

[44] Al-Fārābī accords to animals the capacity to cooperate for the sake of contributing to the common good of their species, including the capacity for some animals to acquire language thereby calling into question any facile demarcation between *zōē* and *bios*. Beginning with Aristotle's distinction between articulate and inarticulate expressions in *De Interpretatione* 16a27–9, al-Fārābī's account of language in non-human animals in his *Long Commentary on the* De Interpretatione (*Sharḥ Kitāb al-ʿIbāra*) is radically innovative for his time, 'Al-Fārābī adds that by "intranscribable or inarticulate sounds", Aristotle means those that have no graphical sign. When Aristotle mentions that these sounds may signify something he is referring to the emotions of non-human animals, such as fear, pleasure or anger, emotional states that non-human animals can communicate among themselves. Hence, given that non-human animals are able to express certain emotions through meaningful sounds and these symbolize something to other members of their species, al-Fārābī concludes that the "sounds of beasts" shall be considered as articulate expressions' (López-Farjeat, 'The Language of Non-human Animals in al-Fārābī and Avicenna', 185).

than simply assuming that religion is diametrically opposed to philosophy, the practice of religion and philosophy are to be conjoined.

By allowing the vipers and weeds into the political conversation as figures of opposition and resistance, the totalising tendency of absolute sovereignty and hence the subsumption of the singular by the universal is effectively resisted.[45] The affirmation of the heterogeneous proliferation of opinions arises with the imagination as a necessary tool for political communication. Religion cannot exist without the imagination. The philosopher-ruler-*imām* is dependent upon the imagination to transmit images to the citizens of the political community. Without the imagination, their relationship is disrupted thereby leading to the demise of the city. The production of images conjoins the philosopher-ruler-*imām* with the political community in such a way that religion arises from the concrete materiality of the imagination.[46] The introduction of the weeds and vipers into the ignorant city serves to express the pervasive nature of the imagination and thereby reaffirms a materialism which decisively calls into question the presuppositions of Platonic and Neoplatonic metaphysics. The vipers and weeds exhibit a necessary ambivalence which discounts their ultimate value but are nevertheless afforded a rank and status within the organisation of the city.[47] If most weeds suffer from a defective imagination by lacking the capacity to sufficiently comprehend the truth, then the image becomes the exclusive source of contention and debate within the ignorant city. These weeds thus appear to be hopelessly confused because they are simply too ignorant to know the difference between truth and falsity and thus presume that they are constantly being deluded given their lack of simple apprehension. A certain toxicity prevails in the suspicion of those ignorant weeds who do not trust the wisdom of the philosopher-ruler-*imām*:

[45] The production of a multiplicity of images affirms a civic pluralism contributing to al-Fārābī's cosmopolitanism; see Parens, *An Islamic Philosophy of Virtuous Religions*, 2–5.

[46] The recuperation of al-Fārābī's cosmopolitanism stems from the retrieval of an occluded materialist tradition inherited from Aristotle and subsequently adopted by Ibn Rushd, Ibn Gabirol, Maimonides, and Gersonides. See especially Dobbs-Weinstein, 'Aristotle on the Natural Dwelling of the Intellect'. For an interpretation of Ibn Sīnā inspired by twentieth-century materialism, see Bloch, *Avicenna and the Aristotelian Left.*

[47] Al-Fārābī's inclusion of such controversial figures reconfigures the ancient map of metaphysics, epistemology, and psychology for the sake of expanding these branches into the cosmopolitical domain. Although we would be remiss to claim that Plato, Aristotle, and Plotinus are exclusively regional philosophers, any metaphysics which subscribes to a hierarchically organised political community by ethnicity, race, or gender may be interrogated with this turn to the democratic city. Despite al-Fārābī's reluctance to affirm democracy as the most perfect city, his cosmopolitanism demonstrates proto-modern tendencies by gesturing towards the promise of democracy as the happiest of all political communities.

> When unable to imagine something sufficiently or to grasp the true topics of contention in the places in which there are topics of contention and when unable to understand the truth, many of them presume that the one who apprehends the truth and says he has apprehended it is lying deliberately in a quest for honor or domination. Or they presume that he is a deluded zealot who also wants to present the truth as false and to vilify the one who has apprehended it. That leads many of them to presume that all people are deluded about everything they claim to have apprehended.[48]

If a city is wholly ignorant and defective, then any bond of trust will be broken between the philosopher-ruler-*imām* and the political community. This delusion culminates in a confused perplexity about all things akin to the Tower of Babel. Moreover, the philosopher-ruler-*imām* naively presumes that these weeds are ignorant simpletons without any hope of redemption through education, 'Due to that it is obligatory for the ruler of the virtuous city to watch over the weeds, keep them busy, and cure each sort by means of what is particularly suited to it – either expulsion from the city, punishment, imprisonment, or assigning them tasks even though they do not strive after them.'[49] Although some weeds are capable of reform, the vipers who demonstrate absolute hostility to political association are conjoined with those individuals who are bestial by nature. Unlike the vipers who at least belong to the city, these beasts (*an'ām*) are not citizens and therefore are absolutely divorced from any form of civic association. Despite the absence of citizenship and civic association, not every beast is qualified as wild. This distinction between those who are included and excluded from the virtuous city alludes to the controversial status of foreigners and slaves. Those foreigners who live at the extremities of the inhabited dwelling-places and who engage in exotic practices such as eating raw meat, grazing on wild plants, or ravishing their prey as do the predatory animals are wild and 'they ought to be treated as beasts'.[50] In contrast, a relatively higher status is accorded to beasts who are domesticated, 'Now any of them who is domestic and useful in some way to the cities is to be spared, enslaved, and used as beasts are used.'[51]

Al-Fārābī does not explicitly address the historical phenomenon of slavery in the *Political Regime*. However, the harm imposed from those who are contrary to preservation of the virtuous city is grave enough that dire measures,

[48] al-Fārābī, *Political Regime*, 125. [106.3–7], 92, tr. Butterworth.
[49] Ibid., 125. [106.15–18], 92.
[50] Ibid., 92. [88.27–8], 76.
[51] Ibid., 92. [88.23–5], 76.

such as enslavement of the conquered, need to be implemented. Given his lack of access to the *Politics*, al-Fārābī's account of slavery invokes the *History of Animals* where Aristotle characterises certain non-human animals as gregarious, independent, and social or political.[52] Therefore, those human animals or beasts that are domesticated by virtue of some degree of civic association are at least presented with the possibility of being spared and enslaved. This description of such a concrete state of affairs does not appear to explicitly prescribe slavery as a historical practice. Like Aristotle who understood the necessity of the slavery for the sake of granting leisure to citizens to conduct political affairs, al-Fārābī brings attention to the usefulness of slaves by virtue of their contributions to the attainment of happiness in the political community. If slaves occupy the status of beasts as *zōē*, then the slave is part of the master and inseparable from his or her ontological and political identity.[53] In this sense, the problem of slavery may be neutralised if we are to attribute the contributions of the slave to the shared teleological paradigm of Aristotle and al-Fārābī where the parts or limbs of the body serve the whole organism and the non-rational part of the soul serve the rational part. Hence, slavery comes to be designated as a useful institution within the political community. Those slaves who are not deemed to be useful are contrary to the divine purpose of the philosopher-ruler-*imām* and the political community:

> When at one time someone exists who is completely disposed by nature for all of the virtues and they are then established in them by custom, this human being surpasses in virtue the virtues found among most people to the point that he almost goes beyond the human virtues to a higher class of humanity. The Ancients used to call this human being divine. The one

[52] 'Some are gregarious, some are solitary . . . And of the gregarious . . . some are political, while others are scattered. Gregarious creatures are among birds, such as the pigeon, the crane, and the swan . . . Political creatures are those among one which there is some one and common function for all; and this property is not common to all creatures that are gregarious. Some political creatures are man, the bee, the ant, and the crane. Again, of these political creatures some submit to a ruler, others are subject to no rule: as for instance, the crane and the several sorts of bee submit to a ruler, whereas ants and numbers of other creatures are subject to no rule' (Aristotle, *History of Animals* 487b33–488a13).

[53] Sara Brill incisively retrieves Pierre Pellegrin's description of the 'fused life' of master and slave to accentuate the pervasive presence of *zōē* in the *Politics*, 'The slave, according to Aristotle, is a partner in the master's life, a *koinōnos zōēs* (1260a40). It is worth emphasizing the organicism at work here. Aristotle will describe the intimacy between master and slave as such that "the slave is a sort of part of the master, a part of his body, as it were, ensouled, yet separate" (125511–12)' (*Aristotle on the Concept of Shared Life*, 210). Cf. Pellegrin, 'Natural Slavery', 98; and Brown, *Slavery and Islam*, 182–3.

> contrary to them and disposed to all of the evil actions, in whom the traits of those evils are established by custom, they almost place beyond the human evils to what is even more evil. They have no name for the excess of his evil and sometimes call them a beast and similar names.[54]

By allusion to those individuals who are incorrigible, al-Fārābī retrieves Aristotle's definition of brutish persons who demonstrate an evil incapable of any kind of reform.[55] The brutish even fall below the category of natural slaves by their incapacity to either deliberate or obey. Therefore, they will not even be able to benefit from natural slavery. Like the vipers, these brutish individuals who stand outside the city constitute a threat to its sovereignty. The preservation of sovereignty is conditioned by this opposition.[56] Hence, even the democratic city, where every citizen is accorded freedom and equality, must be measured against the relative unfreedom and inequality of those beast-like individuals. The popular sovereignty of the democratic community is constitutively defined in relation to that which is absolutely antithetical to its own existence. If the democratic city comes to be identified by its relative pacifism insofar as those who rule are elected

[54] al-Fārābī, *Selected Aphorisms*, 12. [33.4–13], 18, tr. Butterworth. Cf. al-Fārābī, *Aphorisms of the Statesman*, 11., 32–3, 110–11, tr. Dunlop. Al-Fārābī retrieves the demarcation between sovereign and beast from *Nicomachean Ethics* 1145a.

[55] 'So, if as is said, people are turned from humans into gods by a surpassing degree of virtue, it would be clear that it would be such active condition that would be placed opposite to one that is animal-like; for just as there is no vice or virtue belonging to an animal, so too neither state belongs to a god, but the one side is something more honorable than virtue, and the other is something of a different kind of vice. But since it is also a rare thing for there to be a godlike man . . . so too an animal-like person is rare among human beings, and is found most of all among the barbarians, though some instances occur on account of diseases or defects. But we also disparage people who surpass the rest of human beings in vice by calling them animal-like' (Aristotle, *Nicomachean Ethics* 1145a23–33). The reference to barbarians contrasting the superiority of the Greeks with the inferiority of non-Greeks might be said to originate from Hippocrates' *On Airs, Waters, and Places* which claims that the inhabitants of Europe are more courageous than Asiatic peoples due to the variable climate. This attribution of natural differences between Greeks and non-Greeks is contributes to al-Fārābī's distinction between citizens and beast-like individuals. Cf. Aristotle, *Politics* 1327b18–35; Lemoine, *Plato's Caves*, 13; and Curzer, *Aristotle and the Virtues*, 382–6.

[56] By retrieving Homer's reproach of the man who has 'no clan, no law, no hearth' as war-like and isolated like a pawn in chess, Aristotle contrasts the absolute sovereign with the beast as those figures which are diametrically opposed to one another, 'he who is cityless, is by nature and not by chance, a being either degraded or else superior to man [the one who is without a City, who is *apolis*, who is apolitical, is either below man or else above man, either an animal or else a god]' (*Politics* 1253a2–7).

by popular vote, then the war-like state of nature which stands outside the boundaries of the city characterises those individuals who are naturally bellicose and hence belligerent. Since nature demonstrates a cyclical pattern marked by generation and corruption and the eternal contest for survival, the Platonic paradigm of the city in speech at least strives to overcome this fate by gesturing towards a future teleological possibility which stands outside the law of nature.[57]

The prevalence of belligerence and bellicosity in the virtuous city effectively leads to its corruption and demise. Al-Fārābī's exposition of ignorant and defective cities concludes with the pessimistic admission that the weeds presume only a relativistic notion of truth which in turn only compounds their delusion:

> And some of them presume that the truth is what appears to each person and what they presume at each moment and that the truth about each thing is what someone presumes it to be. And some of them exert themselves in making it seem whatever has been presumed to have been apprehended up to this point is completely false and that even if there is something accurate and true, it has not yet been apprehended.[58]

Given the predominance of such ignorant cities, we may compare the conclusion of the *Political Regime* with the *Virtuous City* which contests a series of arguments identified with scepticism. The practice of scepticism is affiliated with sophistry by their common aim to banish the need for philosophical dialectic. In the *Political Regime*, scepticism is applied to the dismissal of the possibility that truth may reside in dreams:

> And some of them imagine – as in a sleeping person's dream or as with a thing seen from afar – that there is a truth here, and it occurs to them that those who claim to have apprehended it have perhaps apprehended it or that there is among them someone who has perhaps apprehended it. In themselves, they sense that it has eluded them either because apprehending it requires a long time as well as toil and hardship whereas they do not

[57] Cf. Derrida, 'We must already anticipate, even if only by a bit; we must move toward the horizon that limits the meaning of the word, in order to come to know better what "democracy" will have been *able* to signify, what it *ought*, in truth, to have meant. We already have some "idea" of what democracy should mean, what it *will have already meant* – and the idea, the ideal, the Greek *eidos* or the *idea* also designates the turn of a contour, the limit surrounding a visible form' (*Rogues*, 18).

[58] al-Fārābī, *Political Regime*, 125. [106.19–25], 93, tr. Butterworth (mod.).

> have adequate time for it nor the power to toil and persevere, because they are busy with pleasures and other such things to which they have become accustomed and which it is hard for them to discard, or because they have sensed that they would not [be able to] apprehend it even if all its cases were made available to them.[59]

Despite the allusion to those prisoners who find themselves rather hopelessly trapped in the cave without any reprieve from the false images and who rather unwillingly toil in their ascent to the truth, a glimmer of optimism resides within those weeds who may be able to learn the art of dialectic to discern the truth within the image. However, most weeds are controlled by their own passions to such a degree that any search for the truth will undoubtedly be futile:

> Sorrow and grief occur to them due to their presuming that it is possible someone else may have seized on it. Due to envy about someone having perhaps apprehended the truth, they form the opinion to struggle by means of sham arguments to make it seem that the one who says he has apprehended it is either deluded or a liar who, in what he purports, is searching for honor, wealth, or some other thing such as to incite passion. Many of these people sense their own ignorance and perplexity. They are pained and hurt by what they feel in themselves, and that grieves and torments them. They find no way to remove this from themselves by means of a science that would seize on the truth, the apprehension of which would earn them pleasure. So they form the opinion to take a respite from that through recourse to the rest of the ends of the ignorant city and to jesting and playful things. They set those down as consolation until death comes to relieve them of their lot.[60]

Ignorance is integral to the composition of the democratic city insofar as some citizens may stive for but nevertheless fail to attain happiness. Although this class of citizens is generally mired in their own ignorance, certain individuals are gifted enough to seek a philosophical education. Therefore, someone who is born with a capacious and creative imagination may finally come to seek and know the truth. The imagination rivals the intellect in its power to discern the truth of the image. By presenting the possibility of the weeds flourishing in the virtuous city, the imagination of the philosopher-ruler-*imām* demonstrates an innate political potential to transform the city.

[59] Ibid., 125. [106.26–107.1–6], 93.
[60] Ibid., 125. [107.7–19], 93.

Al-Fārābī does not determine which political community is most amenable to the imagination. However, most images in their diverse and variegated forms are produced and created by the democratic city. By reference to Plato's description of the democratic city as a multifaceted cloak, the cloak as an image may be construed as seductive and yet deceptive by concealing the imperfections of the city. Rather than bringing attention to its potential for seduction and deception, the multifaceted cloak is valorised for its positive connotations contributing to the diversity of the city. The cloak as a singular image thus conjoins unity with multiplicity.[61] Since the democratic city is defined by the freedom of its citizens to pursue their own individual appetites, it becomes especially difficult for citizens to focus upon a specific virtue contributing to the attainment of happiness of the city as a whole. Following Plato's account of imperfect cities in *Republic* VIII, this quest for self-fulfilment may inevitably come into conflict with the welfare of the city.

Both the *Political Regime* and *Virtuous City* are guided by an optimism presenting a Platonic framework for the attainment of happiness in the virtuous city with the introduction of the philosopher-ruler-*imām*. However, al-Fārābī rather cautiously concludes with the corruption of the city hastened by the ignorance of the weeds and the malevolence of the vipers and beasts.[62] Nevertheless, the ignorance of the weeds may be countered by the promise that some weeds may realise their potential and eventually break free from their self-incurred tutelage. The activity of philosophy is always circumscribed by this movement from ignorance to knowledge. Ignorance motivates the practice of philosophy as the pursuit of wisdom. Here we may begin to envision a search for truth originating from those images which extend from the philosopher-ruler-*imām* to each and every citizen. Even those citizens who appear to be ineducable are to be exposed to persuasive images for the sake of their own pedagogical value. In contrast to Plato

[61] 'Democracy seems – and this is its appearing, if not its appearance and its simulacrum – the most beautiful (*kallistē*), the most seductive of constitutions (*politeiōn*) (557c). Its beauty resembles that of a multi- and brightly colored (*poikilon)* garment . . . Because of the freedom and the multicoloredness of a democracy peopled by such a diversity of men, one would seek in vain a single constitution or *politeia* within it. Given over to freedom, to *exousia* this time, democracy contains all the different kinds of constitutions, of regimes, or states (*panta genē politeiōn*)' (Derrida, *Rogues*, 26).

[62] The ignorance of the weeds and malevolence of the vipers supports the assessment of al-Fārābī as a political realist; see especially Mahdi, *Alfarabi and the Foundations of Islamic Political Philosophy*, 139–46; Butterworth, 'Alfarabi's Goal'; 'What Might We Learn from al-Fārābī about Plato and Aristotle with respect to Lawgiving?'; and Parens, 'Escaping the Scholastic Paradigm', 214–16.

who distinguishes between gold, silver, bronze, and iron souls in his city in speech, al-Fārābī entertains the possibility that some weeds may become philosophers and hence rulers of the virtuous city.

Liberty and Justice for All

With the presence of weeds within the democratic city, a relative freedom, equality, and justice may be attained among all citizens. Freedom and equality as a terminological pair deserve further scrutiny in the constitution of the democratic city. The relationship between freedom and equality is aporetic insofar as the conditionality of equality is to be contrasted with the unconditionality of freedom.[63] Education within the democratic city is determined by the common power of the imagination, which in turn promotes a relative equality contributing to the general happiness of all citizens. Although the democratic city ultimately remains imperfect, it is the best of the imperfect cities, 'this is the most admirable and happy city.'[64] Despite its apparent imperfections, virtue and happiness are inextricably conjoined in the democratic city. The function of education is to provide equality among the citizens by virtue of the power of the image to teach and persuade. The diversity of images utilised for such a purpose reflects the constitution of the democratic city composed of the most virtuous citizens (*al-afāḍil*) of many kinds. Here, the diversity of the democratic city serves as a microcosm for the diversity of the entire inhabited world by being composed of 'countless similar and dissimilar groups (*ṭawā'if*)'.[65] By the power of the philosopher-ruler-*imām* in each political community to impart such persuasive images, the democratic city 'develops into many cities, distinct yet interwoven (*dākhila ba'ḍuhā fī ba'ḍ*) with the parts of one interspersed among the parts of the others'.[66] The

[63] See Jacques Derrida's account of antimony, 'The persistence, the ineluctable return, in truth, of a sort of aporia or, if you prefer, of an antinomy at the heart of every -nomy, that is, at the source of every autoimmune process. This antimony at the heart of the democratic has long been recognized. It is classical and canonical: it is the one between freedom and equality – that constitutive and diabolical couple of democracy. I would translate this into my own language by saying that equality tends to introduce measure and calculation (and thus conditionality) whereas freedom is by essence, unconditional, indivisible, heterogeneous to calculation and measure' (*Rogues*, 47–8). Cf. Hadad, *Derrida and the Inheritance of Democracy*, 7–9.

[64] '*al-madīna al-mu'jaba wa-l-madīna al-sa'īda*'. al-Fārābī, *Political Regime*, 115. [100.18], 87, tr. Butterworth (mod.). Cf. Khalidi, 'Al-Fārābī on the Democratic City', 384.

[65] al-Fārābī, *Political Regime*, 113. [99.19], 86, tr. Butterworth.

[66] Ibid., 115. [100.26–8], 87, tr. Butterworth (mod.). Cf. Khalidi, 'Al-Fārābī on the Democratic City', 385.

democratic city is informed by multiculturalism insofar as religions originate in a given geographical and climactic region. The ethnic and religious diversity of the democratic city clearly warrants attention, 'the nations emigrate to it and reside there, and it grows beyond measure. People of every race multiply in it . . .'[67] Hospitality and toleration are among those virtues exhibiting its unique cosmopolitan character. The hospitality of the virtuous city remains so utterly pervasive that 'foreigners cannot be distinguished from the residents'.[68] Despite Plato's prohibition against intermarriage, al-Fārābī privileges intermarriage between diverse ethnic groups for the sake of strengthening the bonds of mutual cooperation. The plurality of images which constitute a flourishing democracy effectively promotes the general happiness of all citizens, 'Everybody loves it and loves to reside in it, because there is no human wish or desire that this city does not satisfy.'[69] In contrast to Plato's critique of democracy, the democratic city composed of philosophers, rhetoricians, and poets retains the possibility of becoming a virtuous paradigm for more defective cities to emulate and follow. Such a community of free individuals mutually cooperating in the pursuit of happiness may therefore be imagined beyond any fixed geographical determination.[70]

If the democratic city is established within specific geographical regions and extended throughout the entire globe by the proliferation of images meant to teach and persuade its citizens, then religion remains the foundation for the democratic city to both recognise and realise the universal values of equality, freedom, hospitality, and toleration.[71] Al-Fārābī positively reconceives the role of religion as beset with the latent potential to promote democracy. For the majority who are guided by images of religion, the philosopher-ruler-*imām* must communicate these images effectively to the citizens for the sake of attaining happiness in the political community:

> The king in truth is the one whose purpose and intention concerning the art by which he governs cities are to provide himself and the rest of the inhabitants of the city true happiness. This is the goal and purpose of the royal craft.

[67] al-Fārābī, *Political Regime*, 115. [100.23–4], 87, tr. Butterworth (mod.).

[68] Ibid., 115. [100.28–9], 87, tr. Butterworth (mod.).

[69] '*kull insān lahu hawā aw shahwa fī shay'in mā qadara 'alā naylihā min hādhihi al-madīna*'. Ibid., 115. [100.21–2], 87, tr. Butterworth (mod.). Cf. Khalidi, 'Al-Fārābī on the Democratic City', 386.

[70] See Khalidi, 'Al-Fārābī on the Democratic City', 391–3.

[71] For al-Fārābī's adoption of political tolerance in the democratic city, see Sweeney, 'Greek Essence and Islamic Tolerance', 57–60.

> It necessarily follows that the ruler of the virtuous city be the most perfect among the inhabitants of the city in happiness since he is the reason for their being happy.[72]

The philosopher-ruler-*imām* establishes a practical means for the attainment of happiness. Philosophy and religion are conjoined for the sake of promoting happiness, 'Therefore it is possible that excellent nations and excellent cities exist whose religions differ, although they all have as their goal one and the same happiness and the very same aims.'[73] Since images can take myriad forms, multiple kinds of political communities shall be entertained according to the religion in question. A plurality of virtuous religions arises from the plurality of images constituting each religion. Religion is composed of opinions and actions as a product of the imagination and is therefore always grounded in geographical and historical contingencies relative to different communities and nations.[74] In contrast to religions which express contingent truths warranted by their own historicity, philosophy demonstrates universal truths of a rational nature. If philosophy and religion are conjoined for the sake of preserving these truths, then the possibility of a global community comes to be inaugurated whereby many different nations and different religions act in unison with one another, 'the excellent universal state will arise only when all the nations in it cooperate for the purpose of reaching happiness.'[75] This introduction of a global community resolves a problem endemic to the vexed relationship between philosophy and revealed religion. The identification of the images of revealed religion with imitative truth ensures the preservation of religion and guarantees the possibility that religion has a claim to truth. Religion serves as the imaginary ground for sustaining happiness within the political community.

This decision to privilege the truth of the image might be said to inaugurate a radical pluralism ignored by those who identify al-Fārābī as strictly a Platonist or Neoplatonist.[76] In a time where the legitimacy of truth is openly contested by images incompatible with the essential democratic values of life,

72 al-Fārābī, *Selected Aphorisms*, 30. [47.11–16], 27, tr. Butterworth. Cf. al-Fārābī, *Aphorisms of the Statesman*, 27., 40, 122, tr. Dunlop.

73 al-Fārābī, *Virtuous City*, V, 17, §2, 278–81, tr. Walzer.

74 al-Fārābī, *Book of Religion*, 1. [43.1–6], 93, tr. Butterworth.

75 al-Fārābī, *Virtuous City*, V, 15, §3, 230–1, tr. Walzer (mod.).

76 For example, see Fakhry, *Al-Fārābī*; and Netton, *Allāh Transcendent*, 99–148. Cf. Galston, 'A Re-examination of al-Fārābī's Neoplatonism'. In contrast, the materialist account of the imagination may serve as a phenomenological prototype for the notion of the life-world

liberty, equality, and the pursuit of happiness, al-Fārābī recognises how happiness within the political community may be attained by affirming diversity within unity (*e pluribus unum*). By presenting the dialectic between the one and the many, the equilibrium between the singular and the universal is integral to the constitution of the virtuous city. This affirmation of pluralism is instrumental for realising that any claim to universal truth is always conditioned by its own historicity.

The attainment of happiness in the virtuous city is realised by recognising how the citizens find themselves immersed in the lived experience of being with one another, 'Furthermore, it will become evident to them in this science that each person achieves only a portion of that perfection, and what she achieves of this portion varies in its extent, for an isolated individual cannot achieve all the perfections by herself and without the aid of many other individuals.'[77] Here justice is determined by how each person achieves a portion of her own perfection by recourse to the mutual assistance of others. The pursuit of rational perfection in this life is associated with the destiny of the human being and their reward in the afterlife. By reference to the Myth of Er in *Republic* X, the just citizens of the virtuous city will receive just rewards in the afterlife. Divine justice in the afterlife comes to be associated with eternal happiness.[78] The justice enacted by those citizens of the democratic city guarantees its happiness. The relatively pacific character of the democratic city also contributes to the general happiness of the citizens insofar as the city practises only defensive war against its aggressors. Although domestic or civil strife remains a distinct possibility within the democratic city, the relative freedom of the citizens to pursue their own interests is to be balanced by the justice applied by the philosopher-ruler-*imām*.[79]

This application of justice is synonymous with the divine rule of law. Al-Fārābī's attribution of justice to God as a divine name (*Allāh*) is administered by the philosopher-ruler-*imām* who 'must act in accordance with *sharī'ah* – to accomplish which he must use his own wisdom, follow custom,

(*Lebenswelt*). Beginning with those images which bear their own historicity, the pedagogical and persuasive power of the image inaugurates the practice of philosophy; see Husserl, *The Crisis of European Sciences and Transcendental Phenomenology*. The phenomenological naturalism of Aristotle anticipates a series of critical moments whereby the historical authority of the image comes to be recognised.

77 al-Fārābī, *Attainment of Happiness*, 18. [14.8–12], 23, tr. Mahdi.

78 Plato, *Republic* 614b–621d.

79 Al-Fārābī privileges the principles of equality and justice for the sake of the governance and management of the democratic city. Both principles reappear in al-Ṭūsī's *Nasirean Ethics* (*Akhlāq-i Nāṣirī*); see Lameer, *The Arabic Version of al-Ṭūsī's* Nasirean Ethics.

and give priority to the maintenance of peace and welfare'.[80] Since wisdom is necessary for the application of justice to the political community, philosophical education is a prerequisite for acquiring wisdom. With the introduction of the first sovereign, the *Virtuous City* presents a criterion for future generations of sovereigns according to six superior qualities:

> 1) They will be a philosopher (*ḥakīm*). 2) They will be learned and versed in the laws (*al-sharā'i'*) and normative practices (*al-sunan*) and modes of conduct (*al-siyar*) that the first sovereigns have set forth (*dabbara*) for the city, and will measure and pattern all their actions fully according to their example. 3) They will excel at deducing (*istinbāṭ*) a new law by analogy where no law (*sharī'ah*) of their predecessors (*salaf*) has been recorded, and will follow in their deductions the example of the first Imāms. 4) They will have excellent deliberation and the capacity to deduce (new laws) in such conditions and circumstances that arise at a particular instance in the present time for which the first sovereigns had no way (*sabīl*) to lay down the law (*yasunnu*) – and will, in deducing (a new law), have in mind the good of the city (*ṣalāḥ ḥāl al-madīnah*). 5) They will excel in guiding (people), by speech to fulfill the laws (*sharā'i'*) of the first sovereigns as well as those laws deduced in conformity with their principles after their time. 6) They will possess physical strength to undertake the task of war, mastering the serving as well as the ruling military art.[81]

The ruler as a philosopher is to be well-versed in the law. If we apply this rule of law to the democratic city, then the law presumes that sovereignty may be equally distributed among a large association of individuals.[82] Here we cannot

[80] Ahmed, *What Is Islam?*, 480. This model of justice is first presented in the pre-Islamic Sasanian Emperor Kushraw I Ānūshīrvān (501–79 CE). Since justice is bound up with the figure of the philosopher-rule-*imām*, we shall compare the pre-Islamic model of justice with the *Virtuous City* which describes such a sovereign 'as a wise man (*ḥakīm*) and a philosopher (*faylasūf*) and an exemplar (*imām*) who employs an intellect of divine quality, and through the emanation from the Active Intellect to his faculty of imagination a visionary prophet (*nabī*): who warns of things to come and tells of particular things which exist at present' (al-Fārābī, *Virtuous City*, V, 15, §10, 244–5, tr. Walzer, mod.).

[81] al-Fārābī, *Virtuous City*, V, 15, §13, 250–3, tr. Walzer (mod.). Cf. Ahmed, *What Is Islam?*, 462–3; and Kraemer, 'The *Jihād* of the *Falāsifa*', 300.

[82] Orwin, 'Democracy under the Caliphs', 182, defines democracy (*madīna jamā'iyya*) as that which shares the same root as *ijtimā'*, the term identical to association or the assembly of a large group of people and hence a plurality of diverse individuals. Therefore, a democracy is not so much one city, but many different cities. Cf. Najjar, 'Democracy in Islamic Political Philosophy', 110.

rule out the possibility that a philosopher-ruler-*imām* might arise from the constitution of the democratic city as a result of his or her own knowledge.[83] The philosopher-ruler-*imām* experiences the truth of the Divine through revelation via the power of the imagination and therefore has the authority to communicate this message to the entire political community. The philosopher-ruler-*imām* must exercise political prudence to determine how the secret of revelation is to be communicated and conveyed to the political community. Within the democratic city where a plurality of truths are generated by multiple images, it may be rather difficult for the citizens to discern between truth and falsity. Therefore, the philosopher-ruler-*imām* assists with the education of the citizens if they are to comprehend the value of the images. Religion thus serves as the primary communicative medium between the philosopher-ruler-*imām* and the citizens of the political community. However, the images may also be educative in their value by conjoining reason with divine revelation so that the citizens recognise their intellectual value.[84]

The relationship between rulers and ruled in the democratic city may leave us with questions as to how the city should be governed, 'If their situation is examined closely, it turns out that in truth there is no ruler among them and no ruled.'[85] However, there must be a member of the city responsible for having authority over the others, 'one inhabitant has authority over another or over someone else only insofar as he does what removes that person's

[83] The idea of social-political hierarchy embedded in a cosmic hierarchy applies to the distinction between exteriority and interiority, the seen and unseen and their characterisation as physical and social space. With the *imām*, this space is conveyed by the philosopher-ruler-*imām* who receives the truth of the Divine and then conveys that truth to the political community. Shahab Ahmed demonstrates how the dialectic of interiority and exteriority reflects this hierarchical distinction, 'To explain: when the vast and divergent data of historical societies of Muslims is analyzed in the light of the foregoing conceptualization of Islam as hermeneutical engagement with a multi-dimensional spatial dynamic of Revelation, we find that the structure of this engagement logically and necessarily generates truth and meaning – that is to say, Islamic Truth and Meaning – in two spatially-differentiated trajectories: I) hierarchy, and II) interiority/exteriority' (*What Is Islam?*, 367).

[84] Cf. ibid., 379, 'This mutual recognition requires, of course, that there be something that makes people mutually recognizable. That something is, by and large, a shared education productive of shared attitudes to the nature of Truth.' If the democratic city is guided by diversity, both intellectual and moral education is a paramount concern. Given the history of Islamic societies in the classical period, the culture of *adab* remained especially prominent in the cosmopolitan culture of ninth- and tenth-century Baghdad; see Makdisi, *The Rise of Humanism in Classical Islam and the Christian West*, 232–47; and Marlow, *Hierarchy and Egalitarianism in Islamic Thought*, 113–16.

[85] al-Fārābī, *Political Regime*, 113. [99.24–5], 86, tr. Butterworth.

freedom.'[86] Al-Fārābī sketches the various kinds of rulers within the democratic city beginning with the ruler who effectively governs the citizens and is thereby 'honored, superior, and obeyed' by protecting the freedom of the people from their enemies. Here we may observe the intersection between democracy and timocracy proceeding from elements of honour and persuading the citizens to become virtuous. However, honour detracts from equality as a primary principle of the democratic city.[87] In contrast to the timocratic ruler, the democratic ruler receives more honour and wealth than they deserve and consequentially the citizens consider themselves superior (*afḍal*) to their ruler. This kind of ruler is the weakest and most easily deposed:

> What the ignorant rulerships are intent on is as numerous as are the ignorant cities. For each ignorant rulership is intent on gaining control over what is necessary; wealth; enjoyment of pleasures; honor, fame, and praise; domination; or freedom. Therefore, these rulerships are bought for money - especially the rulerships that come about in the democratic city. For no one there is more deserving of rulership than another. So when rulership in it is surrendered to someone, it is either because the inhabitants granted it to them or that they took money or some other recompense from them.[88]

The third and final kind of democratic ruler constitutes a mean between previous extremes as their equal. However, who is the ruler who prides herself upon being equal to the citizens by equitably apportioning justice to them?[89]

[86] Ibid., 113. [99.14–15], 86.

[87] Al-Fārābī does not address whether honour and equality can effectively co-exist in the democratic city. Sophia Vasalou deftly explicates the ethics of honour presented in al-Ghazālī's *On the Condemnation of Status and Dissimulation* from his multivolume magnum opus, the *Revival of the Religious Sciences* (*Iḥyā' 'Ulūm al-Dīn*), 'A lordly element expresses itself as a powerful desire for perfection for its own sake, which in turn manifests as an insatiable desire for domination (*istīlā'*) that is satisfied either by actually exercising power over existents or (where this is not possible) by making them objects of knowledge. Hence indeed our ardor for probing wondrous and mysterious things (*asrār 'ajā'ib*); for by knowing an object, one dominates it. Our desire for honor is connected to this deeper drive and represents a desire to exercise power over one of the two classes of mundane entities, namely souls, the other being, bodies' (*Virtues of Greatness in the Arabic Tradition*, 37).

[88] al-Fārābī, *Political Regime*, 116. [101.9–17], 87–8, tr. Butterworth (mod.). Cf. Orwin, 'Democracy under the Caliphs', 177–8.

[89] Alexander Orwin claims that a democratically elected ruler is unlikely given the account of the democratic city in the *Political Regime*. Since only a praiseworthy ruler will pass down his office to his descendants, Orwin concludes that al-Fārābī's democratic city is in fact a monarchy, most likely a hereditary monarchy, if the succession is peaceful ('Democracy under the

To resolve this question, we shall conclude our inquiry into the democratic city by returning to *Aphorisms of the Statesman*, which proposes two kinds of justice. The first kind of justice is distributive by sharing goods, including security, wealth, and honour, among the citizens of the city. These goods are distributed according to the rank, status, and merit of each citizen. Presumably, the lawgiver or philosopher-ruler-*imām* is responsible for determining how the goods of the city are distributed insofar as each citizen receives his or her proper share (*qisṭ*). Al-Fārābī's exposition of this first kind of justice is followed by a second, more general kind:

> Justice may be spoken of, in another more general way (*naw'*), namely a human being practicing acts of virtue, any virtue whatever, with respect to what is between him and someone else. The justice having to do with dividing and the one having to do with preserving what has been divided is a species of the more general justice, and the more particular is called by the name of the more general.[90]

This general kind of justice (*'adl*) extending beyond the mere sharing of goods to a love (*maḥabba*) for one's neighbour effectively binds the citizens together in solidarity with one another as the most universal virtue of political life. The introduction of justice at this most general level for the sake of educating the potential philosopher-ruler-*imām* sets the stage for its application to the global political community. The composite character of each individual citizen and the internal harmony of their own soul mirrors the external harmony of the city and the cosmos. With the distinction between a specific kind of justice identified with legal proportionality and a general kind of justice identified with practising acts of virtue, justice becomes the *sine qua non* condition for

Caliphs', 178). The ruler is a king with limited power who merely presides over the people in an advisory status not unlike the royal rule of the United Kingdom. However, how are we to distinguish between al-Fārābī's democratic city and the global political community identified with the entire inhabited world? If democratic rule is the only kind of government identified with a city rather than a nation or association, then is democracy exclusively restricted to the city? The democratic city is continually growing and therefore will inevitably expand to become many cities (see al-Fārābī, *Political Regime*, 115. [100.23–4], 87). The unique diversity of the democratic city appeals to everyone, including neighbouring cities and nations, insofar as every other city and nation values its association. This genuinely cosmopolitan vision of the democratic city gestures to a vast multi-ethnic metropolis.

90 al-Fārābī, *Selected Aphorisms*, 64. [74.16–21], 42, tr. Butterworth. Cf. al-Fārābī, *Aphorisms of the Statesman*, 60., 55, 144, tr. Dunlop. See also Khadduri, *The Islamic Conception of Justice*, 83–8.

the flourishing of the democratic city. Here the distinct possibility that equality (*musāwāt*) may reside among all citizens is not discounted. By heeding Socrates' advice to Glaucon in *Republic* VII, the realisation of liberation from ignorance and hence happiness and freedom is available to not just a few of citizens of the city but to all who seek such a possibility:

> Perhaps you've forgotten, my friend, the intent of the lawgiver who wants to found the ideal city. His purpose is not to make any one class of people happier than the rest. Rather, happiness is to be spread to *all* in the city. He wants to hold the citizens together by persuasion and necessity and let them all benefit from the city and to benefit from each other, not to please themselves individually but to help bind the society into a harmonious unity.[91]

Rather than presenting a strict demarcation between the ruling elite (*al-khāṣṣa*) and common citizens (*al-'āmma*), the disposition to become a philosopher-ruler-*imām* is tempered by the labour to assume that position thereby effectively enabling even the weeds to become potential rulers of the city. The democratic city thus presents the most distinct realisation of a cosmopolitanism rooted in the principles of freedom, equality, and justice for all.[92]

[91] Plato, *Republic* 319e.

[92] Louise Marlow argues that al-Fārābī effectively distinguishes between the ruling elite (*al-khāṣṣa*) and the commoners (*al-'āmma*), 'the former being composed of those who possess superior knowledge and understanding . . . while the latter do not possess such gifts' (*Hierarchy and Egalitarianism in Islamic Thought*, 54). The *'āmma* are depicted as being kept in an orderly state by the law administered by the *khāṣṣa*. However, Shahab Ahmed asserts that hierarchy does not promote inequality since the 'distinguishing human quality is knowledge which is something potentially susceptible to acquisition by all people and by means of textual and experiential education (according to differential aptitude)' (*What Is Islam?*, 376). Given Marlow's distinction between egalitarianism identical to the notion of equality in Islam and the impingement of that ideal from external social and political forces, Ahmed concludes that 'hierarchy is at least every bit as Islamic as is the egalitarianism which we habitually associate with Islam' (ibid.).

5
Cosmopolitan Virtues

An Ethics of Hospitality

The cosmopolitan virtues of generosity (*jūd*), hospitality (*ḍiyāfa*), and solidarity (*'aṣabiyya*) interwoven into the multicoloured cloak of the democratic city only come to be further accentuated by their intersection with the civic virtues of benevolence, concord, and friendship. Moreover, civic friendship assumes a cosmopolitan direction by expanding the political community beyond mere intimates and associates. The solidarity which arises from such a civic or political friendship among strangers exceeds the relative cultural and geographical boundaries of any local or regional community.[1] The *Virtuous City* accordingly presents three kinds of perfect societies; great, medium, and small as the foremost expression of this solidarity.[2] Here the allusion to a great society encompassing all the societies of the world may be identified with the advent of the global community (*ma'mūra*). If we are to assume the existence of the democratic city and its requisite expansion as the foremost expression of cosmopolitanism, we shall aim to explicate a certain affiliation between hospitality, generosity, and solidarity contributing to the realisation of this global community.

Among those virtues identified with the theory and practice of cosmopolitanism, hospitality informs a regimen of cultural practices in pre-Islamic Arabia contributing to the expansion of Islam as a unifying religious and political force. The ecumenical orientation of hospitality is indistinguishable from the practice of ethics and integral to the inception of culture where a certain *ēthos* is associated with the specific character of a place

[1] See Aristotle, *Nicomachean Ethics* 1154b21-9.
[2] al-Fārābī, *Virtuous City*, V, 15, §2, 228-9.

(*topos*).[3] Beginning with the formation of nations in the *Political Regime*, the unity between hospitality and ethics informing the inception of cosmopolitanism is determined by natural temperaments, states of character, and conventions of language. The difference between nations arises from the natural differences of the heavenly bodies which position themselves towards the earth in such a way as to incline towards or away from the equator.[4] These meteorological differences in turn condition differences in water, air, and soil which promote differences in plants and non-rational animals. Since humans derive their nutrition from plants and animals, natural differences in human temperament and states of character arise among nations depending upon their geographical location on the earth. The emergence of human temperament and character is also wholly dependent on the order and ranking of the heavenly bodies within the cosmos. By tracing the arc of the human condition originating in and from the motions of the heavenly bodies and ultimately returning to them, al-Fārābī presciently sketches how a culture of hospitality arises in relation to those departed souls from previous generations of communities:

> When a group passes away, and their bodies are nullified, and their souls are delivered and made happy, then other people follow after them, take their place in the city, and perform their activities; the souls of these [people], too, are delivered. When their bodies are nullified, they come to the rankings of those in this group who have passed away. They are neighborly to them in the way that what is not corporeal is neighborly.[5]

The neighbourliness of these departed souls invokes Plato's Myth of Er, the warrior who originates from the region of Pamphylia, along the south coast of Asia Minor. Upon his death, Er reports to his comrades about the fate of

[3] 'Hospitality is culture itself and not simply one ethic amongst others. Insofar as it has to do with the *ethos*, that is, the residence, one's home, the familiar place of dwelling, in as much as it is a manner of being there, the manner in which we relate to ourselves and to others, to others as our own or as foreigners, *ethics is hospitality*; ethics is so thoroughly coextensive with the experience of hospitality' (Derrida, *On Cosmopolitanism and Forgiveness*, 16); see also Derrida, 'Une hospitalité à l'infini'. For the intersection between ecumenical and phenomenological approaches to hospitality, see Kearney and Semonovitch, *Phenomenologies of the Stranger*, and especially Treanor, 'Putting Hospitality in its Place'.

[4] Charles Butterworth notes that this reference to the spheres within the elliptical circle and their inclination towards or away from the equator is derived from *Generation and Corruption* 2.10.336a31–336b11; see al-Fārābī, *Political Regime*, 61n29.

[5] al-Fārābī, *Political Regime*, 85. [82.8–14], 71, tr. Butterworth.

all mortals.[6] The hospitality invoked by conjoining the living with the dead through the practice of reverence for those departed souls and hence the transmission of cultural inheritance from one generation to the next ultimately extends to the pleasure derived from communing with the dead through their intellects:

> Whenever one of those who came after attaches to them, the pleasure of the one now attaching increases due to their encountering those who passed away. And the pleasures of those who passed away increase through joining with those who attach to them because each one intellects their essence and intellects the same as their essence many times. What is thereby intellected increases as the ones now present attach to them in future time. So there will be a boundless increase of pleasures for each one with the passing of time. That is the condition of each group. This, then, is the ultimate true happiness that is the purpose of the active intellect.[7]

This recollection of the departed souls of the past is one method by which individuals of any given political community participate in the universality of the Active Intellect (*al-'aql al-fa''āl*). The strikingly Platonic character of the deliverance of these departed souls to another place is equated with *eudaimonia* whereby the soul properly becomes its own. Given the purification of the soul and the separation of the body from the intellect, al-Fārābī explicitly warns his readers that those souls who are not perfected by their actions in this life will be nullified and not experience the true and ultimate happiness identified with the Active Intellect, 'Thus the souls of these people remain material (*hayūlāniyya*) and do not come to perfection such that they are separate from material; so when their material is nullified,

[6] Plato, *Republic* X, 614b–621d. See Baracchi, *Of Myth, Life, and War in Plato's* Republic, 327a, 'Er, the warrior, who once died in war is now more fully uncovered as Socrates, as the philosopher returning in yet another guise – and his story as the recapitulation of Socrates' deeds and discourses, of the dialogue as a whole. One of Socrates' features that can be inferred from the very beginning of the action is his literally "cosmopolitan" equanimity, his situating himself above and beyond ethnic-cultural identification, and therefore, his ability equally to appreciate "the procession of the native inhabitants" and "the one the Thracians conducted". Er, on the other hand, is "by race a Pamphylian" (614b). Literally, he is, by race, of mingled tribes or races. Er is all races, every-kind-utterly singular and at the same time, not further identified, undifferentiated in his uniqueness' (170). Pamphylia, a compound of 'all' (*pan*) and 'tribe, breed, or nation' (*phylos*) may be quite literally translated as 'all nations' (*panpyhlos*) to indicate its cosmopolitan *ēthos.*

[7] al-Fārābī, *Political Regime*, 85. [82.16–25], 71–2, tr. Butterworth (mod.).

they are also nullified.'[8] By the convergence of the natural temperaments of the inhabitants of the city with the historical fate of the community, the *Political Regime* charts the journey of each individual soul beginning with the aspirational paradigm of the philosopher-ruler-*imām* qua demiurge who works on behalf of the citizens to imitate the intelligibles of the First Cause. The logic of imitation effectively conjoins the philosopher-ruler-*imām* to the First Cause and the ruler to the ruled, 'Thus the parts of the city are then tied to one another, in consonance with one another, and ranked with some having precedence and others being subordinate.'[9] Hospitality may only arise through such a civic unity. The citizens develop this capacity for imitation with the citizens from other cities and nations by means of the imagination. Moreover, the pervasiveness of the image becomes a binding force within the political community by enabling a multiplicity of perspectives and hence a civic pluralism betokening hospitality, 'Thus it may be possible for the religions of virtuous nations and virtuous cities to differ, even if they all pursue the very same happiness.'[10] Such an attunement to the respective differences between various religions via the power of the imagination serves as an explicit admission of hospitality.

The practice of hospitality proceeding by way of the imagination also extends to the advent of language as a distinct cultural phenomenon arising from the geographical and climatic vagaries of a pre-Islamic Arabia. Al-Fārābī's *Book of Letters* describes how language arises in relation to place by distinguishing those citizens who inhabit cities and those citizens who inhabit the wilderness. The inhabitants of the wilderness are exclusively responsible for determining the primary language for all the citizens of the nation:

> Therefore, whenever nations contain both groups, it is better to take the language of the nation from the inhabitants of the wilderness, and preferably those among them who inhabit the interior parts of the country. For those who inhabit the peripheries are more likely to mingle with neighboring nations, so that their languages mixes with those others, and they are more likely to imagine the linguistic barbarisms of their neighbors.[11]

The demarcation between citizens and foreigners is a prerequisite for the law of hospitality to be practised between nations. The origin and development

[8] Ibid., 86. [83.19-20], 72.
[9] Ibid., 87. [84.4-6], 73.
[10] Ibid., 90. [86.1-2], 75.
[11] al-Fārābī, *Book of Letters*, 134., 14, tr. Khalidi.

of language arising from a specific place is delimited by geography for the sake of its own preservation. Those inhabitants who reside within the wilderness of any given nation by virtue of their interiority are primarily responsible for preserving language and hence the cultural inheritance of a place if a cosmopolitanism among nations is to be established. Language emerges as a relatively homogenous cultural phenomenon before it comes to be transmitted and translated into heterogeneous cultures from other nations. The historical development of the Arabic language and the emergence of Arab culture arising from those nomads who practised hospitality in their encounters with those from neighbouring regions comes to be accentuated. Language cannot come to exist in its own right without demarcating between the domestic and foreign.[12] Therefore, hospitality arises from the intersection between language and place in the constant and infinite negotiation between same and other.[13] The phenomenon of hospitality is endemic to those regions of the city exposed to foreign nations and those regions of wilderness where language is thereby preserved:

> They learned their language and the eloquent part of it from the inhabitants of the wilderness rather than the town dwellers, and especially from the people of the interior regions and from the wildest and roughest of them, and the least submissive and compliant, namely [the tribes of] Qays, Tamīm, Asad, and Ṭayy, followed by Hudhayl. These include most of those from whom the language of the Arabs was taken.[14]

Language is derived from a specific geographical place before its dissemination into foreign regions being communicated to other cultures through the arts of rhetoric, poetry, recitation, linguistics, and writing. These arts function as a universal expression of a specific language and hence become the ambassadors of the respective culture due to their intersection with the common affairs of the multitude. In art, the boundary between guest and host is effectively dissolved for the sake of promoting the universality of human expression:

[12] It is the same linguistic inflection point from which Jacques Derrida develops his account of hospitality, 'We only ever speak one language since it returns to the other, it exists asymmetrically, always for the other, from the other, kept by the other. Coming from the other, remaining with the other, returning to the other' (*Monolinguism of the Other or Prosthesis of Origin*, 40).

[13] See Derrida, 'Hostipitality [Seminar]', 363–5.

[14] al-Fārābī, *Book of Letters*, 135., 15, tr. Khalidi.

> They are also one of them, since their utmost goal is also their goal in their art, which is also their art in genus and species, except that it is the most sublime art of that genus and species. Thus, the leaders of the multitude, who preserve for them those things that make them the multitude and use them with respect to the things that make up the multitude, are also of the multitude.[15]

The practical arts also serve as the foundation for the sciences of mathematics and physics. The application of sophistical and dialectical methods to mathematics and physics leads to the science of political affairs. This progressive development originating from the practical arts and extending to the sciences of mathematics, physics, and politics ultimately culminates in the art of philosophy, 'Theoretical science is completed, the mathematical methods are all distinguished, theoretical philosophy and universal practical philosophy are perfected, and they cease to contain any object of examination. It becomes an art that is only learned and taught, and it is taught both to a select audience and commonly to all.'[16]

Moreover, al-Fārābī distinguishes between philosophical instruction for the few which proceeds by demonstrative methods and philosophical instruction for the many which proceeds by dialectical, rhetorical, or poetical methods for the sake of distinguishing between esoteric and exoteric knowledge. The preservation of philosophy and hence the attainment of happiness in the virtuous city is ultimately dependent upon this distinction which effectively prepares the citizens to become potential rulers. If one is to become a philosopher and hence a lawgiver (*nawāmīs*), then one must be properly trained not merely in the demonstrative methods of applying philosophical truths but be gifted enough to translate the intelligibles (*ma'qūlāt*) received by the Active Intellect into images (*mithālāt*) which may be universally understood by those citizens of the particular political community. The philosopher who becomes the lawgiver thus serves as an intermediary between esoteric and exoteric knowledge.[17] A foremost requirement for assuming this intermediary status beyond the innate capacity of the intellect and an expanded capacity of the imagination is the cultivation of hospitality on behalf of the philosopher as the lawgiver who must not only receive the divine message as a guest but ultimately transmit the divine message as a host. The relationship between host and guest operative within hospitality becomes united in the philosopher

[15] Ibid., 139., 17.
[16] Ibid., 143., 19.
[17] See Azadpur, *Reason Unbound*, 65–71.

as lawgiver who receives these demonstrative truths through the divine intermediary of the Active Intellect either in a waking state or in sleep and dreams prior to disseminating them to the citizens of the political community:

> The art of lawgiving consists of the ability to represent imaginatively what is difficult for the multitude to conceive of the theoretical intelligibles. It also consists in the ability to infer each of the beneficial political actions in attaining happiness, and the ability to persuade with respect to all the theoretical and practical matters that the multitude should be taught using persuasive methods.[18]

The relative ambivalence of the philosopher as lawgiver who performs the roles of host and guest extends to the other common tropes of the foreigner, stranger, and the other. The philosopher-ruler-*imām* is akin to the demiurge as an intermediary between the sensible and intelligible domains who always works on behalf of the people and therefore must negotiate the tenuous relationship of host and guest by both receiving and disseminating the divine message.

Generosity of the First Cause

Hospitality ever so gradually comes to be affiliated with the cosmopolitan virtues of generosity and solidarity. Generosity may be easily confused with the practice of hospitality.[19] Therefore, we shall attempt to demarcate them by introducing generosity as a phenomenon which emanates exclusively from the Neoplatonic One or First Cause qua gift to the philosopher-ruler-*imām*. In the *Political Regime*, the First Cause is identified with generosity (*jūd*) through the activity of emanation:

> Therefore, that existence emanates from its existence to something else is in its substance; and the existence by which it becomes substantiated in its essence is the very existence by which something else attains existence from it . . . Therefore the existence of what exists from it does not become subsequent to it in time at all; rather, it is subsequent to it only in all the rest of the modes of being subsequent.[20]

[18] al-Fārābī, *Book of Letters*, 144., 119, tr. Khalidi.
[19] See Siddiqui, *Hospitality and Islam*, 29.
[20] al-Fārābī, *Political Regime*, 28. [48.20–32], 43, tr. Butterworth.

Since the First Cause exists for its own sake and those things that emanate from it follow from its substance, generosity may be conceived as related essentially to the activity of emanation and as a predicate attributed to the First Cause. While existence is anterior to those things which emanate from the First Cause, the activity of emanation cannot be distinguished from the substance of the First Cause and follows from its essence. The relationship of generosity to divine predication is subsequently addressed if only to indicate that the essence of the First Cause is to be determined as an absolutely simple substance:

> It ought not to be presumed that the kinds of perfections signified by its many names are many kinds into which it is divided and by all of which it is made substantial. Rather, those many names ought to signify a single substance and a single existence that is not at all divided . . . Of the names that signify perfection and excellence in the things around us, some signify what it is in its essence and not insofar as it is related to another thing – like being, oneness, and what is similar to that. Others signify what it is in relation to something else external to it – like justice and generosity.[21]

The *Political Regime* defines the essence of the First Cause as a single substance which cannot be divided. Generosity is predicated as a relation between the First Cause and those existents produced by the activity of emanation. However, the *Virtuous City* reaffirms the ambivalent relation of generosity and justice to the First Cause as identical to its substance. Moreover, the generosity which inheres in the substance of the First Cause is akin to justice. Generosity as an activity of emanation thereby becomes equivalent to the essence of the First Cause as a substance:

> Inasmuch as the substance of the First is a substance from which all the existents emanate, while it does not neglect any existence beneath its existence, it is generous, and its generosity (*jūd*) is in its substance; and inasmuch as all the existents receive their order of rank from it, and each existent receives from the First its allotted share of existence in accordance with its rank, the First is just, and its justice is in its substance. This does not apply to anything apart from its substance.[22]

Generosity inheres in the substance of the First Cause and therefore cannot be demarcated from its essence. This activity of giving without expectation of

[21] Ibid., 29. [49.7–12], 30. [49.19–23], 44.

[22] al-Fārābī, *Virtuous City*, I, 2, §2, 94–6, tr. Walzer.

reciprocity as an expression of generosity invites a comparison to the logic of the gift.[23] In contrast to the virtue of justice, which inheres in the substance of the First Cause apportioning by equal measure what is to be given and received, generosity as gift and donation enacts the divine abundance of the First Cause through the ongoing and infinite process of emanation. If we are to further situate generosity in relation to Neoplatonism beginning with the identity between the One and the First Cause, the generosity which emanates from the First Cause may exist independently as a divine predicate by its dissemination.[24] Therefore, generosity is always a radical exorbitance, a donation circumscribing the relationship between donor and recipient, host and guest. Without eliding the significance of the donor–recipient relationship to generosity, al-Fārābī also attributes justice to the substance of the First.

The attribution of generosity and justice to the First Cause has evident theological precedent in the Qur'ān where generosity is synonymous with charity and genuine nobility. The Prophet Muḥammad transposes generosity from the ostentatious expression of wealth and abundance to an inner motivation aligned with humility, 'Believers, you must not make your charity vain by grudging and making disagreeable remarks, as one who expends of his wealth simply for the pleasure of an ostentatious display, and not from his belief in God and the Last Day.'[25] Generosity is informed by deliberation and hence the apportioning out of wealth according to a specific measure. Here generosity might serve to indicate that the existence which emanates from the First Cause provides each specific being with a measure according to its own hierarchical position in creation.

Given the intersection between Neoplatonism and *kalām* in the *Theology of Aristotle* and *Book of Causes*, generosity bears a semantic resonance with justice. Both generosity and justice are meted out by a divine authority. In lieu of ostentation or miserliness, generosity is guided by a pious motive aimed at the mean between extremes, 'The true servants of the Merciful God are . . . those who, when they spend, are neither prodigal nor miserly, but who ever take the constant mean between the two.'[26] Al-Fārābī's *Directing Attention to the Way of Happiness* (*Risālat al-Tanbīh 'alā Sabīl al-Sa'āda*) inspired by the words of the Prophet Muḥammad presents generosity as the mean between stinginess and profligacy, 'Generosity is produced by a median state between saving and spending wealth. Too much saving and too little spending produce

[23] See Derrida, 'The Time of the King'.

[24] See Morewedge, 'The Neoplatonic Structure of Some Islamic Mystical Doctrines'.

[25] Qur'ān 2:264; Izutsu, *Ethico-religious Concepts in the Qur'ān*, 77.

[26] Qur'ān 25:67; Izutsu, *Ethico-religious Concepts in the Qur'ān*, 78.

stinginess, which is ignoble, whereas too much spending and too little saving produce profligacy. Whenever these dispositions are present, the very same actions result.'[27] The virtue of justice and the subsequent explication of the noble dispositions and median actions which result from justice are not simply imitated and reproduced, but instead retrieved and reconfigured with explicit attention to the cultivation of affection as a noble disposition.[28] The introduction of affection merits further attention as the basis for the expansion of friendship and hospitality. The display of affection through friendship is born out of an unconditional hospitality to the guest.[29]

With the affinity established between generosity and justice as attributes of the First Cause, hospitality becomes synonymous with the practice of cosmopolitanism beginning with the attitude of the religious believer and citizen towards the foreigner or stranger. If we are to recall al-Fārābī's democratic city where 'strangers cannot be distinguished from residents', the utter exorbitance of this remark, which effectively erases the distinction between foreigner and resident, enemy and friend, recalls Aristotle's neologism that friendship exceeds justice.[30] In *Directing Attention to the Way of Happiness*, hospitality is invoked as a propaedeutic for those aspiring to perfect themselves for the sake of happiness:

> Happiness is a certain end (*ghāya mā*) that everyone desires (*yatashawwaquhā*), and everyone who strives to attain it does so precisely because it is a certain perfection (*kamāl mā*), requires no explanation since it is completely well-known (*fī ghāyat al-shuhra*). The human being desires every perfection and every end precisely because it is a certain good (*khayr mā*), which is necessarily something choice-worthy (*mu'thar*). Now, while the ends that are desired because they are good and choice-worthy are many, happiness

27 al-Fārābī, *Directing Attention*, 16.2 [61.9–12], 110, tr. McGinnis and Reisman.

28 Ibid., 16.6 [62.13–18], 111.

29 Given al-Fārābī's career as a patron of the royal court, it is not difficult to envision why these dispositions and virtues may be retrieved. Perhaps al-Fārābī recognised the sycophantic paradigm in Baghdad court culture insofar as any hospitality granted in the relationship between hosts and their guests, between the princes and their patrons, reflects the delicate art of negotiation and compromise; see especially Kramer, *Humanism in the Renaissance of Islam*, 1–30; and Netton, *Al-Fārābī and His School*, 18–30.

30 al-Fārābī, *Political Regime*, 115. [100.28–9], 87, tr. Butterworth (mod.); Aristotle, *Nicomachean Ethics* 1154b21–9. Jacques Derrida's *Politics of Friendship* interrogates Carl Schmitt's friend–enemy distinction by retrieving Aristotle, Montaigne, Kant, Nietzsche, and Blanchot. Indeed, al-Fārābī deserves to be included in such a list by introducing the democratic city as the foremost expression of his cosmopolitanism.

> is the most appropriate (*ajdā*) of the preferred goods. Therefore, it is clear that happiness is the greatest in goodness among the goods, and that among the things people choose (*mu'tharāt*), it is the most perfect (*akmal*) and choice-worthy of all the ends towards which the human being strives.[31]

Al-Fārābī implores his readers to study and practise philosophy if one is to attain happiness by distinguishing between the 'study' of philosophy concerned with first principles and the 'practice' of philosophy obtained by the knowledge of things that can be acted upon. Hospitality may be comprehended as an expression of the divine love of the First Cause practised by adopting a specific ethical orientation. The composition of the democratic city embodies the *ethōs* of hospitality. Although the democratic city is identified with imperfection, the democratic city possesses the potential to perfect itself by adopting the virtue of hospitality as a mean between the vices of sycophancy and churlishness. Hospitality as a noble disposition is the requisite measure of those virtues needed to attain happiness in the democratic city insofar as it requires prudence and discernment to receive those who are other than oneself. Despite Aristotle's relative omission of hospitality from his ethical writings, we should not neglect its critical relevance as a condition for friendship beginning with his cosmopolitan remarks about fellow travellers.[32] In *Directing Attention to the Way of Happiness*, al-Fārābī rather curiously alludes to hospitality as a moral virtue by identifying it with the noble disposition of 'displaying affection':

> Displaying affection, which is a noble disposition, comes about in a person's interactions with another through a median state with respect to whatever words or actions please the other. Too much of it results in sycophancy, whereas too little results in churlishness - even worse, if it has caused the other pain, the person has become antisocial. We could apply the same model of a median state, excess, and deficiency to other actions.[33]

Perhaps this allusion stems from *Nicomachean Ethics* IV.6 which explicitly refers to the existence of a 'nameless disposition' approximating but not

[31] al-Fārābī, *Directing Attention*, 1. [47.1–48.2], 104, tr. McGinnis and Reisman (mod.); Mattila, *The Eudaimonist Ethics of al-Fārābī and Avicenna*, 24, tr. Mattila (mod.).

[32] Aristotle, *Nicomachean Ethics* 1155a21. Given Aristotle's status as a *metic* and al-Fārābī's status as a court patron, this allusion to hospitality as a friendly 'display of affection' among fellow travellers comes to be further developed and refined by al-Tawḥīdī's concept of friendship (*ṣadāqa*) as a social and cosmopolitical objective; see Alshaar, *Ethics in Islam*, 158–95.

[33] al-Fārābī, *Directing Attention*, 16.6 [62.13–18], 111, tr. McGinnis and Reisman.

identical to friendship.[34] To resolve this lacuna, we shall aim to defend the view that Aristotle's 'nameless disposition' is the most likely candidate for hospitality:

> But it is different from friendship because it is without feeling and without affection for one's associates, for without liking or disliking, but just by being this sort of person, one is accepting of each thing in the way one ought to be. Such a person will do things the same way toward those he knows and those he does not know, those he is accustomed to be around and those he is not accustomed to be around, except for doing them in the way that is fitting in each case, since it is not appropriate to be considerate in the same way of both customary associates and strangers, nor to do what causes them pain in the same way.[35]

Given the multiple references to customary associates and strangers which merit our attention, hospitality corresponds to other noble dispositions, namely, generosity, self-control, urbanity, and honesty. These noble dispositions come to be implemented on behalf of the common good, 'Since we attain happiness only when we come to possess the noble dispositions, and since the noble dispositions become our property only through the discipline of philosophy, it necessarily follows that philosophy is the means by which we attain happiness.'[36] The practice of hospitality requires that one first learn philosophy and hence cultivate proper discernment to perceive what is correct. However, discernment does not only apply to those who are innately disposed to philosophy. Instead, the exposition of these noble dispositions highlights the potential of all citizens to perform virtuous actions and attain happiness. Therefore, we should not limit the practice and perfection of the noble dispositions to only philosophers, 'Every person, from the moment he exists, is by discernment, the way they should be, and it is through the very same potentiality that these three are not the way they should be.'[37] By invoking Aristotle's moral virtues, al-Fārābī underscores how every person is disposed with the innate intellectual aptitude to discern the mean benefiting the entire community. Hospitality may emerge under such conditions and give rise to the democratic city. However, we cannot be certain that the democratic city

[34] Aristotle, *Nicomachean Ethics* 1126b20.

[35] Ibid., 1126b27–9.

[36] al-Fārābī, *Directing Attention*, 31. [77.5–8], 117, tr. McGinnis and Reisman.

[37] Ibid., 7. [52.16–19], 106. His presentation of the moral virtues reflects his treatment of the voluntary intelligibles in *Attainment of Happiness*, 24. [18.1–20.4], 26–7.

will effectively evolve into a peaceful community or devolve into civil strife. Given that the democratic city depicts the cosmopolitan culture of ninth and tenth-century Baghdad, hospitality is paramount to its survival and flourishing.[38] Indeed, it may be rather difficult to discern between democracy and hospitality itself.[39] If hospitality functions as a religious and ethical precept for welcoming the stranger, then democracy is the natural expression of hospitality where all voices are to be effectively heard. In this sense, the democratic city bears both a utopian and proto-utopian promise.[40]

For the sake of our exposition, we shall briefly entertain the utopian potential of democracy as synonymous with an ethics of hospitality. Hospitality is decisive to the constitution of the democratic city as a condition for ethics and hence the politics of democracy. Moreover, hospitality may be construed by its exclusively secular orientation thereby preserving the expansion of hospitality from theocracy.[41] The secular orientation of hospitality demonstrates a cosmopolitan commitment to the imagination as a precondition for the practice of democracy to flourish.

[38] See Orwin, 'Democracy under the Caliphs,' 184–6; and Burns, 'Alfarabi and the Creation of an Islamic Political Science', 378.

[39] Democracy is constituted by an internal ambivalence to degenerate and thus become a pale imitation of itself or aspire to a 'democracy to come'. Responding to a paper by Richard Kearney, Derrida pursues a line of thinking which conjoins democracy with hospitality according to their aporetic structure. Hospitality is aporetically conditioned by certain culturally specific laws and norms such as the right to egress and asylum despite its determination as a pure regulative idea, 'I would simply say that, if I want to improve the conditions of hospitality, and I think, we would agree about that, if I want to improve the conditions of hospitality, the politics of hospitality, I have to refer to pure hospitality, if only to have a criterion to distinguish between the more limited hospitality and the less limited hospitality. So I would need what Kant would call the regulating idea of pure hospitality, if only to control the distance between in-hospitality, less hospitality, and more hospitality. This could also lead us beyond Kant's own concept of hospitality as a regulating idea' (Kearney, 'Desire of God', 133).

[40] Rather than simply devaluing the democratic city (cf. Orwin, *Redefining the Muslim Community*, 181–6) or affirming its radical utopian potential (cf. Khalidi, 'Al-Fārābī on the Democratic City'), we shall instead seek to investigate how democracy contains within itself the principle of auto-immunity, self-immolating and sacrificing itself on behalf of the Other; see especially Derrida, *Rogues*, 45. Hence, democracy is always beset with the real possibility of its own destruction. How are we to isolate the principle of anarchy residing within pure democracy and hence the democratic city as an imperfect regime? Does such a political association always entail the lack of a governing hierarchical principle by virtue of popular rule? Is the democratic city a democracy in name only?

[41] See Fraenkel, 'Theocracy and Autonomy in Medieval Islamic and Jewish Philosophy'; and *Philosophical Religions from Plato to Spinoza*, 154–64.

Solidarity in the Virtuous City

To trace the manifestation of hospitality in a concrete political sense, we shall first turn to the role of solidarity within the inception of the virtuous city. Both hospitality and solidarity effectively engage the imagination in such a way which exceeds the boundaries of the political. With hospitality, the imagination engages the singularity of the Other prompting a responsibility to the Other as a neighbour or stranger. In contrast, with solidarity, the imagination comes to recognise that a necessary plurality constitutes each and every manifestation of singularity. Solidarity appears to imply a veritable erasure between singularity and plurality. However, such an erasure is not enacted on a concrete material basis. Rather, the inversion of this difference only takes place at the level of education where the practice of hospitality and solidarity is consistent with the cultivation of the intellect and moral character developed by the arts of poetry, music, rhetoric, and philosophy.[42]

Although solidarity (*'aṣabiyya*) does not appear as a technical term in al-Fārābī's political writings, we shall nevertheless aim to disclose how the practice of solidarity is always intimately conjoined to a more expansive notion of collective identity.[43] Beginning with his *Book of Letters*, which introduces the role of religion as binding the multitude together, we shall strive to make apparent the material conditions which give rise to solidarity. The origins of religion and hence the expansion of various branches of religion leading to a diversity of religions is historically subsequent to the practice of philosophy, 'Religion, if rendered human, comes after philosophy, in general, since it aims simply to instruct the multitude in theoretical and practical matters that have been inferred in philosophy, in such a way as to enable the multitude to understand them by persuasion or imaginative representation, or both.'[44] Religion functions as a

[42] George Makdisi cites al-Ḥasan ibn Sahl, the prime minister of the caliph, al-Ma'mūn, advising his sons, 'Learn to speak eloquently; for it is through speech that man is superior to the other animals; and the more eloquent you are in speaking, the more worthy you are of humanity' (*The Rise of Humanism in Classical Islam and the Christian West*, 95). To discern the advent of solidarity necessitates a retrieval of the culture of *adab* and the relationships between teachers and disciples which lead to the common pursuit of knowledge. The intellectual conditions of ninth- and tenth-century Baghdad were ripe for such a solidarity whereby one could recognise the common humanity of oneself in others. Surely, al-Fārābī recognised the value of solidarity in his travels by his own choice of dress as a Ṣūfī no-man and hence every-man. Perhaps this modesty afforded relations with those who lacked education as well as those who were as intellectually cultivated as himself in the pursuits of philosophy; see Netton, *Al-Fārābī and His School*, 4–7; al-Fārābī, *Al-Fārābī on the Perfect State*, 4.

[43] See Brunkhorst, *Solidarity*; and Roth, 'Solidarity and Responsibility'.

[44] al-Fārābī, *Book of Letters*, 108., 1, tr. Khalidi.

pedagogical tool. By instruction through rhetoric and the exposition of similes and images, the multitude begins to understand how they may relate to one another as citizens in the virtuous city. Moreover, religion is a propaedeutic to citizenship. The solidarity of the citizens is strengthened by images provided through religious education in addition to other forms of instruction. One such form of instruction effecting solidarity is music.

The political function of music is broached in the concluding section of al-Fārābī's *Great Book of Music* (*Kitāb al-Mūsīqī al-Kabīr*).[45] Music may bring the city to perfection by enacting solidarity between the citizens but may also contribute to its destruction through the promotion of factionalism. In what follows, we shall first investigate how music serves to perfect and complete the virtuous city by retrieving Plato's exposition of its pedagogical function in *Republic* III. Beginning with the youth who are exposed to lawful music, music brings harmony to the city and hence solidarity by first creating a well-balanced soul, 'because rhythm and harmony most of all insinuate themselves into the innermost part of the soul and most vigorously lay hold of it in bringing grace with them'.[46] The proper education attained through rhythm and harmony enables the youth to discern what is beautiful and good by nature. Therefore, music as condition for the study of philosophy may be compared with the role of religion as a means of instructing the multitude through the exposition of images. Those citizens who possess the art of music are prepared to engage in the art of politics. The relationship between music and politics appears within the context of Plato's discussion of sharing women and children which is designed to erase familial ties and rivalries arising from nepotism. After Socrates' assertion that the possession of women, marriage, procreation, and children must be arranged in accordance with the maxim that friends hold all things in common, Socrates gestures that the city will undergo a cycle of continuous growth upon its founding, 'And hence, the regime, once well started, will roll on like a circle in its growth.'[47] However, Socrates later recants on such a gesture if only to indicate the harms imposed by music contributing to civic strife. Hence, the guardians must ensure that there is 'no innovation in gymnastic and music contrary to the established order'.[48] Both gymnastics and music have inherent powers to move the citizens in such a way that they will be disposed to be better or worse. Socrates declares, 'For beware

[45] See especially Klein, 'Imagination and Music'; and Shedai, *Philosophies of Music in Medieval Islam*, 51-65.

[46] Plato, *Republic* 401d.

[47] Ibid., 424a.

[48] Ibid.

of change to a strange form of music as endangering the whole. For never are the tropes of music moved without the greatest political laws being moved, as Damon says, and I am persuaded.'[49] Music must be lawful to educate the youth as potential guardians for the sake of contributing to the composition of the city. Therefore, music performs a legal function within the city which effectuates solidarity by harmonising the dispositions of the citizens to contribute to its well-being. The youth shall only be exposed to lawful music in the hope that such lawfulness will inform other activities which the youth as potential guardians may engage in, 'setting right anything in the city that may have been previously neglected'.[50]

The power of music is recognised for the potential to effect solidarity.[51] Excellent melodies may be useful in cultivating virtue and attaining happiness in the political community. Since one of the defining traits of melodies is their capacity to cause human passions, the passions caused by music are not exclusive to the arts of rhetoric and poetry, but also include the art of political affairs. Such melodies include 'those that strengthen them, such as anger, enmity, etc.; those that weaken them, such as fear and mercy; and finally, those that mix the first two kinds, and so incline towards moderation'.[52] Here one may imagine how melodies which combine both positive and negative passions are juxtaposed with one another to produce moderation in the soul. The political function of music harmonises the soul by promoting the virtue of moderation. If moderation serves as a political tool for bringing the citizens together in harmony with one another, then music may be understood as an underlying source of civic solidarity. In addition, we may also consider solidarity as conjoined to the definition of humanity (*insāniyya*) insofar as the

49 Ibid., 424c.

50 Ibid., 425a.

51 Thérèse-Anne Druart summarises the introduction to al-Fārābī's *Kitāb al-Mūsīqī al-Kabīr* by bringing necessary attention to the political potential of three kinds of music: '1. Melodies that convey pleasure and delight in the sound heard. Such melodies also produce a state of rest and relaxation, but nothing else. 2. Melodies that in addition provide imaginings and yield representations of things and imitations of them. Such melodies are like visual decorations and pictorial representations. 3. Melodies that derive from sounds expressing affections or passions and states of being, be they pleasant or painful. Such sounds are common to human beings and irrational animals and differ from the sounds human beings and animals use as signs for communication. The melodic expression of passions and feelings may either reinforce them in exciting them or weaken them in providing a musical substitute when their usual proper completion cannot be reached' ('What Does Music Have to Do with Language, Logic and Rulership?', 207). Cf. al-Fārābī, *Kitāb al-Mūsīqī al-Kabīr*, 59.

52 Druart, 'What Does Music Have to Do with Language, Logic and Rulership?', 208. Cf. al-Fārābī, *Kitāb al-Mūsīqī al-Kabīr*, 1178.

universal character of humanity is identified with the practice of reflection, volition, and ethical action.[53] If each of the three conditions for the practice of philosophy contribute to the cultivation of humanity and solidarity, then reflection may be equated with critical self-examination to foster the spiritual path of illumination. The student of philosophy engages in reflection by logical and dialectical training. Al-Fārābī distinguishes between theoretical and practical intelligibles which entail some form of volition. Reflection which involves thinking about first principles in a logical manner when conjoined with volition results in ethical actions.[54] Al-Fārābī's *Directing Attention to the Way to Happiness* accordingly presents the value of proper reflection and volition for the sake of happiness:

> Thus, the noble disposition and the powerful mind together constitute human excellence, in the sense that anything's excellence is what imparts to it goodness and perfection in its being and goodness in its actions. When both [the noble disposition and the powerful mind] are present, we have goodness and perfection in our being and action. It is through them, then, that we become noble, good, and virtuous, that the way we behave in our lives becomes virtuous, and that our modes of comportment become praiseworthy.[55]

The practice of philosophy is guided by Socratic self-examination and the quest for the good, the true, and the beautiful. A noble disposition and a powerful mind bring necessary order to the world and promulgate the values of humanism and cosmopolitanism. Music undoubtedly contributes to the expansion of both values. In addition to composing the *Great Book of Music*, al-Fārābī was a particularly skilled musician in his own right performing in the royal courts of the day and hence keenly aware of its seductive power to harm

[53] See Kraemer, *Humanism in the Renaissance of Islam*, 115, 120, for the identification of humanity with solidarity. Cf. Daiber, 'Humanism', 297–8, 'Reflection, volition and ethical behaviour in the process of approximation to God appeared as instruments of a society, which Fārābī considers to be joined by the attribute, *insānīya*, "humanness" across the boundaries between peoples and nations. The species "humanity" or "humanness" became the basis for the peaceful coexistence of peoples and nations. This sounds like the principle of solidarity, which more than 400 years after Fārābī became a central theme in the "Introduction" (*Muqaddima*) to world history, written by the most important Islamic historian, Ibn Khaldūn; the principle of solidarity appears as *ʿaṣabīyya*, a sense of community that exists among the nomads in an authentic manner; it is a prerequisite for social union. This is true not only for Muslims but for all humanity.'

[54] al-Fārābī, *Attainment of Happiness*, 2. [24–31], 26–31.

[55] al-Fārābī, *Directing Attention*, 10. [54.19–20–55.1–5], 107, tr. McGinnis and Reisman.

potential rulers of the city.[56] Nevertheless, music is comprehended charitably as a universal language akin to philosophy. The mathematical origins of music come to be disclosed by the power of melodies to arouse these positive and negative passions. The remarkable ambivalence of music contributes to both the generation and corruption of the city as a political organism.

Beginning with al-Fārābī's allusions to *jihād* in *Aphorisms of the Statesman*, solidarity comes to be affiliated with loyalty to family members before extending to members of a clan or tribe, to citizens of a community, and even strangers and foreigners in a global community.[57] *Jihād* may be defined by the external struggle of factionalism between individuals, groups, or nations leading to enmity and war and the internal struggle between the various parts of the soul.[58] If we are to assume that soul is literally at war with itself, we cannot effectively distinguish such a striving for unity from the disunity, division, and difference which marks the condition for solidarity in the political community.[59] The inception of community is necessarily inscribed by a solidarity which simultaneously unites and divides. Here *jihād* may also be transposed as a term to describe the internal conflict arising between a commitment to divine law (*sharī'a*) and juridical law (*sunna*). Since the term is often misappropriated for political purposes to refer exclusively to offensive war, several scholars attribute a juridical distinction between the brotherhood

[56] Ian Richard Netton recounts the story of a mysterious musician which appears twice in the *Rasā'il* of the Ikhwān al-Ṣafā', 'Then a man of shabby appearance dressed in shabby clothes, entered and the major-domo (*ṣāḥib al-majlis*) placed him higher than all of them. Their faces exhibited their disquiet at that. The major-domo wished to demonstrate [the new guest's] superiority and calm the others' anger. So he asked him to let them hear something of his art. The man took out some pieces of wood which were with him, put them together and stretched [some] strings over them. He then played in such a way that it made all who were in the majlis laugh from the pleasure, and happiness and delight seized their souls' (*Al-Fārābī and His School*, 6–7; and Ikhwān al-Ṣafā', *Rasā'il*, vol. 1, 185, 289).

[57] al-Fārābī, *Selected Aphorisms*, 58. [66.4–8], 37, tr. Butterworth. Cf. al-Fārābī, *Aphorisms of the Statesman*, 54., 50, 137–8, tr. Dunlop. In contrast, the most prominent proponent of solidarity within medieval Islam, the fourteenth-century historian Ibn Khaldūn, presents solidarity as a kind of social glue aimed at preserving and protecting the structure of the family by promoting group loyalty.

[58] The ancient Greek heritage of Heraclitus and Plato frames our understanding of *jihād* in order to address the perpetual war between the parts of the soul: 'The focus on becoming in its exuberance and excess leads, in turn, to the emergence of a further related theme, namely that of conflict, and more pointedly, of war. Alone, the concern with war pervasive in the Platonic dialogue, if scarcely studied, would warrant, in fact, call for an attunement to this motif and its thematization. But more importantly, as Heraclitus also intimated, there seems to be an essential connection between the broad figure of becoming and the figure of war' (Baracchi, *Of Myth, Life, and War in Plato's* Republic, 9).

[59] Plato, *Republic* 470c–d.

of Islam (*dār al-islām*) and the realm of war (*dār al-ḥarb*).[60] The rationale for this distinction hinges upon the necessity of war to compel those unbelievers by force or consent to submit to belief in one God. Although we shall not determine whether the Qur'ān explicitly sanctions offensive *jihād*, the threat of paganism permits the dualism between the realms of belief and unbelief, darkness and light, good and evil, to saturate the imagination of the believer. In this sense, the believer develops 'a spirited hostility toward the darkness within oneself and toward the darkness outside. *Jihād* covers precisely these two senses of struggle.'[61] Despite this exposition of *jihād* in light of the Qur'ān, al-Fārābī does not justify offensive *jihād* as a resolute defence of Islam.[62] Rather, *jihād* is presented as a moral contest (*al-ijtihād*) between reason and passion reminiscent of *Nicomachean Ethics* VII:

> There is a difference between the one who is self-restrained and the one who is virtuous. That is, even if the one who is self-restrained does virtuous actions, one does good things while having a passion and longing for evil. One contends against their passion and resists what their trait and their yearning inspire them to do. One does good things and is irritated at doing them. The one who is virtuous follows what their trait and their yearning inspire him to do. One carries out good things while having a passion and a longing for them, and is not irritated at [doing] them; rather, on takes pleasure in them.[63]

[60] Joshua Parens presents a prescient summary of the contemporary theological and juridical debate, 'The realm of Islam is the realm in which Muslims have achieved political authority; the realm of war is the realm in which they have not. We need not descend into extensive detail here about what constitutes political authority, especially all of the various details about the various forms of submission. Contemporary scholars stress often that it is a juridical rather than a Qur'anic distinction' (*An Islamic Philosophy of Virtuous Religions*, 59). For the relevance of *jihād* to al-Fārābī's political philosophy, see Dunlop, *The Fuṣūl al-Madanī of al-Fārābī*, 1–22, who defends the claim that al-Fārābī supports *jihād* with philosophy. In contrast, Kraemer, 'The *Jihād* of the *Falāsifa*', 291–2, argues that al-Fārābī supports philosophy with *jihād*. Lambton, *State and Government in Medieval Islam*, 317–18, and Butterworth, 'Al-Fārābī's Statecraft', 93, contend that al-Fārābī promotes harmony between philosophy and religion with regard to *jihād* whereas Parens, *An Islamic Philosophy of Virtuous Religions*, 55–76, claims that al-Fārābī uses philosophy to criticise *jihād*. Sweeney, 'Philosophy and *Jihād*', conclusively demonstrates that al-Fārābī is criticising philosophy with *jihād*.

[61] Parens, *An Islamic Philosophy of Virtuous Religions*, 60.

[62] See Qur'ān 8:38, 9:29, 16:98–100, 37:23–8, 39:71.

[63] al-Fārābī, *Selected Aphorisms*, 14. [34.9–18], 18–19, tr. Butterworth (mod.). Cf. al-Fārābī, *Aphorisms of the Statesman*, 13., 33, 112, tr. Dunlop. See Parens, *An Islamic Philosophy of Virtuous Religions*, 65, 'This combat between reason and desire Alfarabi refers to as "the virtue of struggle" (*faḍīlah al-ijtihād*). This is clearly and correctly an allusion to the internal *jihād* praised so highly by the Qur'an and the Sufis.'

The individual restrains his or her passion in the struggle to live with constancy and integrity. Therefore, *jihād* may be exercised for the sake of promoting the internal cohesion and solidarity between the various parts of the soul. In contrast, the manifestation of *jihād* as an external struggle is identified with war and conquest. *Aphorisms of the Statesman* refers to those rulers and governors of the city who carry out *jihād*, 'One is the king in truth; he is the supreme ruler and the one in whom six stipulations come together: wisdom, complete prudence, excellent persuasion, excellent imaginative evocation, bodily capability for struggle, and having nothing in his body that prevents him from carrying the things pertaining to struggle.'[64] This external struggle may be orchestrated by a single sovereign. However, if no human being exists in which all the qualities of the perfect sovereign come together, then these qualities are dispersed among multiple sovereigns in the aristocratic rulership of the virtuous. Moreover, in the case that an aristocracy is untenable, the possibility is entertained that the rulership of the virtuous is replaced by the rule of law (*mulk al-sunna*) governed by a king according to the law (*malik al-sunna*).[65] Finally, a fourth type of rule may be necessary in the absence of a kingship, namely, collective leadership according to the law (*ru'asā' al-sunna*). The fourth type of rule may be said to replicate the Nocturnal Council of the *Laws* insofar as the external expression of *jihād* is motivated by the benevolence of those sovereigns who strive to promote solidarity.[66]

War remains a purpose for the existence of the second-best city and hence serves as a means for enacting solidarity. In his *Summary of Plato's* Laws, al-Fārābī identifies a certain need that impels the members of tribes and clans to begin to legislate themselves:

> He explained further with respect to traditional laws how they come about and that they were only the traditional laws sons had [derived] from the ways of life of their fathers. Then, later on, when those traditional laws led to solidarity, need compelled [them] first to a lawgiver of a general law that would unite the different ways of life, the members of numerous households, and the descendants of numerous ancestors with regard to a single thing encompassing their well-being.[67]

[64] al-Fārābī, *Selected Aphorisms*, 58. [66.4–8], 37, tr. Butterworth. Cf. al-Fārābī, *Aphorisms of the Statesman*, 54., 50, 137–8, tr. Dunlop.

[65] al-Fārābī, *Selected Aphorisms*, 58. [66.12–18], 37–8, tr. Butterworth. Cf. al-Fārābī, *Aphorisms of the Statesman*, 54., 50–1, 137–8, tr. Dunlop. See also Kraemer, 'The *Jihād* of the *Falāsifa*', 300.

[66] See Sweeney, 'Philosophy and *Jihād*', 562–72; and Mufti, *The Art of Jihad*, 90–6.

[67] al-Fārābī, *Summary of Plato's* Laws 2.2 [681a–682e], 145, tr. Butterworth.

Given that members of diverse tribes and clans may come together to share a common dwelling, the solidarity which already resides among them by virtue of their own tribalism requires legislation to prevent strife. All forms of strife, including civil and foreign, are characterised by a struggle for victory leading to the domination and conquest of the vanquished, 'Then he explained the struggle for domination that stems from solidarity, the hatred, and the [desire] for coercion that the inhabitants of one city have with respect to those of another. And [he explained] that these things do not present any usefulness since they are not in accordance with the law.'[68] Therefore, such a strife may only be effectively tempered by legislation. Akin to the stages of civic growth and decline portrayed in Plato's *Republic*, the relations between different clans or tribes is marked by solidarity by reversion to the harms of civil war. The solidarity that exists within the clan or tribe may be cemented by alliances between them within the city for the sake of fighting a common enemy. The prospect of a foreign war may increase the solidarity between clans and tribes. However, without a common enemy, the inclination to reassert some form of tribal solidarity prevails. The need for legislation to control this inclination to belligerence leads to the creation of laws to eliminate fighting between clans and tribes within the city. Since common law can only serve to eliminate civic strife, another form of law is needed, namely a divine law, which unites all clans and tribes under a common purpose, the persecution of war with the aim of establishing global peace. Peace can only be achieved by the prosecution of a war to end all wars, 'When it is lawful, one, two, or many kings may join together against a single city and compel it to accept the divine law.'[69] If we are to assume that the divine law refers to *sharīʿa*, then the prosecution of foreign wars for the sake of establishing global peace and hence a global community entails a necessary conversion to one faith by compulsion if the whole world is to live under one law.[70] Al-Fārābī does not explicitly designate that the whole world should be governed by a single sovereign. Here the reference to many kings or sovereigns implies the possibility of some form of democracy compatible with the existence of a constitutional monarchy. Although domination is a much easier means to establishing a global community than freedom, the

[68] Ibid., 2.3 [682c–e], 145.

[69] Ibid., 3.4 [683c–686c], 145.

[70] 'One wonders what the purpose of the law will become once it has achieved its purpose of eliminating strife. In other words, once it has accomplished its intermediate purpose of eliminating domestic strife, what will come of its ultimate purpose of facilitating foreign war? . . . The law expresses its wish to be intellect (*Minos*) by its aspiration to world rule. Intellect is truly cosmopolitan; thus the law aspires to be truly cosmopolitan' (Parens, *Metaphysics as Rhetoric*, 74–5).

harms of domination upon free and virtuous persons are accordingly recognised, 'Then he explained that just as domination and coercion are exceedingly fine for those who are slaves and evil, domination and coercion are exceedingly bad for those who are free and virtuous.'[71] Therefore, the expansion of virtue and happiness to these conquered foreign lands is more aligned with a soft despotism where those conquered peoples are presented with the opportunity for self-improvement akin to the citizens who are reformed by the Nocturnal Council. It is apparent that al-Fārābī weighs the moral differences between the domination exercised by absolute sovereignty and the prospect of choice afforded by constitutional rule:

> Then, he explained that domination taking place in this manner is more appropriate and easier in many respects than rule by means of choice since by confronting the inhabitants of the city with domination, it is possible for the one who sets down traditional laws to make the inhabitants upright in the briefest period. In contrast, the one who does not dominate but proceeds in accordance with the path of freedom, cannot do without gentleness; and gentleness takes more time.[72]

The virtue of gentleness serves as an expression of the etiquette and decorum identified with the cultivation of *adab*. Rather than blindly ignoring the will of the people for the sake of the ruled merely following the letter of the law, the directive of the Athenian Stranger is affirmed to implant the law in the hearts of the people:

> Then he explained how the law should be implanted in the hearts of the people, giving as an example a doctor who treats children with gentleness. He mentioned that doctors have servants who imitate them. Likewise, there are judges who emulate legislators in giving guidance. It is obligatory on them to employ extreme gentleness in restoring traditional laws and preserving them for the people.[73]

This attention to the virtue of gentleness also translates to those members of Plato's Nocturnal Council who are tasked with guiding the citizens to embody the law. This council of judges serve a restorative function aimed at rehabilitation rather than the administration of punitive measures. The existence of

[71] al-Fārābī, *Summary of Plato's* Laws 4.6 [710e–713a], 151, tr. Butterworth.
[72] Ibid., 4.5 [710e–713a], 150–1.
[73] Ibid., 4.14 [719e–720e], 152.

such judges respects the individuality accorded to each citizen to arrive at his or her own interpretation of the law by exhorting them through preludes which affirm morally praiseworthy behaviour, 'Then then there is another kind of prelude not belonging to the genus of these three, namely the praiseworthy and noble moral habits that legislators and judges extol and that the ignorant and children follow so as to be become habituated to these moral habits.'[74] Although the cultivation of such moral habits may be practised at the behest of legislators and judges, a conversion to moral rectitude is more easily achieved by divine law. Hence, religion serves as the predominant unifying source for effecting solidarity by obedience to the divine law. Moreover, the possibility is not discounted that multiple religions may exist under the aegis of a global community:

> Let him set down the traditional laws appropriate for making them upright. Then let him devote most of his concern to the issue of temples and esteemed places on earth so that they not change. For changing them will corrupt people's hearts, and corrupting their hearts will, in turn, throw the affairs of the city into disorder.[75]

With the admission of temples and other esteemed places on earth, the limits of the political community may be effectively expanded to include a multiplicity of religions. The existence of multiple religions portends the existence of multiple administrators or friends of the city (*aṣḥāb al-siyāsāt*) responsible for governing each group of people in a manner pertaining to their specific religious orientation 'thereby preventing dissension from arising as a result of badly governing them'.[76] If religions are inherently multiple with each nation possessing its own distinctive religious character, then the religion of each nation is to be optimally preserved to ensure solidarity between all nations. Indeed, if we are to speak of a virtuous city which extends across the entire inhabited world, such a city would be constituted by an internal diversity among its parts ensuring that the distinct harms of political oppression would not prevail.[77]

[74] Ibid., 4.16 [722c–723b], 153.
[75] Ibid., 8.7 [835d–844d], 169.
[76] Ibid.
[77] This diversity within unity synonymous with the democratic city is characterised by Joshua Parens as the 'multiplicity argument', 'Leaving aside that important qualification of "all", namely, "most", Alfarabi goes on to argue that the basis of these shared acts and opinions is human beings' shared "human nature" (*al-ṭabī'ah al insāniyyah*) (45, 34.14; Yasin, p. 83). Yet, it should be obvious that the view that we share some acts and opinions in common need not entail the view that all of our religions should be the same, or that Alfarabi aims

Here we might compare the inception of solidarity in al-Fārābī's virtuous city by recourse to the origination of political communities presented in Ibn Khaldūn's *Muqaddima*. Solidarity is constituted by a respect for the differences between nations and therefore inculcates a spirit of a shared humanity. The apparent conjunction between humanity (*insāniyya*) and struggle (*jihād*) as expressions of solidarity (*'aṣabiyya*) importantly anticipates Ibn Khaldūn's own account of civic and dynastic expansion in its multifaceted cultural and geographical complexity.[78] While al-Fārābī's *Book of Letters* presents a relatively regional anthropology by describing the origins of the Arabic language, Ibn Khaldūn's *Muqaddima* documents how the natural geography of the desert environment prompts the disposition to seek human culture and society and contends that the strong bonds of brotherhood in Arab nomadic cultures gives rise to the filial bond of solidarity oriented by ever-expanding spheres of obligation ranging from cities to nations and dynasties to all of humanity.[79] In contrast to al-Fārābī, Ibn Khaldūn distinguishes between three kinds of political communities: the first arising from Revelation or divine order, the second arising from human or secular order, and the third arising from their unity.[80] The first political community identified with the divine order replicates the Neoplatonic schema of emanation outlined in the *Virtuous City* and *Political Regime*. Since the paradigm for the human or secular order is premised upon divine order as its counterpart, their relationship mandates an account of religion as a binding force.[81] If solidarity arises primarily in nomadic societies which privilege the merits of rugged individualism leading to tribal affiliation,

at a relatively homogeneous virtuous regime of the inhabited world. On the contrary, he immediately follows up his references to such a shared nature and its entailed shared acts and opinions with references to the ruler's need to attend to the differences between "every group in every nation" (*kull ṭā'ifatin min kulli ummah*)' (*An Islamic Philosophy of Virtuous Religions*, 79). The multiplicity argument contributes to this solidarity between nations by respecting those differences within universality.

78 Ibn Khaldūn, *Muqaddima*, I.306–17, 343–55. Cf. Mahdi, *Ibn Khaldūn's Philosophy of History*, 209–16; and Khalidi, *Arabic Historical Thought in the Classical Period*, 222–31.

79 Ibn Khaldūn, *Muqaddima*, I.279–82, 313–18. Here we may compare Ibn Khaldūn's notion of solidarity with the Stoic cosmopolitanism of Hierocles where 'our place within the human community is described as being like the center of a number of concentric circles on which lie other human beings' (Goldin, 'Conflict and Cosmopolitanism in Plato and the Stoics', 279).

80 Ibn Khaldūn, *Muqaddima*, I.251–309, 282–346.

81 We cannot deny the hierarchical nature of al-Fārābī's paradigm. However, we shall strive to examine where such a hierarchy begins to invert itself, most strikingly with his account of the imagination, the weeds, and democracy which may indicate either the rise or demise of the political community. If we are to return to the formation of nations, we may also begin to see a common bond between the role of religion and the role of solidarity.

then religion is to be understood 'as a spiritual feeling of brotherhood', most likely found among the multitude in cities.[82]

Al-Fārābī's *Book of Religion* (*Kitāb al-Milla*) explicitly identifies religion with what is best for the multitude. The formation and organisation of political communities is inaugurated by religion which brings the multitude together in solidarity through shared images.[83] Religion is distinguished from philosophy as particular images are contrasted with universal concepts. Therefore, religion attends to the multiplicity of opinions rather than the unity identified with philosophy as an investigation into first principles, 'Religion is opinions and actions, determined and restricted with stipulations and prescribed for a community by their first ruler who seeks to obtain through their practicing it a specific purpose with respect to them or by means of them. The community may be a tribe, city, or district, a great nation or many nations.'[84] If religion is concerned with the determination of particulars, namely, opinions and actions derived from shared images, then we may begin to see how religion applies to the multitude where multiple opinions and actions exist. It is the duty of the first ruler to effectively utilise opinions and actions to ensure the attainment of happiness within the political community. Since these opinions and actions are determined by the ruler to benefit the political community, some form of solidarity may ensue:

> The descriptions of the things compromised by the opinions of religion ought to be such as to bring the citizens to imagine everything in the city – kings, rulers, and their servants; their ranks, the way they are linked together, and the way some yield to others; and everything prescribed to them – so that what is described will be likenesses the citizens will follow in their ranks and actions. These, then, are the opinions that are in religion.[85]

Religion proceeds by images and thereby brings solidarity to the political community by binding the actions of the ruler to the ruled. The philosopher-ruler-*imām* determines the opinions and actions of the multitude by the persuasive communication of these images. The actions of the philosopher-ruler-*imām* invoke the activity of the First Cause and perform both a religious

[82] See Mahdi, *Ibn Khaldūn's Philosophy of History*, 196.

[83] The *Book of Religion* is characterised by its relative austerity by comparison to the *Book of Letters*, purportedly al-Fārābī's most schematic work; see Parens, *An Islamic Philosophy of Virtuous Religions*, 88.

[84] al-Fārābī, *Book of Religion*, 1. [43.1–6], 93, tr. Butterworth.

[85] Ibid., 2. [45.41–5], 95.

and political function. In fact, at this stage, religion can neither be separated nor distinguished from law and jurisprudence:

> 'Religion' (*milla*) and 'creed' (*dīn*) are almost synonymous, as are 'law' (*sharī'a*) and 'tradition' (*sunna*). Most often, the latter two signify and apply to the determined actions in the two parts of religion. It may be possible, as well, for the determined opinions to be called 'law', so that 'law', 'religion' and 'creed' would be synonymous, given that religion consists of two parts: specifying opinions and determining actions.[86]

Religion thereby determines how the community is to be ruled. In contrast to those universal first principles supported by logical demonstration, religion proceeds by dialectic and rhetoric to verify opinions for the sake of the citizens of the political community. The function of religion informs the constitution of the political community at the most intimate level of the family, clan, or tribe. While political science may be conceived as a branch of philosophy limited to universals and patterns, religion transmits these universals and patterns through particular images which suit the multitude. Perhaps we might come to comprehend religion quite literally as the bond or binding of ruler to ruled expressing the harmony between the one who is serving and the ones who are served.[87] With religion as its vehicle, the art of politics aims to attain solidarity among all members of the political community, 'In addition, it brings about cognizance of their harmony, of how they are linked together, how they are organized, how their actions are organized, and how they mutually support one another so that despite their multiplicity, they might be like one thing.'[88]

Given the prominence afforded to the role of the individual in the acquisition of knowledge, the essential nature of the human being prior to the social bond of cities and states is also informed by how individuals find themselves attuned to specific kinds of environments which give rise to language, 'It is clear that the public and the multitude precede the select in time. Likewise, the shared cognitions, which are the preliminary opinions of all, precede the practical arts and the cognitions which pertain to each art, which are collectively common cognitions. The public and the multitude are the first to originate and come to be.'[89] Beginning with the most intimate unit of community, namely the family, language arises from the communication between individuals, 'If

[86] Ibid., 4. [46.18–22], 96.
[87] See Derrida, 'Faith and Knowledge', 16.
[88] al-Fārābī, *Book of Religion*, 20. [63.16–19], 110, tr. Butterworth.
[89] al-Fārābī, *Book of Letters*, 114., 4, tr. Khalidi (mod.).

a human being needs to acquaint another with what is in their mind or their intention, they will first use a sign to indicate what they want from whomever they seek to make understand, provided the other person is in a position to see their sign, later on they will use sound.'[90] By the formation of simple gestures and sounds, the individual communicates with other individuals. By way of the emergence of language, language expands from the family to the tribe to the nation, 'The first letters and expressions are signs for sensibles (*maḥsūsāt*) that can be pointed to and to intelligibles (*ma'qūlāt*) derived from sensibles that can be pointed to. For each universal intelligible has particulars that differ from the particulars of another intelligible.'[91] Here the art of rhetoric also assists with the development of language insofar as it makes available common images that can be understood by the multitude and hence communicated among them, 'Clearly the intelligible meanings of this nation are entirely rhetorical, since they are all arrived at by preliminary opinion. Their premises, expressions, and arguments, are all rhetorical at first, for the rhetorical ones precede the rest.'[92]

The art of rhetoric subsequently gives rise to the arts of poetry and music enabling a necessary solidarity to be established within and among nations. By retrieving the filiation of poetry and music, the potential to bring distinct communities together in their multiplicity is retained through the capacity of listeners to hear the same melodies. If the art of music gives rise to solidarity, then musical instruction also entails that the student of music cultivate an understanding of how the individual parts of melodies are to be ordered to contribute to the composition of the whole melody. The origins of language and hence the formation of political communities gesture to how solidarity is conjoined with justice on a global scale.[93] Since justice entails an innate recognition of reciprocity between citizens as equal, such a reciprocity is in turn grounded in an altruism aimed at preserving the solidarity of the political community.[94] Even after the historical and political demise of the 'Abbāsid Caliphate, solidarity remained a potent secular force expressed by the natural

[90] Ibid., 116., 5.

[91] Ibid., 119., 6.

[92] Ibid., 129., 10–11.

[93] See especially Nusseibeh, 'To Justice with Love', 186, 'For, on the other hand, the basic glue binding a polity is this instinct, and it is significantly a glue in which "the other" – even though it is a specific other as its basis, a blood relative, the object of one's affection, or a loved one – counts at least as much as oneself, if not more.' Cf. Mian, 'Love in Islamic Philosophy', 399–401.

[94] The relationship between solidarity and justice invokes the Stoic notion of affiliation (*oikeiōsis*) and anticipates Rousseau's *amour de soi*, 'If the direct relationship between persons who help each other is very close, so that it leads to close contact and unity, the ties

disposition of displaying affection for another. Beginning with family members and close friends, solidarity expands to those inhabitants of the political community who are physically and geographically far apart. Therefore, a cosmopolitan conception of political association begins to emerge by virtue of this vision of an 'imagined community'.[95]

are obvious and clearly require the (existence of a feeling of solidarity) without any outside (prodding). If, however, the relationship is somewhat distant, it is often forgotten in part. However, some knowledge of it remains and this causes a person to help his relatives for the known motive, in order to escape the shame he would feel in his soul were a person to whom he is somehow related be treated unjustly' (Ibn Khaldūn, *Muqaddima*, I.235, 264.8).

[95] See especially Anderson, *Imagined Communities*; Oklopcic, *Beyond the People*; and Taylor, *Modern Social Imaginaries*. Here we may compare Ibn Khaldūn's account of solidarity with the role of the imagination contributing to the proliferation of a multiplicity of religions in al-Fārābī's *Book of Letters*, 154., 23–4. For the affinity between al-Fārābī and Ibn Khaldūn, see Walzer, 'Aspects of Islamic Political Thought'.

6
Cosmopolitical Imaginaries

The Invention of Imagination

At the beginning of the *Harmonisation* al-Fārābī declares his intention to bring the respective philosophies of Plato and Aristotle into harmony 'in order to make the agreement between the beliefs of them apparent, and to remove doubt and suspicion from the hearts of those who look into their books, and to explain the places of uncertainty (*mawāḍi' al-ẓunūn*) and the sources of doubt in their treatises'.[1] His conspicuous reference to the knowledge of the two sages rather than their beliefs and opinions recapitulates Aristotle's distinction between knowledge and opinion. If the logical art of demonstration is identified with knowledge insofar as it proceeds by means of necessary and universal premises to arrive at certainty (*yaqīn*), then the arts of dialectic, sophistry, rhetoric, and poetics merely engage generally accepted opinions for the sake of engendering belief (*ẓann*), 'Now a belief is true and accurate when it corresponds to the way the thing expressed is.'[2] The beliefs pertaining to these arts are to be retrieved for the sake of explicating the respective philosophies of Plato and Aristotle, 'For that is among the most important [things] to be intent upon explaining and among the most beneficial to wish to expound upon and elucidate.'[3] This gesture of reconciliation is rooted in the need to

[1] al-Fārābī, *Harmonisation*, 1. [1b10–12], 125, tr. Butterworth.

[2] Ibid., 2. [1b25], 126.

[3] Ibid. See López-Farjeat, 'Al-Fārābī's Psychology and Epistemology', 'Dialectic engenders belief (*ẓann*) through arguments built upon generally accepted opinions; sophistry is a logical art that makes general opinions appear true; rhetoric persuades by means of appealing elocutions; poetics persuades by means of alluring or repulsive images; finally, demonstration, the highest of the logical arts, leads to certainty by means of universal and necessary premises. The non-demonstrative logical arts – dialectic, sophistry, rhetoric, and poetics – engender opinion in different degrees whereas, in contrast, demonstration

defend philosophy as an authentic science for the sake of establishing universal truths. Al-Fārābī subsequently warns his readers not to be misguided by those spurious opinions which may lead one to accept the opinions of Plato and Aristotle at face value without further inquiry. Instead, the discernment of their universal truths requires mutual intellectual labour:

> But when various intellects come to be in agreement – after reflecting on, pondering, investigating, examining, criticizing, disputing, and bringing up opposing passages – there will then be nothing more correct than what they believe in, testify to, and agree upon. And we find the various tongues unrestrained about the eminence of these two sages in philosophy. They are cited as examples, and high consideration is bestowed on them. They are described as the ultimate in profound wisdom, subtle knowledge, remarkable inferences, and fathoming the delicate meanings that lead to purity and truth in everything.[4]

How is such a meeting of various intellects to be envisioned if not by recourse to a political community where philosophy is privileged as a common good? Al-Fārābī explicitly contrasts those members of a political community who rather 'slavishly adhere to a single opinion and defer to a leader to precede them and direct them in what they agree upon', with these various intellects who by virtue of the free contestation of beliefs and opinions eventually arrive at consensus.[5] Moreover, the existence of such a political community is not limited to citizens and residents who speak a single language, rather 'various tongues [are] unrestrained about the eminence of these two sages in philosophy'.[6] Philosophy as a resolutely cosmopolitan enterprise thereby exceeds geographical, cultural, and linguistic boundaries. The multivalent character of philosophy extending far beyond the ancient Greek heritage thus invokes the possibility that such human intellectual achievement can be realised both regionally and internationally among multiple political communities.[7]

engenders certainty. However, in some places al-Fārābī admits that it could be the case that these non-demonstrative arts would lead to assent to beliefs in a way very close to certainty.'

4 al-Fārābī, *Harmonisation*, 4. [3a5–13], 128, tr. Butterworth.

5 Ibid., 4. [2b24–5], 127.

6 Ibid., 4. [3a8–9], 128.

7 See Vallat, 'Principles of the Philosophy of State', 338, 'According to al-Fārābī, the only way to make this possible is to provide everyone with the appropriate form of philosophical teaching, because becoming human is to act in accordance with what makes us unique among all natural species. And this is the capacity to think rightly, a capacity that only

Since this chapter examines the decisive contributions of the imagination to the generation of the virtuous city, we shall seek to envision how the practice of philosophy might foster the inception of a global community. It is only by virtue of the imagination that such a remote possibility may come to fruition. The imagination effectively enables those citizens of the virtuous city to recognise the universal importance of philosophy as means to attaining happiness. If such happiness is to be realised, then the imagination is cultivated and exercised by engaging in a regimen of civic education which prepares both philosophers and non-philosophers in the arts of rhetoric and persuasion. The realisation of the virtuous city is determined by the enactment of the imagination beginning with the philosopher-ruler-*imām* who receives and translates intelligibles from the Active Intellect into images which can then be communicated to the citizens. The reception, translation, and transmission of these images by means of rhetoric and persuasion effectively promotes the acquisition and cultivation of civic and cosmopolitan virtues contributing to the flourishing of the political community. Since 'the noble and just things which the political art examines [are by no means homogenous] but admit of much dispute and variability', the imagination as a political instrument presents the opportunity for all citizens to enact their natural disposition to attain happiness.[8] The universal attainment of happiness as the aim of the virtuous city is only made possible through the collective exercise of the imagination.

Given the relative unity accorded to metaphysics and ethics, we shall return to the insistent emphasis accorded to the attainment of happiness for all citizens

truth, that is, demonstrative philosophy, can properly channel and lead to its end. But peoples are different through their particular natural traits and cultures. Truth, remaining essentially the same, must therefore take on the appropriate shape to fit each people. Theoretically, there can by as many inflections of such a true philosophical teaching as there are peoples on earth apt to be taught.'

8 Aristotle, *Nicomachean Ethics* 1094b15–17. Al-Fārābī admits that the moral virtues or voluntary intelligibles demonstrate an extensive range and variability in their acquisition dependent upon differences in time and place, 'Those of them that come to exist are for the most part realized by the agency of whoever rules and does them. Yet because of the obstacles standing in their way – some of which are natural and others voluntary, resulting from the wills of other individuals – sometimes none of them at all is realized. Furthermore, they suffer not only *temporal variations*, so that they may exist at a certain time with accidents and states different from those that accompany them at another time before or after; their states also differ when they exist in different *places*' (*Attainment of Happiness*, 24. [18.13–18], 26, tr. Mahdi.).

of the political community.[9] As we shall demonstrate below, the power of the imagination contributes to a radically egalitarian account of the virtuous city originating in the vicissitudes of the given life-world. Since the imagination is afforded an intermediary status between the intellect and sense-perception, we shall specifically retrieve its material affinity with sense-perception and its contribution to the *sensis communis* (common sense). With the introduction of the common sense, the respective domains of psychology and epistemology may then be applied to political science for the sake of interrogating the distinction between the one and the many, philosophers and non-philosophers, rulers and ruled. These distinctions, as we shall see, are elided in the democratic city as a point of contrast with Platonic and Neoplatonic metaphysics. The practice of imagination thereby comes to be inextricably connected with an explicitly democratic form of politics. An ethics and politics of cosmopolitanism thus remains indistinguishable from the practice of philosophy in a democratic community. To envision the ambitious implications of such a cosmopolitanism, we shall return to Aristotle's exposition of the imagination as conceived in both *De Anima* and *Rhetoric*. By doing so, we shall aim to investigate how the phenomenological materialism of the imagination fosters the inception of a global community.[10]

In *De Anima* III.9, Aristotle underscores the pervasive importance of the imagination by virtue of conjoining the faculties of sense-perception and intellection as the intermediary between them. The imagination is distinguished by the respective powers of discrimination and motion with respect to place.[11]

9 Beginning with Strauss's foundational essay, 'Farabi's Plato', Mahdi, *Alfarabi and the Foundations of Islamic Political Philosophy*, Galston, *Politics and Excellence*, and Butterworth, 'Alfarabi's Goal', contend that al-Fārābī is a political philosopher *par excellence* by privileging his political texts as holding the esoteric key to deciphering his philosophy as a whole. Gutas, 'The Meaning of *Madanī* in al-Fārābī's "Political Philosophy"', and Reisman, 'Al-Fārābī and the Philosophical Curriculum', have consistently refuted Strauss's exoteric/esoteric distinction which mistakenly conflates his political philosophy with his metaphysical, logical, rhetorical, and musical treatises.

10 Joshua Hall attributes a phenomenological materialism to al-Fārābī which most importantly precedes Ibn Rushd by arguing that the *Virtuous City* 'offers a materialist critique that prefigures critical theory and post-structuralism and thereby provides guidelines for how to more effectively engage monotheistic communities in the pursuit of social justice – including along the axes of race, gender, and sexual orientation' ('Alfarabi's Imaginative Critique', 175).

11 Aristotle, *De Anima* 432a15–18. The imagination falls between both thinking and perceiving as a middle-voiced phenomenon simultaneously both active and passive and thereby occupies an ambivalent role in Aristotle's explanatory model of animal and human behaviour. Cf. Polansky, *Aristotle's* De Anima, 504, '*Phantasia* has close connection to the sensitive part without being simply the same as it, and *phantasia* differs from the calculative, spirited,

Since perception of motion, rest, shape, magnitude, and number are common to the faculties of sense-perception, Aristotle gestures to a unified faculty or common sense to which all the proper objects of sense-perception are directed.[12] However, there is no common faculty independent of the faculties of sense-perception. Instead, the particular senses are unified insofar as each individually contributes to the collective faculty of common sense.

Aristotle's exposition of sense-perception demonstrates how the perceiving soul is capable of self-awareness. The awareness of perception may appear to be self-evident for human beings and portends the existence of a unified awareness affiliated with the exercise of imagination. To further illustrate his account of self-awareness, Aristotle distinguishes between the activities of hearing and sounding, 'Whenever that which is capable of hearing is hearing and that which is capable of sounding is sounding, then the hearing in its being active and the sounding in its being active come into being simultaneously.'[13] Although what it is to hear and what it is to sound are respectively different, their activity appears to be one and the same. How are the activities of hearing and sounding conjoined insofar as what sounds is properly heard? Aristotle introduces a faculty which simultaneously enables the unity of hearing with that which sounds, 'Now if harmony is a sort of voice and there is a way in which voice and hearing exist as one, and harmony is a *logos*, then it is necessary that hearing also has to be some sort of *logos*.'[14] The faculty of hearing is configured in such a way that the sensible object transmits sound according to a specific kind of harmony or ratio which corresponds to the activity of hearing.

Although there may be a precise mathematical and musical sense by which *logos* may be understood as both harmony and ratio, *logos* should not be isolated from the faculty of sense-perception. If we are to speak of *logos* exclusively as a rational faculty, then we risk devaluating its semantic resonance in relation to the practical disciplines of ethics, political science, rhetoric, and poetics. The faculty of sense-perception also bears an affinity with the faculty of the intellection by its power to discriminate between appearances, 'perception when directed at its proper objects is always true and is present in all animals, but it is possible to think things through also falsely,

appetitive, rational, and irrational parts of his predecessors, being a distinctive faculty itself. Yet if *phantasia* is made too separate from the other faculties, especially sense perception, it would not exist at all and could hardly do its functions; hence the perplexity regarding it.'

12 Aristotle, *De Anima* 424b22–425a14.

13 Ibid., 425b29–426a1.

14 Ibid., 426a27–8.

and this is present in no animal in which there is not also reasoning.'[15] By drawing a distinction between the activities of reasoning and perceiving, Aristotle appeals to the power to critically judge appearances as true or false as a power exclusive to reasoning. However, the activity of perceiving already exercises its own kind of discernment which may be said to contribute in some way to the activity of reasoning. Here the contribution of sense-perception to the activity of reasoning is mediated by the imagination to present a judgement about what may or may not be the case, 'For imagination is different from both perceiving and thinking things through, and it does not come about without any perceiving, and without it there is no responsive supposition that something is the case.'[16] After contrasting reasoning and sense-perception with regard to truth and falsity, Aristotle concludes that the imagination is different from both faculties but intimately united to them insofar as the imagination has the power to exercise interpretation by discerning the image received according to a given disposition. In this case, the reception of an image and its discernment should not be conceived as distinct activities, but rather as one activity whereby the thing as an image or appearance first comes to be disclosed and discerned as a thing.

Aristotle defines the imagination as a certain function of the soul, 'according to which we say a certain appearance comes into being before us'.[17] Imagination is compared with sense-perception by its power to move and be moved by an image insofar as the image may be discerned to be either true or false:

> Since it is possible when one thing is being moved for another thing to be moved by it, but imagination seems to be a certain motion and not to come into being without the power of perceiving, but in beings that perceive and from the things of which there is no perception, and since it is possible for a motion to come about by the activity of the power of perceiving and necessary for it to be similar to perceiving, then this motion would be neither possible without the power of perceiving nor present in beings that do not perceive, and that which has it may act and be acted upon in various ways and the motion may be either true or false.[18]

[15] Ibid., 427b8–14.

[16] Ibid., 427b14–16. Thomas Kjeller Johansen entertains the possibility that the *phantasia* should be characterised as an affection by reference to *Physics* 202a22–5, 'Change may be understood, then, as an affection (*pathos*) in the patient. This is not an inappropriate distinction of *phantasia* since it is a change in the perceiver caused by the activity of perception' (*The Powers of Aristotle's Soul*, 205).

[17] Aristotle, *De Anima* 428a1–2.

[18] Ibid., 428b10–19.

By highlighting the role of locomotion for the constitution of the imagination, namely, the power to act and be acted upon, the imagination through the appearance of images remains inseparable from the power to be affected by them. The faculties of sense-perception, thinking, and imagination demonstrate an inextricable interconnectivity and integration whereby it becomes difficult if not impossible to exclusively distinguish between them.

With this caveat in mind, we shall now turn to the *Rhetoric* to discern the function and role of imagination in the reception, transmission, and communication of affects. By retrieving the affects as phenomena integral to the constitution of ethico-political life, we shall strive to recuperate the occlusion of the imagination and, more precisely, its intersection with the passive or material intellect (*nous pathētikos*) as inherited through the Platonic-Christian framework of medieval scholasticism. To engage in such a brief introduction to the *Rhetoric* may also serve to underline its relevance for developing an account of politics rooted in the materialist tradition whereby the *De Anima* and the *Nicomachean Ethics* are to be read and interpreted in their relative inseparability.

Between Word and Image

The *Rhetoric* is explicitly conjoined with the *Poetics* as inclusive to the Organon throughout the medieval Islamic heritage.[19] However, its relative historical importance may be said to extend to ethico-political life by conjoining the affects of the soul from *De Anima* with those dispositions integral to the cultivation of moral character in the *Rhetoric* and *Nicomachean Ethics.* Here one cannot discount the role of the affects for the constitution of the image and its transmission into speech. The imagination and its contribution to shaping ethico-political life is crucially informed by this intersection between affects and images.

In *Rhetoric* III.1, Aristotle retrieves the materiality of the affects and their efficacy for producing images in political speech. Demonstrative speech contributes to the aims and objectives of a virtuous political community through the interconnection between speech, image, and affect, 'the subject of speech, however, has some small necessary place in all teaching: for to speak in one way rather than another does make some difference in regard to clarity, though not a great difference; but all these things are forms of outward show and

[19] Deborah Black's *Logic and Aristotle's* Rhetoric *and* Poetics *in Medieval Arabic Philosophy* defends their inclusion in the Organon to present an epistemological interpretation of the *Rhetoric* and *Poetics.*

intended to affect the audience.'[20] Speech serves as a guiding principle for the production of the image. Therefore, certain forms of speech are developed to produce the proper image for a respective audience. Although demonstrative speech is merely one species of rhetorical speech, the capacity for speech to produce images informs every form of rhetorical speech. If we are to situate the introduction of demonstrative speech in relation to Aristotle's definition of rhetoric, then demonstrative speech presents possibilities inherent to rhetoric itself as a way of seeing and hence expressing the world through speech.[21] Demonstrative speech is especially unique as a form of speech designed for public exhortation aimed at expressing praise and blame. Since praise and blame are distinguished according to their positive and negative aims, demonstrative speech may be further demarcated into affects which aim to uplift and thereby empower the audience through praise and affects which aim to cause distress to the audience through blame. The speaker is thus confronted with the ambitious task of expressing both praise and blame through the medium of those images produced by the imagination. Such an image brought forth by demonstrative speech produces a distinctive affect among the audience. Hence, the function of demonstrative speech to literally inform the image is determined by the power of its affective appeal.

The imagination of the speaker produces images which become imprinted within the imagination of the audience. Each image accordingly bears a specific temporal and spatial register in terms of its magnitude as a quality relative to time, place, and circumstance for the sake of embellishing the subject of the speech.[22] An increase in the relative magnitude of the speech and hence the intensity of the image which is spontaneously produced only further stimulates the imagination of the audience. The imagination is determined by its power to act and be acted upon insofar as the image remains inseparable from the 'affect which lies in our power whenever we choose'.[23] Their relative inseparability only comes to further magnified with the constitution of both honour and shame. The imagination cannot be separated from the constitution of specific affects and contributes to the formulation of opinions, 'when we form an opinion that something is threatening or frightening, we

[20] Aristotle, *Rhetoric* 1404a6–8.

[21] Martin Heidegger describes demonstrative speech as 'the possibility of seeing what is given at the moment: what speaks for a matter that is the topic of discourse, the possibility of seeing at each moment what can speak for a matter' (*Basic Concepts of Aristotelian Philosophy*, 78).

[22] Aristotle, *Rhetoric* 13621b, 1362a17.

[23] Aristotle, *De Anima* 427b19–20.

are immediately affected by it.'[24] Although opinions may appear to be dependent upon the imagination since they are formulated by the distinct influence of the speaker, opinions also retain their own autonomy from the imagination insofar as they remain separate from affect for the sake of deliberation. The activity of deliberation engages the imagination by producing mental images. The one who deliberates must be aware of how affects condition deliberation and hence judgement, 'for it is wrong to warp the jury by leading them into anger or envy or pity'.[25] Both deliberation and judgement demonstrate the value of the intellectual virtues of practical wisdom and contemplation to the imagination. One cannot successfully deliberate between images for the sake of choosing a future course of action without exercising practical wisdom. Given the explicit legal and political context for the application of practical wisdom, demonstrative speech invokes the deliberation of mental images. Moreover, demonstrative speech addresses the role of the listeners to engage in the activity of contemplation. A speech comes to be judged as ugly or beautiful by the measure of its capacity to invoke contemplation. In this sense, demonstrative speech fulfils an explicitly theoretical aim which may also be attributed to the inception of philosophy through the cultivation of wonder. Hence, one could imagine a speech producing certain mental images which may be worthy of contemplation. Despite the contemplative value of a speech invoked by a speaker, the pivotal role attributed to the production and expression of emotion may outweigh its rational importance. Therefore, demonstrative speech shapes the affective ground of deliberation, contemplation, and judgement.

We shall conclude our brief overview of the relationship between imagination and demonstrative speech by retrieving how the speaker appeals to their audience to generate opinions by using lexical strategies to produce images which evoke certain affects. Affects may unite the audience for the sake of attaining politically expedient ends such as evoking the fear of punishment. Aristotle appeals to fear as a species of pain produced by those negative mental images anticipating a harmful outcome, 'Let fear be defined as a sort of pain or agitation derived from the imagination of a future destructive or painful or evil.'[26] Fear functions as a powerful political tool for shaping public opinion. Fear is conjoined with shame as 'an impression about a loss of reputation', since 'honor and reputation are among the most pleasant things, through each person

[24] Ibid., 427b22–3.
[25] Aristotle, *Rhetoric* 1354a5.
[26] Ibid., 1382a32.

imagining that they have the qualities of an important person'.[27] Despite its classification as a loss of reputation and honour and hence as a form of individual punishment bestowed on behalf of the community, shame demonstrates a positive valence for the sake of educating the population and therefore should be accorded a positive pedagogical value. Al-Fārābī importantly modifies Aristotle's account of shame by highlighting its value as a moral virtue alongside liberality, wittiness, humility, respectfulness, gentleness, and moderation:

> Actions that are good are equilibrated actions intermediate between two extremes, both of which are evil: one being an excess, the other a deficiency. Similarly, virtues are traits of the soul and states intermediate between two traits, both of which are vices, one of which is greater and the other lesser like moderation, for it is intermediate between avidity and insensibility to pleasure.[28]

In his *Summary of Plato's* Laws, al-Fārābī explicitly contrasts shame with its contraries, 'shame is praiseworthy, but, in excess, it becomes impotence and blameworthy.'[29] Shame is identified with impotence as a blameworthy action but also may be aligned with temperance and moderation. The Athenian Stranger of the *Laws* identifies shame with that which stands opposed to our greatest pains and fears and our greatest desires and pleasures. Shame resembles the moral virtues of courage and moderation. However, shame is generated from an opinion of oneself and at best is only 'the concealment of our own defectiveness''[30] Despite the Stranger's denigration of shame as merely a shame as a quasi-virtue, al-Fārābī intentionally recuperates the moral value of shame as worthy of exhortation.[31] Shame comes to be identified with the role

[27] Ibid., 1384a14, 1371a16.

[28] al-Fārābī, *Selected Aphorisms*, 18. [36.9–15], 20, tr. Butterworth. Cf. al-Fārābī, *Aphorisms of the Statesman*, 16., 34, 113–14, tr. Dunlop.

[29] al-Fārābī, *Summary of Plato's* Laws, 22. [d129.22–3], 137, tr. Butterworth.

[30] Benardete, *Plato's* Laws, 50.

[31] What prompts al-Fārābī to transform shame into an active disposition identified with virtue? In contrast to his *Summary of Plato's* Laws, the *Book of Rhetoric* (*Kitāb al-Khaṭāba*) identifies shame as an affect that accompanies an enthymeme used to argue against or persuade an opponent, 'The orator may seek to show the superiority of his moral character and the faulty character of his adversaries, not in the manner about which he is speaking, but he shows his superior moral character and the faulty character of his adversaries in other things that are outside of the matter about which they are discoursing, as Galen did when he showed his superior moral character by talking about the excellent moral character of his father and his country and the lack of moral excellence in his opponents by mentioning the lack of moral excellence in their ancestors and countries' (al-Fārābī, *Book of Rhetoric* 258a22–9, tr. Ezzaher, 30).

of the law and the lawgiver to exhort the citizens to follow a given course of action and hence to obey the law. Rather than compulsion or prescription, the moral exhortation of the lawgiver emphatically urges the citizens to uphold their legal and political duties. Shame works in conjunction with both civic law and divine law to ensure the cultivation of virtues among the citizens. Although al-Fārābī does not mention the role of the divine law (*sharī'a*) in his account of shame, the philosopher-ruler-*imām* is divinely guided to exhort the citizens to follow the laws (*sunan*) by providing images (*mithālāt*) through demonstrative speech to deter blameworthy actions and guarantee that the citizens follow the law. The potential legislator must be trained in the art of rhetoric to effectively convey the moral value of shame. Hence, a distinctive pedagogical regimen must be invoked to teach rhetorical skills if shame is to be effectively conveyed with the imagination as political strategy of persuasion. Shame is conditioned by the productive role of the imagination to generate those affectively resonant images. Here we should not discount the power of images to persuade the audience to adopt a specific judgement by manipulating those affects identified with shame. The exposition of the intersection between imagination and the affects is integral to formulating rhetorical judgements. By bringing to light the role of the imagination for the sake of rhetorical judgements, the cultivation and development of persuasive images through demonstrative speech is the most common method for attaining the desired political end of the legislator.[32]

Beyond All Borders

The advent of the global community is decisively informed by the rhetorical power of the imagination. The philosopher-ruler-*imām* explicitly invokes the rhetorical strategies of demonstrative speech to effectively communicate those images received from the Active Intellect for the sake of pedagogy and persuasion. By retrieving the powers of discernment and locomotion which are contingent upon the imagination to bring images together into a coherent whole, al-Fārābī affirms the pervasive material presence of the imagination as the necessary condition for the attainment of happiness in the political community. The distinction between theoretical and practical philosophy is effectively called into question with the role of the imagination as a bridge

[32] Cf. 'We might mitigate the historical and generic trouble that Aristotle's account presents if we note the fluidity of his conception of epideictic and understand his account as describing a particular function of discourse, the phantasmatic function' (O'Gorman, 'Aristotle's "Phantasia" in the *Rhetoric*', 27).

between metaphysics and ethics. If both ethics and politics are defined by an investigation into relative truths contingent upon human experience, then the science of metaphysics is commonly identified with first principles and hence necessary and universal truths. The *Virtuous City* demonstrates their correspondence beginning with the robust intersection established between the disciplines of metaphysics, rational theology (*kalām*), and psychology.[33] After presenting a survey of the different kinds of knowledge in relation to the science of metaphysics, al-Fārābī remarkably retrieves the faculty of nutrition as the foundation for the other faculties, namely, sense-perception, imagination, appetite, and reason.[34] Although the faculties of sense-perception and appetite retain a higher level of complexity by virtue of their respective functions, the faculty of nutrition determines how the nature of the soul is both constituted and sustained. Therefore, the faculties of sense-perception and appetite are dependent upon the faculty of nutrition by their power to relate to stimuli in their surrounding environments. The complex perceptual and appetitive apparatus of the animal soul conditioned by receiving sensibles through sense organs and ultimately pursuing or avoiding them according to pleasure and pain accentuates the supreme importance of nutrition as an occluded source for the constitution and sustenance of all organic life.

In the *Virtuous City*, the imagination is further determined by how the senses respond to both positive and negative stimuli by identifying these stimuli with impressions which one may either pursue or avoid. The imagination effectively places those stimuli in relation to one another to influence a specific course of action. Since the imagination is situated between sense-perception, appetite, and reason, the imagination is the bridge that retains the stimuli by virtue of the strength of their impressions before they come to be judged to be either true or false by the rational faculty. The faculty of imagination genetically emerges from the faculties of nutrition, sense-perception, and appetite as branches stemming from the same tree:

[33] The *Virtuous City* includes a hierarchical classification of ideal and less than ideal cities. Following Plato, who presents those cities that depart from the ideal city in speech, al-Fārābī ranks each city according to the knowledge of the prophet-philosopher-ruler to effectively rule by aiming towards happiness and the relative character of the citizens who are ruled.

[34] The nutritive faculty remains the first principle (*archē*) for constituting and determining the life of the soul, 'In the history of western philosophy, bare life as such is identified at a decisive moment. It is the moment in which Aristotle, in *De anima*, isolates the most general and separable meaning of "living being" (*zōon*) among the ways in which the term is said' (Agamben, 'On Potentiality', 230).

> Then afterwards another faculty arises in him by which he retains the impressions (*rusūm*) of the sensibles in the soul when these sensibles are no longer perceived, this being the faculty of imagination (*al-quwwa al-mutakhayyila*). By this faculty, he connects some of the sensibles with each other and disconnects others in different connections and disconnections, some being false, some true.[35]

Although al-Fārābī and Aristotle privilege the imagination as an intermediary between sense-perception and reason, al-Fārābī specifically highlights the absence of sensibles as enabling the work of the imagination. The imagination effectively organises the sensibles through the activity of recollection (*dhikr*) and thus serves as a protype for the faculty of reason (*al-quwwa al-nāṭiqa*) by its power to imitate, recollect, organise, and relate the sensibles to one another. Whereas the faculties of sense-perception and appetite originate from nutrition, the faculty of reason originates from the imagination and this specific power to discriminate between sensibles. Despite Aristotle's reluctance to identify the faculty of imagination with the faculty of reason, al-Fārābī's association of the imagination with discrimination and judgement highlights the material basis of imagination extending beyond the realm of mere recollection to include communication through pedagogy and persuasion:

> It retains the sensibles (*maḥsūsāt*) when they are no longer presented to sense-perception, and by its very nature controls the sensibles and exercises judgement over them: for it separates them from each other and connects them with each other in various ways, so that it happens that some of the things imagined (or 'represented') agree with those perceived by the senses and others differ from them.[36]

Here al-Fārābī refers to the faculties of imagination and reason as sharing an affinity between one another by virtue of their proximity to that which is true or trustworthy (*ṣādiq*). Since images can be judged to be either true or false, reason works with the imagination to make possible the knowledge of good and evil.[37] The material basis of the relationship between imagination and reason is identified with the nature of belief, namely, how beliefs are composed by the retention, recollection, and organisation of present and absent sensibles. In addition to recollecting absent sensibles, the imagination possesses the

[35] al-Fārābī, *Virtuous City*, V, 10, §1, 164–5, tr. Walzer.
[36] Ibid., IV, 10, §4, 168–9.
[37] Ibid., IV, 10, §1, 164–5.

power to engage in the imitation and reproduction of images, 'But in addition to the preservation of the impressions of the sensibles and their association with one another it displays a third activity, namely "reproductive imitation" [*mimēsis*] (*muḥākāt*). This faculty is different from the other faculties of the soul, being capable of "imitating" the sensibles which have remained preserved in it.'[38] The activity of imitation is integral to the political function of the imagination. The reproduction of images for the sake of communicating with the citizens is instrumental to the role of the philosopher-ruler-*imām*. Although the ruler is often identified with the rational and intellectual faculties, we should not underestimate how the imagination pervades both faculties by influencing any decision or judgement reached. Once a judgement is rendered, those beliefs may be conveyed as opinions to the multitude either by pedagogy or persuasion.

If we are to assume that reason or the intellect is identified with the philosopher-ruler-*imām*, al-Fārābī interrogates the hierarchical classification of the faculties of the soul by privileging the role of the imagination, particularly its mysterious imitative and reproductive powers.[39] By the retention of this rather enigmatic function to imitate and thereby reproduce images, the imagination is identified with the divine activity of the One transmitted through the Active Intellect (*al-'aql al-fa''āl*) in a prophetic vision to the philosopher-ruler-*imām*.[40] Despite Aristotle's claim that prophetic vision occurs among the ordinary rather than the best and the wisest, the activity of prophetic vision is retrieved for the sake of establishing a connection between the prophet and ruler as one person within the political community.[41] This account of the philosopher-ruler-*imām* should be placed within the Neoplatonic schema of

[38] Ibid., IV, 14, §2, 210–11.

[39] 'Unless . . . philosophers become kings in the cities or those whom we now call kings and rulers philosophize truly and adequately and there is a conjunction of political power and philosophy . . . there can be no cessation of evils . . . for cities nor, I think, for the human race' (Plato, *Republic* 473c11–d6).

[40] Al-Fārābī claims that his account of prophetic vision follows from *De Anima*; see *Political Regime*, 79. [79.13–18], 69. Craig Streetman's 'If It Were God Who Sent Them . . . Aristotle and al-Fārābī on Prophetic Vision' concludes that Aristotle remains rather sceptical if not indifferent to the authenticity of prophetic vision given his own critique of prophetic dreams (212). While the imagination figures prominently in *Parva Naturalia* and *De Anima*, scant attention has been devoted to the function of the imagination in *De Divinatione per Somnum* (*On Prophecy in Sleep*). For the influence of al-Fārābī's prophetic imagination upon Maimonides, see Melamed, *The Philosopher-King in Medieval and Renaissance Jewish Political Thought*, 34–5.

[41] Aristotle, *De Anima* 426b22–4.

emanation whereby the 'First Cause, First Intellect, or First Existent' effectively produces the prophetic vision by way of emanation through the Active Intellect:

> When it happens that the faculty of imagination (*al-quwwa al-mutakhayyila*) imitates those things with sensibles (*maḥsūsāt*) of extreme beauty and perfection, the person who has that sight comes to enjoy overwhelmingly and wonderful pleasure, and one sees wonderful things which can in no way whatever be found among other existents. It is not impossible, then, that when one's faculty of imagination reaches its utmost perfection that one will receive in their waking life from the Active Intellect (*al-'aql al-fa''āl*) present and future particulars of their imitations in the form of sensibles, and receive the imitations of the transcendent intelligibles (*ma'qūlāt*) and the other glorious existents and see them. This person will obtain through the particulars which they receive 'prophecy' (supernatural awareness) (*nubuwwa*) of present and future events, and through the intelligibles which they receive prophecy of things divine. This is the highest rank of perfection which the faculty of imagination can reach.[42]

Although the Active Intellect may be identified with the Aristotelian Unmoved Mover as the principle of intelligibility and the primary cause of human intellection, al-Fārābī explicitly retrieves the Platonic demiurge who is responsible for ordering matter in such a way as to bring the sensible cosmos into existence. The divine authority of the Active Intellect as an innovator of matter extends to the power of the imagination within the prophet to envision the conjunction between intelligibles and sensibles for the sake of portending present and future events.[43] The imagination of the prophet as an innovator of matter literally brings images into being and therefore may be analogously compared to the creative activity of

[42] al-Fārābī, *Virtuous City*, IV, 14, §9, 222–5, tr. Walzer (mod.).

[43] Both *Theologia Aristotelis* (*Theology of Aristotle*) and *Liber de Causis* (*Book of Causes*) contribute to this tendency to Platonise Aristotle and were widely circulated throughout the formative period of Islamic philosophy, 'Whoever looks into his statements on lordship [*al-rubūbiyya*] in the book known as the *Theology*, will no longer be confused about his affirming [the existence] of the Artisan, the Innovator of this world. Indeed, in these statements, the issue is too manifest to be concealed. There he explains that primary matter has been innovated by the Creator, may he be glorified and magnified out of nothing, and that it has become corporeal by the Creator, may his majesty be magnified, and by his will, then set in order' (al-Fārābī, *Harmonisation*, 56. [16a25–16b10], 155, tr. Butterworth). Cf. Adamson, *The Arabic Plotinus*; and Taylor, 'A Critical Analysis of the Structure of the *Kalām fī mahd al-khair* (*Liber de Causis*)'.

the Active Intellect. By virtue of this dissemination of images to the multitude, the prophet also becomes akin to the activity of emanation identified with the Neoplatonic One and the Active Intellect. Al-Fārābī's *Harmonisation* retrieves the *Theology of Aristotle* to describe this efficient cause of all creation insofar as 'the one [that] exists in all multiplicity and the multiplicity in which the one does not exist is absolutely unlimited'.[44] However, such an account of emanation does not strictly subscribe to the Neoplatonic schema of the One–Intellect–Soul triad. Instead, al-Fārābī's cosmology consistently privileges the analogy between the order of the cosmos and the organic parts of a living body as a consequent of an Active Intellect which brings all of existence into motion in a manner reminiscent of the Unmoved Mover.[45] Insofar as the Active Intellect exists as the formal 'light' for all rational beings to be enlightened, the intellect of the prophet comes to be identified with the material status of the passive intellect *who receives intelligibles via* the acquired intellect:

> Then, there emanates from the Active Intellect (*al-'aql al-fa''āl)* to the passive intellect (*al-'aql bi-l-quwwa)* the faculty by which one is able to seize on the definition of things and actions and direct them toward happiness. This emanation proceeding from the Active Intellect to the passive intellect by the intermediary of the acquired intellect (*al-'aql al-mustafāḍ)* is revelation (*waḥy*). Because the Active Intellect is an emanation from the existence of the first cause, the first cause is what brings revelation to this human being by the intermediary of the Active Intellect.[46]

If the Active Intellect is responsible for the transmission of intelligence, then the passive intellect which becomes activated by the Active Intellect requires the assistance of the imagination. The imagination is accordingly classified by its intermediary status in the transmission of intelligence:

> For when the faculty of imagination (*al-quwwa al-mutakhayyila*) is extremely powerful in a human being and developed to perfection, and when the sensibles which reach it from the outside do not overpower it so as to absorb it completely and do not make it work in the service of the rational faculty (*al-quwwa al-nāṭiqa*), and when there is, on the contrary, in it, a considerable surplus enabling it to perform its specific activities, then its state in waking

[44] al-Fārābī, *Harmonisation*, 56. [16b.18–20], 156, tr. Butterworth.
[45] See Janos, *Method, Structure, and Development in al-Fārābī's Cosmology*, 191–2.
[46] al-Fārābī, *Political Regime*, 80. [79.26–80.7], 69, tr. Butterworth (mod.).

> life while being kept busy by these two activities is like its state during sleep when it is relieved of them.[47]

The imagination as an intermediary between sense-perception and reason comes to be accentuated to such a degree so as to attain its own perfection. Despite al-Fārābī's observation that the imagination 'is the matter for the rational faculty', the imagination should not be construed as merely passive.[48] The materiality of the imagination retains its own dynamism to enrich and expand itself as it receives intelligence from the Active Intellect and transmits that intelligence to the passive intellect. If for every thought there is a corresponding image, then the imagination performs an essential material role by imitating and reproducing images for the sake of the common sense and the acquired intellect.[49] Such images are required for the prophet to effectively deliberate and choose the action most beneficial to the political community:

> Now the faculty of imagination (*al-quwwa al-mutakhayyila*) imagines many of the things supplied by the Active Intellect (*al-'aql al-fa''āl*) (by means of) visible sensibles (*maḥsūsāt*) which imitate them. These objects of imagination are in turn impressed on the faculty of common sense (*al-ḥiss al-mushtarak*), once their impressions (*rusūm*) are present in the faculty of common sense, the faculty of sight is affected by those impressions, and they are impressed on it. From such impressions within the faculty of sight arise impressions of them in the shining air which connects the sight which proceeds from the eye with the ray of vision. Once these impressions have appeared in the air, the image of the air is in turn again impressed on the faculty of sight which resides in the eye, and that impression is reflected back to common sense and to the faculty of imagination. And since all these states are continuous, the objects of that kind which the Active Intellect has supplied become visible to the person.[50]

Thus, the imagination not only works intimately with the Active Intellect but impresses those images upon the faculty of the common sense. The common sense as an internal sense corresponds to the faculty of sight as an external sense enabling images to be transmitted from the imagination of the prophet

47 al-Fārābī, *Virtuous City*, IV, 14, §8, 220–3, tr. Walzer.
48 Ibid., IV, 10, §9, 174–7.
49 Cf. Aristotle, *De Anima* 431a16.
50 al-Fārābī, *Virtuous City*, IV, 14, §8, 222–3, tr. Walzer.

to the imagination of the audience beholding the image.[51] Al-Fārābī identifies those internal senses corresponding to the five external senses in order to delineate their function as species of sense-perception:

> The latter are the five senses known to everyone, and they are located in the eyes, the ears, and the rest. Each of the five senses perceives the sensible that is proper to it. The main power (*ra'īs*) is the one in which all the perceptions of the five senses are gathered together, the five senses being like its reporters. It is as if the five senses were all its advisers, each responsible for a different kind of information from one of the regions of the kingdom (*mamlaka*). The main power is like the king (*al-malik*) at whose court the advisers gather the news from all regions of the kingdom.[52]

Following the Platonic analogy of the soul, al-Fārābī describes how each of the five senses corresponding to each sensible reports to the philosopher-ruler-*imām*, in this case, the figure of the king, to communicate the news gathered from each region of the kingdom. Here the king is rather conspicuously placed within the faculty of sense-perception identified with the common sense (*al-ḥiss al-mushtarak*). In contrast to the Platonic model of the philosopher-king who occupies the role of reason or the intellect, the king as the faculty of common sense which effectively brings the other senses together is responsible for securing their power insofar as the respective senses emanate from them. Although the precise relationship between the imagination and the common sense remains unclear, the common sense demonstrates an intimacy with the imagination to such a degree that the imagination assumes the same privileged rank and thus inaugurates a new material paradigm for political rule.[53] Al-Fārābī is wholly responsible for jettisoning this decisive

[51] Daniel Heller-Roazen remarks that 'the classical Arabic thinkers, al-Fārābī among them, are the first to identify the "internal senses" (*ḥawās bātina hushim panimim*)' (*The Inner Touch*, 145).

[52] al-Fārābī, *Virtuous City*, IV, 10, §3, 166–9, tr. Walzer (mod. Heller-Roazen, 148).

[53] The political writings of al-Fārābī were composed during a critical turning point in Islamic history, namely, the brief rise of Shī'ism, particularly a moderate Imāmite Shī'ism and Zaydism imposed by the dynasty of the Persian Būyid sultans and of extremist Ismā'īlī Shī'ism represented politically by the Fāṭimid dynasty. One of the differences between Ismā'īlī and Imāmite Shī'ism is that the former maintained that the *imām* whom al-Fārābī identifies with the philosopher-ruler-*imām* existed not only as a perfect man but as the incarnation of God. It may be dubious to claim al-Fārābī subscribes to such a belief. However, the *imām* in the virtuous city demonstrates the extraordinary creative potential to not merely imagine a utopia but ultimately bring such a utopia into existence; see Campanini, *An Introduction to Islamic Philosophy*, 13; and Black, *The History of Islamic Political Philosophy*, 56–74.

turn away from the transcendent power of the Active Intellect and towards the concrete material immanence of political rule associated with the power of the imagination. This shift towards a new materialist paradigm of political rule is perhaps most concretely exemplified by the prophetic transmission of knowledge to the political community.

Both Aristotle and al-Fārābī agree that the philosopher-ruler-*imām* must be in an awakened and vigilant state to most effectively discern the transmission of such a revelation (*waḥy*). After receiving the revelation, the philosopher-ruler-*imām* may then properly discern how the revelation is to be concretely transmitted by images. Following *On Prophecy in Sleep* (*De Divinatione per Somnum*), al-Fārābī highlights the role of theoretical wisdom and practical wisdom in the contemplation and deliberation of the revelation.[54] Since the revelation is received by the philosopher-ruler-*imām* as an involuntary intelligible and is therefore concerned with eternal and universal truth as an object of theoretical wisdom, the philosopher-ruler-*imām* is tasked with the transmission of the revelation to a historically contingent political community. Practical wisdom must be effectively exercised to deliberate about how to apply the intelligible to a concrete political situation by working in conjunction with the image received and reproduced by the imagination. With regard to the practical deliberation of the philosopher-ruler-*imām*, al-Fārābī retrieves the power of the imagination to evoke the desired political end by assisting the activity of practical wisdom with determining the persuasive efficacy of the image:

> And among them is for there to be two whose goal is one in itself. One of the two is more complete in imaginatively evoking that goal, more perfectly virtuous, possessing practical wisdom (*ta'aqqul*) by which he infers everything for the sake of arriving at that goal, and finely prepared so as to use someone else to attain the goal. The one is a ruler over the second who does not have that.[55]

The imagination accurately imitatively reproduces the intelligible and translates the intelligible into an appropriate sensible for the sake of producing the desired political end. In doing so, imagination performs a threefold function in the reception of the intelligible, the imitative reproduction of the intelligible into a sensible image, and the transmission of the sensible image. Therefore, al-Fārābī resolves a historical lacuna by presenting the first comprehensive

[54] See especially Walzer, 'Al-Fārābī's Theory of Prophecy and Divination'.

[55] al-Fārābī, *Selected Aphorisms*, 60. [68.10–14], 39, tr. Butterworth (mod.). Cf. al-Fārābī, *Aphorisms of the Statesman*, 56., 52, 138–9, tr. Dunlop.

analysis of the productive power of the imagination foretelling even Kant's own presentation of the transcendental schematism.[56]

In a departure from those intelligibles which cannot be directly translated into political action, the active power of the imagination imitatively reproduces those voluntary intelligibles for the sake of transmitting them as sensible images. This gesture only further highlights the intersection between the imagination and practical wisdom. The philosopher-ruler-*imām* must exercise practical wisdom to deliberate about how the sensible images and symbols will be applied to a specific city or nation for the sake of persuasion, 'Now, these things are reproduced by imitation for each nation and for the people of each city through those symbols which are best known to them. But what is best known often varies among nations, either most of it or part of it. Hence these things are expressed for each nation in symbols other than those used for another nation.'[57] Given the correspondence of political science with practical wisdom and metaphysics with theoretical wisdom, the *Political Regime* develops an account of the imagination in relation to the truth of any given cognition, 'To form a concept of them is to have their essences sketched in the human soul as they exist in truth. To imagine them is to have their images, their likenesses, and the objects representing them sketched in the human soul.'[58] Although the imagination presents only an indirect access to intelligibles via imitation, images are a requisite condition for disclosing the truth which resides within each cognition.

The relative fecundity of the imagination responsible for imitating and reproducing images promotes both pluralism and relativism in its application to specific political communities and different nations. In his *Book of Letters*, al-Fārābī concludes that religion follows from philosophy, and that religion is in fact an imitative substitute for philosophy. Therefore, religion must proceed through persuasive images.[59] Since the imagination of the philosopher-ruler-*imām* reproduces an image which organically relates to the essence or truth of the intelligible, 'the things by which they are represented are many and

[56] 'Synthesis in general, as we shall hereafter see, is the mere result of the power of imagination (*Einbildungskraft*), a blind but indispensable function of the soul, without which we should have no knowledge whatsoever, but of which we are scarcely ever conscious' (Kant, *Critique of Pure Reason*, A78/B103, 112).

[57] al-Fārābī, *Virtuous City*, V, 17, §2, 280–1, tr. Walzer.

[58] al-Fārābī, *Political Regime*, 89. [85.7–10], 74, tr. Butterworth.

[59] al-Fārābī, *Book of Letters*, 108–11., 1–3. Cf. 'So far as Spirit in religion pictures itself to itself, it is indeed consciousness, and the reality enclosed within religion is the shape and guise of its image-thinking (*Vorstellung*)' (Hegel, *Phenomenology of Spirit*, 412).

different. Some are closer to what is represented and others more distant.'[60] Therefore, the communication of the image is only a relative truth. As long as the citizens affirm the relative truth of images and abide by them, then the philosopher-ruler-*imām* has successfully performed his or her own essential function. Insofar as this is the case, the *Virtuous City* also acknowledges that religion and rhetoric inhabit the same domain in their movement away from the first principles of logical demonstration to contingent and inductive principles derived from images and symbols:

> But when they are known through symbols which reproduce them by imitation, grounds for objection may be found in these symbols, in some less, in others more, and grounds for objection will be more easily seen in some and less in others. It is not impossible that among those who know these things through such symbols, there is someone who puts their finger on the grounds for objection to those symbols and holds that they are inadequate and false.[61]

Both pluralism and relativism are affirmed by this exposition of the referential and symbolic function of images.[62] Hence, images have a claim to another kind of truth that transcends mere logical demonstration. The philosopher-ruler-*imām* effectively discerns the intelligibles received from the Active Intellect and imaginatively transforms them into an image or symbol transmitted to the citizens of the political community. Despite al-Fārābī's omission of any strict logical criterion for distinguishing images from one another according to their degree of truth, the imagination of the philosopher-ruler-*imām* reproduces intelligibles as accurately as possible and translates them into images for the sake of persuasion. The philosopher-ruler-*imām* thus serves as a teacher by prudently presenting the right image at the right time to the right citizens:

> Since it is difficult for the public to understand these things in themselves and the way they exist, instructing them about these things is sought by other ways – and those are ways of representation. So these things are represented to each group or nation by things of which they are more cognizant.

[60] al-Fārābī, *Political Regime*, 90. [85.26–8], 74, tr. Butterworth.
[61] al-Fārābī, *Virtuous City*, V, 17, §3, 280–1, tr. Walzer (mod.).
[62] Katharine Loevy decisively concludes that 'There is no universal nation, because geography, religion, and imagination are not universal, but there can be a more universal political entity composed of several nations, and this would be more perfect than the nation because it would reflect more clearly the universality of the human essence' ('Al-Farabi's Images', 76).

> And it may be possible that what one of them is more cognizant of is not what another is more cognizant of.[63]

Here we are presented with the possibility of different kinds of citizens receiving different kinds of truths. The image may be transformed into different modes of symbolic expression which most accurately correspond to the geographical place and historical time of the political community. The image bears within itself its own spatial and temporal historicity. Hence the imagination should not be exclusively comprehended in terms of its political valence. Since there is no one universal history, history begins with the 'first natural cause for the difference in nations'.[64] The geographical and historical variations attributed to political communities and nations is determined by the given climate and those plants and animals located in specific climactic zones. If history is primarily determined by geography and hence fluctuations in climate, then language is also derived from the same set of natural conditions to become the primary means by which images are to be communicated as tools of persuasion. Therefore, the philosopher-ruler-*imām* effectively deliberates about those images corresponding to the geographical and historical circumstances of the political community. In doing so, the philosopher-ruler-*imām* must be properly educated to discern between the various kinds of images and their relative power of persuasion.

Following the regimen of education sketched throughout the *Republic*, *Attainment of Happiness* addresses how belief and opinion precede knowledge and truth in the education of the philosopher-ruler-*imām*, 'Until they acquire the theoretical virtues, they ought to be instructed in things theoretical by means of persuasive methods. They should comprehend many theoretical things by way of imagining them.'[65] If the philosopher-king is to be educated to properly discern between the truth and falsity of images, then the philosopher-ruler-*imām* must similarly identify the truth that resides in the image through the cultivation of the power of intellect and the reliance upon logical demonstration.[66] The education of the philosopher-ruler-*imām* only comes to fruition with the concomitant education of the citizens who receive those images most pedagogically suitable to a particular community or nation.

The phenomenological power of the image extends from the philosopher-ruler-*imām* to each and every citizen. Even those citizens who appear to be

[63] al-Fārābī, *Political Regime*, 90. [86.11–18], 75, tr. Butterworth.
[64] Ibid., 65. [70.10–12], 61.
[65] al-Fārābī, *Attainment of Happiness*, 40. [30.12–14], 35–6, tr. Mahdi.
[66] See Plato, *Republic* 382a4–c3.

ineducable, often derisively referred to as 'weeds', are at least to be exposed to persuasive images for their pedagogical value.[67] In contrast to Plato who distinguishes between gold, silver, bronze, and iron souls constituting the various classes of society in his city in speech, al-Fārābī refrains from presenting any absolute demarcation between classes of society to privilege the possibility of universal education.[68] Even certain 'weeds' retain the possibility of becoming philosopher-ruler-*imāms* by virtue of such an education beginning with their persuasion by images and concluding with the truth of logical demonstrations and a knowledge of essences:

> Whoever is like this has his level of imagination elevated to things that the arguments he brings forth do not show to be false. If he is persuaded in thus being elevated, he is left there. But if he is not persuaded by that either and falls upon topics he can contend against, he is elevated to another level. It goes on like this until he is persuaded by one of these levels. But if he does not chance to be persuaded by one of the levels of imagination, he is elevated to the ranking of truth and made to understand those things as they are (*al-ashyā' 'alā mā hiya*). At that point, his opinion becomes settled.[69]

The imagination performs an explicitly political function by granting promise to the attainment of happiness in the political community. Those weeds who are purportedly identified as sceptics (*mustarshidūn*) are the nascent philosophers who are asking for guidance and seeking the truth. Given his exposition of the prophetic vision of the philosopher-ruler-*imām* attained via the Active Intellect, al-Fārābī subsequently invokes the power of those images (*mithālāt*) within Plato's Allegory to foster the inception of philosophy. Beyond the strict demarcation of intellect and sense-perception established by the Divided Line, the imagination as a source of their mediation (*tawassaṭa*) explicitly conjoins them. It is precisely this possibility to be 'elevated to the ranking of truth and made to understand those things as they are' which first comes to be disclosed

[67] 'Another sort has already imagined the things we have mentioned, except that they are not persuaded by what they have imagined. So, for themselves and for others, they show those things to be false by arguments. In doing so, they are not contending against the virtuous city. Rather, they are asking for guidance and seeking truth' (al-Fārābī, *Political Regime*, 123. [104.28–105.2], 91, tr. Butterworth).

[68] See Plato, *Republic* 415a1–415d4.

[69] al-Fārābī, *Political Regime*, 123. [105.3–10], 91, tr. Butterworth.

through the activity of the imagination.[70] The imagination thus makes itself apparent at those critical junctures where nothing else than the fate of political community comes to be contested. In this sense, the inception of philosophy by virtue of the imagination always bears its own trace by calling us from the past to a hitherto unknown future and hence a cosmopolitanism to come.[71]

[70] Ibid., 123. [105.3–10], 91.

[71] John Sallis eloquently brings attention to the inherent political implications of the imagination, 'Imagination gathers up the various visible moments, both those actually seen and those only implied by what is seen, and by taking up this manifold of visible moments, it brings to presence the city itself, posits it as actually there. But being-present, being-there, is not a matter of being visible to our sensible vision. Rather, the city shows itself as being there by being brought forth nonsensibly by imagination. The city itself remains invisible, and yet imagination attests to its being there, to its actual presence' (*Ethicality and Imagination*, 109).

Coda: Community

In our hyper-technological age, cosmopolitanism as a latent possibility and urgent promise remains endemic to contemporary political discourse. The spectre of cosmopolitanism persistently haunts those governments which embody the institutional practices of the modern nation-state. With the historical cataclysm of global warfare and increasing economic disparities between the Northern and Southern hemispheres, the displacement of entire populations of peoples as refugees fleeing political persecution, social oppression, and climate change has become an urgent matter for political deliberation. Cosmopolitanism combats both the scourge of nationalism and xenophobia through a renewed ethical commitment to the practice of an unconditional hospitality by welcoming the foreigner and the stranger, the immigrant and the refugee.[1] However, how are we to put into practice such a radical form of hospitality in light of the bleak political climate which persistently threatens its realisation? Bertolt Brecht's poem 'To Posterity' (*Nachgebornen*) appropriately laments:

> Truly, I live in dark times!
> The simplest word is foolhardy.
> A smooth brow

[1] The history of cosmopolitanism is punctuated by a contradictory logic beginning with the Stoic and Pauline traditions before culminating in Immanuel Kant's essay 'Perpetual Peace' and therefore cannot be separated from the practice of ethics and the experience of hospitality, 'Hospitality is culture itself and not simply one ethic amongst others. Insofar as it has to do with the *ethos*, that is, the residence, one's home, the familiar place of dwelling, inasmuch as it is a manner of being there, the manner in which we relate to ourselves and to others, to others as our own or as foreigners, *ethics is hospitality*; ethics is so thoroughly coextensive with the experience of hospitality' (Derrida, *On Cosmopolitanism and Forgiveness*, 16–17).

Betokens callousness. He who laughs
Has merely not heard
The terrible tidings.[2]

Perhaps these dark times are not exclusively limited to Brecht but extend into our own century where the truth often remains distorted by those who simply explain away unpleasant facts and unjustified concerns. With the proliferation of misinformation, the prospect of engaging in a genuine dialogue to arrive at the truth has become further challenged by increasing political polarisation. How are we to formulate a collective response to Brecht's poem in a political climate characterised by the pessimism of deep despair? The history of modernity remains radically ambivalent and hence Janus-faced bequeathing to its inheritors the inspiring ideas of global fraternity and universal justice, on the one hand, and the dangerous agendas of nationalism and xenophobia, on the other.[3] Despite the paroxysm of two world wars and the resurgence of regional warfare prompted by ethnic rivalries and neocolonial agendas, the promise of cosmopolitanism gained political traction after World War II when various global citizenship organisations were established, including the International Registry of World Citizens in 1949 which claimed over 900,000 members.[4] Albert Camus, Karl Jaspers, and Albert Einstein inspired by Stoic cosmopolitanism and the early German Romantics who embraced the unity of humanity were among the first intellectuals of their generation to advocate for the possibility of a global political community to be established among all peoples.[5] Alongside Brecht, Hannah Arendt is undoubtedly influenced by the cosmopolitan tradition. However, Arendt remains justifiably sceptical about the prospects of any form of cosmopolitanism portending to a world government. Arendt's essay addressed to Jaspers, 'Karl Jaspers: Citizen of the World', stridently critiques the political paradigm of cosmopolitanism, 'Nobody can be a citizen of the world as she/he is a citizen of her/his country.'[6] Upon concluding that any world government whatever its form

[2] Brecht, 'An Die Nachgebornen ("To Posterity")', 227. Brecht composed his poem between 1934 and 1938 in the disconsolate years leading up to World War II.

[3] Fred Dallmayr presents probing and prescient reflections regarding the past and future of cosmopolitanism in *Being in the World*, 30–58.

[4] For a concise history of the International Registry of World Citizens, see Davis, *My Country Is the World.*

[5] See Jaspers, *The Origin and Goal of History*; Warf, 'Nationalism, Cosmopolitanism, and Geographical Imaginations'; and Hayden, 'Albert Camus and Rebellious Cosmopolitanism in a Divided World'.

[6] Arendt, *Men in Dark Times*, 81.

would be 'a forbidding nightmare of tyranny', Arendt distinguishes between philosophy which 'conceives of the earth as the homeland of humankind with one unwritten law, eternal and valid for all' and politics which 'deals with human beings, nationals of many countries and heirs to many pasts; its laws are the positively established fences which hedge in, protect, and limit the space in which freedom is not a concept, but a living, political reality'.[7]

How are we to abide by Arendt's distinction between philosophy and politics today? Is the paradigm of cosmopolitanism simply an impractical utopian ideal in an age of globalisation punctuated by increasing political, economic, health, and environmental crises which continue to threaten the stability and integrity of the nation-state? As we reflect upon those historical events which challenge the idea of national sovereignty, why is the West consistently thematised as the foremost proponent of this cosmopolitan paradigm?[8] With the admission that hospitality should inaugurate each and every dialogue, a certain theological orientation comes to be associated with the West as the regional designation for the advent of monotheism. Despite the historical contributions of monotheism to the expansion of a global ecumenism, Judaism, Christianity, and Islam often find themselves held hostage by virulent forms of orthodox fundamentalism thereby only hastening the divide between a radically secular cosmopolitanism and theocratic forms of nationalism.[9]

Since the publication of Arendt's 'The Decline of the Nation-State and the End of the Rights of Man' in her *Origins of Totalitarianism* in 1951, numerous countries throughout the globe have collectively observed the frightening rise of xenophobia targeted directly at refugees and immigrants.[10] Given the history of colonialism, citizens from countries throughout the Global South are confronted with the daily prospect of increasing economic inequality and the necessity to migrate in order to simply survive. How are we to respond

[7] Ibid., 81–2.

[8] The 'West' remains a conceptually problematic term given the complex degree of cultural assimilation and interdependence between disparate and diverse cultures which have come to constitute such a historical designation; see Said, *Orientalism*, 31–48. Tamara Albertini analyses five common 'orientalisms' pertaining to the study of Islamic philosophy in 'Reintroducing Islamic Philosophy'.

[9] See Balibar, *Secularism and Cosmopolitanism*, 94–109. To combat the ignorance of orthodox theocracy, one might merely heed the initial words uttered by the angel Gabriel in 610 CE which initiated a series of divine revelations to the Prophet Muḥammad, namely, 'Read! In the name of your Lord who has created all things' (Qur'ān 96:1). This imperative is similarly invoked in Augustine's own hearing of God's words '*tolle lege*' ('take up and read') in *Confessions* XIII.12.

[10] Arendt, *Origins of Totalitarianism*, 267–302.

to the plight of the immigrant and the refugee in a historical moment ripe with possibility but also inscribed by a perpetual state of emergency with the lingering presence of international conflicts throughout the Middle East and Eastern Europe compounded by the unfolding catastrophe of global climate change? With the contemporary resurgence of nationalism contributing to the destabilisation of parliamentary republics throughout Europe, how are we to defeat the most virulent forms of tribalism, racism, and xenophobia which undoubtedly aim to persecute and hence occlude the non-Western 'other'?[11]

If this history of persecution and occlusion is endemic to the 'grand narrative' of the West, what may be said about the cultivation of an ethics of hospitality within those cultural traditions affiliated with the inception and expansion of Islam? Perhaps one needs to look no further than the Qur'ān 4:36 where the hosting of wayfarers or travellers (*ibn al-sabīl*) is presented as a religious and moral duty, 'Worship God and associate nothing with Him, and to parents do good, to relatives, orphans, the needy, the near neighbour, the neighbour far away, the companion at your side, the traveller, and those whom your right hand possess. Indeed, God does not like those who are self-deluding and boastful.' Despite the reluctance of certain Western nations to welcome refugees, several countries which contain the largest number of refugee populations currently reside in the Islamic world.[12] The practice of hospitality embodied by the openness to hosting asylum seekers fleeing persecution and civil unrest is among the most profoundly cosmopolitan gestures of our time. The great economic cost to those countries who have chosen to practise hospitality by opening their borders to vulnerable refugee populations undoubtedly illustrates the difference between cosmopolitan rhetoric and action.

Here we may return to a dialogue between Jacques Derrida and Mustapha Chérif which invokes the need to interrogate the European intellectual construct of Islam by challenging the accepted contrast between Islam and the West. Since the Greek and Islamic traditions are intimately conjoined at multiple historical moments, our own retelling of this cosmopolitan narrative has been guided by the aim 'to rediscover the sources and the moments in which those currents, far from being in contrast, truly fertilized each other . . . There are many Islams, there are many Wests.'[13] To commence

[11] See George Makari's autobiographical prologue 'Out of Beirut' in *Of Fear and Strangers*, xi–xxii.

[12] For example, 7 per cent of the Turkish population claims refugee status compared to 0.5 per cent of the UK; see UN Refugee Statistics: www.unrefugees.org/refugeefacts/statistics/.

[13] Chérif, *Islam & the West*, 39.

such a dialogue, it may be prudent to simply put into practice Chérif's admission that 'universal civilization belongs to everyone and is owned by no one. Indeed, every true civilization is pluralist, and every universal must be accessible to all.'[14] Rather than simply eliding the existence of irreducible differences between Islam and the West, our aim has been to reframe this contentious debate away from culturally conservative historians who steadfastly maintain the clash of civilisations hypothesis for the sake of entertaining a more expansive and inclusive historical interpretation by re-conceiving the northern and southern shores of the Mediterranean as a unity composed by two complementary halves.[15]

The phenomenon of migration and the seeking of asylum for political refugees is endemic to this history. If we turn to the Hebraic heritage, the Book of Numbers describes God ordering Moses to institute cities of refuge or asylum.[16] Throughout the Middle Ages, this divine injunction literally came to be adopted throughout Western Europe with the Great Law of Hospitality whereby cities as an expression of their sovereignty would open up their churches and synagogues as sanctuaries for the sake of securing immunity or

[14] Ibid., 37. Cf. Jacques Derrida's prescient remarks about the urgency of retrieving a democratic paradigm inherent to the Islamic heritage to critically inform the scope of the current investigation, 'One of the two tasks would be of the order of theoretical or hermeneutical knowledge. It would consist in an enormous, urgent, and thorough historical study of everything that does and does not authorize in different readings of the Koranic heritage, and in its own language, the translation of a properly democratic paradigm. But it would be essential to study and to take seriously into account (something for which I have neither the time nor the competence), beginning with Greece of Plato and Aristotle, with the political history and discourse of Athens, but also of Sparta, of Hellenism and Neoplatonism, what gets passed on, transferred, translated from Europe by pre- and post-Koranic Arabic, as well as by Rome' (*Rogues*, 31).

[15] Chérif, *Islam & the West*, xvi. See Lewis, *The Crisis of Islam*; Huntington, *The Clash of Civilizations and the Remaking of the World Order*; Roy, *The Failure of Political Islam*; and Mamdani, *Citizen and Subject*. With respect to the irreducible differences between each religious tradition, Pierre Claverie, the murdered Bishop of Oran, speaks eloquently of reverencing the unique in the other when he observed of Christian-Muslim dialogue that to 'really have common ground we must leave behind the illusion that our different worlds refer the same realities. I prefer to say a priori that the other is other . . . I will never be the other, nor in the place of the other, however much I may desire to enter into communion with him, to know him, to love him; it's impossible! Encounter, co-existence, dialogue, friendship are only possible on the basis of difference being recognized and accepted. To love the other in their difference is the only possible way of loving. Otherwise, we tear each other apart' (McGee, 'Pierre Claverie and the Truth That Unites Us').

[16] Numbers XXV.9–32.

survival for refugees.[17] According to the law of *auctoritas*, we may also identify numerous examples of kings and lords from the Italian Renaissance who were obligated to shield their refugees and guests from other warring states, including a certain story about our cosmopolitan interlocuter, Dante, who was banished from Florence and then welcomed in Ravenna.[18] The serendipity of Dante's biographical experience as a political exile deserves to be retold for the sake of historical contrast with al-Fārābī who was travelling from Damascus to Ascalon when he was purportedly robbed and killed by highwaymen.[19]

This history of political exile and banishment is nothing new to the practice of philosophy as a life of self-examination in its ancient and medieval iterations. To be a lover of wisdom, one must 'honour truth even above friends'.[20] Al-Fārābī's profound knowledge of the Platonic and Aristotelian heritage would no doubt lead him down the same path of ostracism and exile. His solemn message expressed as a moral injunction echoes the fate of the accused Socrates, 'Therefore it is wrong for the virtuous man to remain in corrupt politics, and he must emigrate to the ideal cities, if such exist in fact in his time. If they do not exist, then the virtuous man is a stranger (*gharīb*) in the present world and wretched (*radī*) in life, and to die is preferable for him than to live.'[21] It is rather remarkable that al-Fārābī employs the term

[17] 'In the medieval tradition, on the other hand, one can identify a certain sovereignty of the city: the city itself could determine the laws of hospitality, the articles of predetermined law, both plural and restrictive, with which they meant to condition the Great Law of Hospitality - an unconditional law, both singular and universal, which ordered that the borders be open to each and every one, to every other, to all who might come, without question or without even having to identify who they are or whence they came' (Derrida, *On Cosmopolitanism and Forgiveness*, 18).

[18] See Paolucci, 'Exile among Exiles'; and Raffa, 'Dante's Poetics of Exile'.

[19] See Took, *Dante*, 323-479. Douglas M. Dunlop observes that al-Fārābī's *Aphorisms of the Statesman* 'speaks emphatically of the duty of emigration (*hijrah*). The word has important religious associations for every Muslim. It may be well that al-Fārābī regarded his departure from Baghdad as his personal *hijrah*' (*Aphorisms of the Statesman*, 15).

[20] Here Aristotle retrieves Plato who cites Socrates in a demonstration of their philosophical inheritance; Aristotle, *Nicomachean Ethics* 1096a12–16; Plato, *Phaedo* 91c, *Republic* 595b–c; Cf. Baracchi, 'The Shining and the Hidden', 223, 'Precisely, there where he seems to be setting friendship (with Plato and the Platonists) aside for the love of truth, Aristotle is in effect recognizing that he and they share a common venture. At stake in the privileging of truth is recognition that others pursue and love it as well, in their own way. And it is crucially because of this commonality that they are our friends.'

[21] al-Fārābī, *Aphorisms of the Statesman*, 88., 72, 164, tr. Dunlop. Cf. al-Fārābī, *Selected Aphorisms*, 93. [95.14–18], 60–1, tr. Butterworth. See Rosenthal, 'The Stranger in Medieval Islam', 36. Cf. Siddiqui, *Hospitality and Islam*, 37, 'the word *gharīb* is used frequently in the *ḥadīth* literature to mean stranger. The concept of hospitality involves the concept of a stranger.

gharīb, a word not located in the Qur'ān but appropriated by *ḥadīth* literature and the Ṣūfī heritage to describe the life of an itinerant wanderer who is not of this world.[22] In his *Attainment of Happiness*, al-Fārābī similarly affirms the life of the true philosopher as a useless life if the most evolved member of the political community is unacknowledged or, even worse, ostracised and exiled, 'If after reaching this stage no use is made of him, that fact that he is *no use* to others is not his fault but the fault of those who either do not listen or are not of the opinion that they should listen to him.'[23] By allusion to *Republic* IX where Socrates invites Glaucon to tend to a city which may be found no place (*a-topos*) on earth, al-Fārābī gestures towards the utterly placeless character of the philosopher as a citizen of the world (*kosmopolitēs*) if only to indicate the intractable cosmopolitanism of philosophy itself as a universal human endeavour.[24] Such a philosophically inclined cosmopolitanism inaugurates a unique vision of political association oriented by the realisation of friendship, solidarity, liberty, equality, and justice on a global scale. Although we cannot possibly capture the historical transmission and appropriation of this vision in its entirety, our modest aim has been to reconstructively *imagine* the uncontestably abundant constellation of dialogue and debate within the Graeco-Roman and Islamic heritage for the sake of renewing the practice of cosmopolitanism today.[25]

But as Rosenthal points out, despite there being strangers everywhere in Muslim societies, "within the community of believers and wherever Muslims were in political control, there was no such distinct category as stranger".' Cf. Derrida, *Hospitality*, 80–1, 'What then does Socrates say (at the moment when, let us not forget, he is risking and is going to lose his life), what does he say in presenting himself *as* a Stranger, at the same time (by fiction) *as if* he were a foreigner and insofar as he is in fact a foreigner accused and summoned to justify himself before the law and judges of the city?'

22 'The messenger of God took me by the shoulder and said: "Be in the world as though you were a stranger or wayfarer." The son of Umar used to say: "At evening do not expect [to live till] morning, and at morning do not expect [to live till] evening. Take from your health for your illness and from your life for your death"' (al-Nawawī, *Al-Nawawī's Forty Ḥadīth*, 122).

23 al-Fārābī, *Attainment of Happiness*, 62. [46.11–15], 49, tr. Mahdi.

24 Plato, *Republic* 592a–b.

25 For example, Ibn Ṭufayl cites al-Fārābī's lost commentary on the *Nicomachean Ethics*, 'Finally, in his commentary on Aristotle's *Ethics*, discussing human happiness, he says that it exists only in this life, and on the heels of that has words to the effect that all other claims are senseless ravings and old wives' tales' (*Ḥayy ibn Yaqẓān*, 14.2–6, 100, tr. Goodman). In contrast, al-Ghazālī subsequently condemns al-Fārābī and those who follow his opinions; see *Incoherence of the Philosophers* (*Tahāfut al-Falāsifa*), 201–25. This probing spirit of dialectical inquiry across generations is quite remarkable and poignantly anticipates Kant's own Enlightenment dictum, '*sapere aude!*'.

If the ancient and medieval history of cosmopolitanism is often conceived as reaching its denouement in the rational humanism of the Italian Renaissance, then the cosmopolitanism of the Islamic Renaissance may be characterised by the pervasive power of the imagination which stretches far beyond the boundaries of the Western world to embrace the new and unchartered expanse of a global community (*ma'mūra*). To heed al-Fārābī's commitment to this cosmopolitan vision as a way of life, we may return to where we began with al-Kindī, reputed as 'the first philosopher of the Arabs' and founder of the first philosophical circle in Baghdad who identifies the pursuit of philosophy with those 'who are not to be ashamed of appreciating the truth and acquiring it wherever it comes from, even if it comes from races distant and nations different from us'.[26] Perhaps this invocation to seek the truth beyond all borders portends both the future and fate of cosmopolitanism.

[26] al-Kindī, *Kitāb fī al-Falsafa al-Ūla*, in *Rasā'il al-Kindī al-Falsafiyya*, vol. 1, 103.4–7; and 'On First Philosophy', in *Al-Kindi's Metaphysics*, 58, tr. Ivry. Finally, we may note that al-Kindī's cosmopolitan invocation in 'On First Philosophy' is immediately preceded by his homage to Aristotle, 'Aristotle, the most distinguished of the Greeks in philosophy, said, "We ought to be grateful to the fathers of those who have contributed to any truth, since they were the cause of their existence; let alone (being grateful) to the sons, for the fathers are their cause, while they are the cause of our attaining truth." How beautiful is that which he said in that matter!' (vol. 1, 103.1–3, 58, tr. Ivry).

Bibliography

Primary Sources

'Abd al-Jabbār, al-Qāḍī, Abū al-Ḥasan al-Asadābādī. *Kitāb al-Uṣūl al-Khamsa, Book of the Five Fundamentals: A Muslim Mu'tazilī Creed – Synopsis of Edition & Translation.* Edited by Gregor. M. Schwarb. http://dx.doi.org/10.17613/dfsx-fb32.

Alighieri, Dante. *Monarchy.* Edited and translated by Prue Shaw. Cambridge: Cambridge University Press. 1996.

Alighieri, Dante. *Purgatorio.* Translated by Jean Hollander and Robert Hollander. New York: Doubleday, 2003.

al-'Āmirī, Abū al-Ḥasan Muḥammad ibn Yūsuf. *Kitāb al-Amad 'alā al-Abad.* Edited by E. Rowson. Leiden: Brill, 1988.

al-'Āmirī, Abū al-Ḥasan Muḥammad ibn Yūsuf. *Kitāb al-Sa'āda wa-l-Is'ād.* Edited by M. Minovi. Wiesbaden: University of Tehran Publications, 1957.

Aristotle. *Opera.* 5 vols. Edited by I. Bekker. Berlin: Akademie, 1831–70.

al-Ash'arī, Abū al-Ḥasan 'Alī ibn Ismā'īl. *Maqālāt al-Islāmīyyīn wa-Ikhtilāf al-Muṣallīn.* Edited by Muḥammad Muḥyī al-Dīn 'Abd al-Ḥamīd. 1st ed. Cairo: Maktabat al-Nahḍa al-Miṣriyya, 1950.

Augustine. *City of God.* Translated by Henry Bettenson. New York: Penguin, 1984.

Augustine. *Confessions.* Vol. 1. Books 1–8. Translated by Carolyn J. Hammond. Cambridge, MA: Harvard University Press, 2014.

Badawī, 'Abd al-Raḥmān, ed. *al-Akhlāq, Ta'līf Aristūtālīs Tarjamat Isḥāq ibn Ḥunayn.* Kuwait: Wikālat al-Maṭbū'āt, 1979.

Bayhaqī, Ẓahīr al-Dīn. *Tatimmat Ṣiwān al-Ḥikma.* Edited by Muḥammad Shafī'. Lahore, 1932.

The Holy Bible. King James Version. New York: World Publishing, n.d.

Cicero. *On Duties*. Translated by Walter Miller. Cambridge, MA: Harvard University Press, 1913.

Cicero. *Tusculan Disputations*. Translated by John Edward King. Cambridge, MA: Harvard University Press, 1927.

Diogenes Laertius. *Lives of the Eminent Philosophers*. Vols. I–II. Loeb Classical Library. Translated by R. D. Hicks. Cambridge, MA: Harvard University Press, 1925.

al-Fārābī, Abū Naṣr. *Alfarabi's Book of Dialectic (Kitāb al-Jadal): On the Starting Point of Islamic Philosophy*. Translated by David M. DiPasquale. Cambridge: Cambridge University Press, 2019.

al-Fārābī, Abū Naṣr. *Alfārābīs Philosophische Abhandlungen*. Translated by Friederich Dieterici. Leiden: Brill, 1892.

al-Fārābī, Abū Naṣr. 'The Book of Letters'. Translated by Muhammad Ali Khalidi in *Medieval Islamic Philosophical Writings*, edited by Muhammad Ali Khalidi, 1–26. Cambridge: Cambridge University Press, 2005.

al-Fārābī, Abū Naṣr. *Commentary and Short Treatise on Aristotle's* De Interpretatione. Translated by Franz Zimmerman. Oxford: Oxford University Press, 1988.

al-Fārābī, Abū Naṣr. 'Directing Attention to the Way of Happiness'. Translated by Jon McGinnis and David C. Reisman in *Classical Arabic Philosophy: An Anthology of Sources*, edited by Jon McGinnis and David C. Reisman, 104–20. Indianapolis: Hackett, 2007.

al-Fārābī, Abū Naṣr. 'The Enumeration of the Sciences'. Translated by Charles Butterworth in *Medieval Political Philosophy: A Sourcebook*, edited by Joshua Parens and Joseph A. Macfarland, 18–23. Ithaca: Cornell University Press, 2011.

al-Fārābī, Abū Naṣr. *Falsafat Aflāṭūn*. Edited by F. Rosenthal and R. Walzer. London: Warburg Institute, 1943.

al-Fārābī, Abū Naṣr. *Falsafat Ārisṭūṭālīs*. Edited by Muhsin Mahdi. Beirut: Dār al-Mashriq, 1961.

al-Fārābī, Abū Naṣr. *Al-Fārābī on the Perfect State: Abū Naṣr al-Fārābī's Mabādi' ārā' ahl al-madīna al-fāḍila*. Translated by Richard Walzer. Chicago: Great Books of the Islamic World Inc., 1998.

al-Fārābī, Abū Naṣr. *The Fuṣūl al-Madanī of al-Fārābī*. Edited and translated by Douglas M. Dunlop. Cambridge: Cambridge University Press, 1961.

al-Fārābī, Abū Naṣr. *Fuṣūl al-Muntaza'a*. Edited by Fauzi M. Najjar. Beirut: Dār al-Mashriq, 1971.

al-Fārābī, Abū Naṣr. *Iḥṣā' al-'Ulūm*. Edited by 'Uthmān Amīn. Cairo: Maktabat al-Anjilū al-Miṣriyya, 1968.

al-Fārābī, Abū Naṣr. *Kitāb al-Alfāẓ al-Musta'mala fī al-Manṭiq*. Edited by Muhsin Mahdi. Beirut: Dār al-Mashriq, 1968.

al-Fārābī, Abū Naṣr. *Kitāb al-Burhān*. In *Kitāb al-Burhān wa-Kitāb Sharā'iṭ al-Yaqīn*. In *al-Manṭiq 'inda al-Fārābī*. Vol. 4. Edited by Majid Fakhry. Beirut: Dār al-Mashriq, 1986.

al-Fārābī, Abū Naṣr. *Kitāb fī al-Manṭiq: al-Khaṭāba*. Edited by Muḥammad Salīm Salīm. Cairo: Dār al-Kitāb, 1976.

al-Fārābī, Abū Naṣr. *Kitāb al-Ḥurūf*. Edited by Muhsin Mahdi. Beirut: Dār al-Mashriq, 1970.

al-Fārābī, Abū Naṣr. *Kitāb al-Jam' bayn Ra'yay al-Ḥakīmayn Aflāṭūn al-Ilāhī wa-Arisṭūṭālīs*. In *Alfārābīs Philosophische Abhandlungen*, edited by Friederich Dieterici, 1–53. Leiden: Brill, 1892.

al-Fārābī, Abū Naṣr. *Kitāb al-Milla wa-Nuṣūṣ Ukhra*. Edited by Muhsin Mahdi. Beirut: Dār al-Mashriq, 1968.

al-Fārābī, Abū Naṣr. *Kitāb al-Mūsīqī al-Kabīr*. Edited by G. A. Khashabah and M. A. al-Hifnī. Cairo: Dār al-Kātib al-'Arabī li-l-Ṭibā'a wa-l-Nashr, 1967.

al-Fārābī, Abū Naṣr. *Kitāb al-Siyāsa al-Madaniyya*. Edited by Fauzi M. Najjar. Beirut: al-Maṭba'a al-Kāthūlīkiyya, 1964.

al-Fārābī, Abū Naṣr. *Kitāb al-Wāḥid wa-l-Waḥda*. Edited by Muhsin Mahdi. Casablanca: Les Éditions Toubkal, 1989.

al-Fārābī, Abū Naṣr. *La politique civile ou les principes des existants* (*al-Mabādi'*). Edited and translated by Amor Cherni. Paris: Libraire Albouraq, 2012.

al-Fārābī, Abū Naṣr. *Le Livre du Régime Politique*. Edited and translated by Philippe Vallat. Paris: Les Belles Lettres, 2012.

al-Fārābī, Abū Naṣr. *Mabādi' Ārā' Ahl al-Madīna al-Fāḍila*. Edited by Friederich Dieterici. Leiden: Brill, 1895.

al-Fārābī, Abū Naṣr. 'On the Intellect'. Translated by Jon McGinnis and David C. Reisman in *Classical Arabic Philosophy: An Anthology of Sources*, edited by Jon McGinnis and David C. Reisman, 68–77. Indianapolis: Hackett, 2007.

al-Fārābī, Abū Naṣr. *Philosophy of Plato and Aristotle*. Translated by Muhsin Mahdi. Ithaca: Cornell University Press, 2001.

al-Fārābī, Abū Naṣr. *The Political Writings: 'Selected Aphorisms' and Other Texts*. Translated by Charles Butterworth. Ithaca: Cornell University Press, 2001.

al-Fārābī, Abū Naṣr. *The Political Writings*. Vol. II, *'Political Regime' and 'Summary of Plato's* Laws*'*. Translated by Charles Butterworth. Ithaca: Cornell University Press, 2015.

al-Fārābī, Abū Naṣr. *Risāla fī al-'Aql*. Edited by Maurice Bouyges, S. J. Beirut: Imprimerie Catholique, 1938.

al-Fārābī, Abū Naṣr. *Risāla fī Quwānīn Ṣinā'at al-Shi'r.* Translated by A. J Arberry. *Rivista degli Studi Orientali* 17 (1938): 267–78.
al-Fārābī, Abū Naṣr. *Risālat al-Tanbīh 'alā Sabīl al-Sa'āda.* Amman: al-Jāmi'a al-Urduniyya, 1987.
al-Fārābī, Abū Naṣr. *Taḥṣīl al-Sa'āda.* Edited by Ja'far al-Yāsīn. Beirut: Dār al-Andalūs, 1981.
al-Ghazālī, Abū Ḥāmid. *The Incoherence of the Philosophers* (*Tahāfut al-Falāsifa*). Translated by Michael E. Marmura. Provo: Brigham Young University Press, 1997.
al-Ghazālī, Abū Ḥāmid. *On Disciplining the Soul* (*Kitāb Riyāḍat al-Nafs*) and *On Breaking the Two Desires* (*Kitāb Kasr al-Shahwatayn*). Translated by T. J. Winter. Cambridge: Islamic Texts Society, 2016.
al-Ghazālī, Abū Ḥāmid. *On the Manners relating to Eating* (*Kitāb Ādāb al-Akl*). Translated by D. Johnson-Davies. Cambridge: Islamic Texts Society, 2015.
al-Ghazālī, Abū Ḥāmid. *Revival of the Religious Sciences* (*Iḥyā' 'Ulūm al-Dīn*). Edited by 'Abd Allāh al-Khālidī. Beirut: Sharikat Dār al-Arqam Ibn Abī al-Arqam, 1988.
Hierocles. *Hierocles the Stoic: Elements of Ethics, Fragments and Excerpts.* Edited by Ira Ramelli. Translated by David Konstan. Atlanta: Society of Biblical Literature, 2009.
Hippocrates. *Hippocrates.* Vol. 1, *Ancient Medicine. On Airs, Waters, and Places. Epidemics 1 and 3. The Oath. Precepts. Nutriment.* Loeb Classical Library. Translated by W. H. S. Jones. Cambridge, MA: Harvard University Press, 2022.
Ibn Abī Uṣaybi'a. *'Uyūn al-Anbā fī Ṭabaqāt al-Aṭibbā'.* 2 vols. Edited by A. Müller. Königsberg, 1884.
Ibn 'Adī, Yaḥyā Abū Zakariyyā'. *The Reformation of Morals.* Translated by S. Griffith. Provo: Brigham Young University Press, 2002.
Ibn 'Adī, Yaḥyā Abū Zakariyyā'. *Tahdhīb al-Akhlāq.* In *Rasā'il al-Bulaghā'*, edited by M. Kurd 'Alī, 483-522. 3rd. ed. Cairo, 1946.
Ibn Bājja, Abū Bakr. *Rasā'il Ibn Bājja al-Ilāhiyya* (*Opera Metaphysica*). Edited by Majid Fakhry. Beirut: Dār al-Nahār, 1968.
Ibn Khaldūn, Walī al-Dīn 'Abd al-Raḥmān. *al-Muqaddima.* al-Dār al-Bayḍā': Khizānat Ibn Khaldūn, Bayt al-Funūn wa-l-'Ulūm wa-l-Ādāb, 2005.
Ibn Khaldūn, Walī al-Dīn 'Abd al-Raḥmān. *The Muqaddimah: An Introduction to History.* Translated by Franz Rosenthal. Princeton: Princeton University Press, 1967.

Ibn Khallikān, Abū al-'Abbās Aḥmad. *Wafayāt al-A'yān*. Vol. 5. Edited by Iḥsān 'Abbās. Beirut: Dār Ṣādir, 1977.

Ibn Miskawayh, Abū 'Alī Aḥmad ibn Muḥammad. *Refinement of Character* (*Tahdhīb al-Akhlāq*). Translated by Constantine K. Zurayk. Chicago: Great Books of the Islamic World Inc., 2002.

Ibn Miskawayh, Abū 'Alī Aḥmad ibn Muḥammad. *Tahdhīb al-Akhlāq*. Edited by Constantine K. Zurayk. Beirut: American University of Beirut Centennial Publications, 1966.

Ibn al-Nadīm, Muḥammad ibn Isḥāq. *The Fihrist: A Tenth-Century Survey of Muslim Culture*. Translated by B. Dodge. New York: Columbia University Press, 1970.

Ibn al-Nadīm, Muḥammad ibn Isḥāq. *Kitāb al-Fihrist*. 2 vols. Edited by G. Flügel. Leipzig, 1871–2.

Ibn Rushd, Abū al-Walīd. *Averroes on Plato's* Republic. Translated by Ralph Lerner. Ithaca: Cornell University Press, 1974.

Ibn Rushd, Abū al-Walīd. *Commentaire moyen à la Rhétorique d'Aristote*. 3 vols. Edited by M. Aouad. Paris: Vrin, 2002.

Ibn Rushd, Abū al-Walīd. *Decisive Treatise and Epistle Dedicatory*. Translated by Charles E. Butterworth. Provo: Brigham Young University Press, 2008.

Ibn Rushd, Abū al-Walīd. *The Decisive Treatise*. Translated by Charles Butterworth in *Medieval Political Philosophy: A Sourcebook*, edited by Joshua Parens and Joseph C. Macfarland, 123–40. Ithaca: Cornell University Press, 2011.

Ibn Rushd, Abū al-Walīd. *Kitāb Faṣl al-Maqāl*. In *Philosophie und Theologie von Averroes*, edited by M. J. Müller, 1–127. Munich: Commission bei G. Franz, 1859.

Ibn Rushd, Abū al-Walīd. *Tahāfut al-Tahāfut* (*The Incoherence of the Incoherence*). Translated by S. Van den Bergh. London: Luzac, 1954.

Ibn Sīnā, Abū 'Alī. *The Metaphysics of the 'Healing': A Parallel English–Arabic Text* (*al-Ilāhiyāt min al-Shifā'*). Translated by Michael E. Marmura. Provo: Brigham Young University Press, 2005.

Ibn Ṭufayl, Muḥammad ibn 'Abd al-Malik. *Philosophus Autodidactus or Ḥayy ibn Yaqẓān*. Translated by S. Ockley. London and Cairo, 1905.

Ibn Ṭufayl, Muḥammad ibn 'Abd al-Malik. *Ibn Tufayl's Hayy Ibn Yaqzān*. Translated by Lenn Evan Goodman. Los Angeles: Gee Tee Bee, 2003.

Ikhwān al-Ṣafā'. *Rasā'il Ikhwān al-Ṣafā'*. 12 vols. Beirut: Dār Bayrūt, 1957.

al-Kindī, Ya'qūb ibn Isḥāq al-Ṣabbāḥ. *Al-Kindi's Metaphysics: A Translation of Ya'qub ibn Ishaq al-Kindi's 'On First Philosophy'*. Translated by Alfred Ivry. Albany: State University of New York Press, 1974.

al-Kindī, Ya'qūb ibn Isḥāq al-Ṣabbāḥ. *Rasā'il al-Kindī al-Falsafiyya.* 2 vols. Edited by M. A. Abū Rīda. Cairo: Dār al-Fikr al-'Arabī, 1950–3.

Maimonides, Moses. *Dalālat al-Hā'irīn.* 3 vols. Edited by S. Munk. Paris, 1856–66.

Maimonides, Moses. *The Guide of the Perplexed.* Translated by Shlomo Pines. Chicago: University of Chicago Press, 1963.

al-Nawawī, Yaḥyā ibn Sharaf. *Al-Nawawī's Forty Ḥadīth.* Translated by Ibrahim Ezzeddin and Denys Johnson-Davies. No. 40. Stuttgart: Ernst Klett Printers, 1976.

Plato. *Platonis Opera.* Edited by John Burnet. Oxford: Oxford University Press, 1950.

Plato. *Plato's Timaeus.* Translated by Peter Kalkavage. Newburyport, MA: Focus Publishing, 2001.

Plotinus. *Enneads.* Edited by Lloyd P. Gerson. Translated by George Boys-Stones, John M. Dillon, Lloyd P. Gerson, R. A. H. King, Andrew Smith, and James Wilberding. Cambridge: Cambridge University Press, 2019.

Porphyry. *Porphyryii philosophi fragmenta.* Edited by Andrew Smith. Fragmenta Arabica, David Wassertein Interpretante. Stuttgart: Teubner, 1993.

Porphyry. *Porphyry: On Abstinence from Killing Animals.* Translated by G. Clark. Ithaca: Cornell University Press, 2000.

Proclus. *Commentary on Plato's* Timaeus*: Proclus on the Causes of the Cosmos and Its Creation.* Vol II. Edited by David T. Runia and Michael Share. Cambridge: Cambridge University Press, 2017.

Proclus. *Procli Diadochi in Platonis Timaeum commentaria.* 3 vols. Edited by E. Diehl. Leipzig: Teubner, 1903–6.

Proclus. *Proclus's Commentary on Plato's* Parmenides. Translated by Glenn R. Morrow and John M. Dillon. Princeton: Princeton University Press, 1987.

Ptolemy. *Ptolemy's* Almagest. Translated by G. J. Toomer. Princeton: Princeton University Press, 1998.

al-Qifṭī, 'Alī ibn Yūsuf. *Tārīkh al-Ḥukamā'.* Edited by J. Lippert. Leipzig: Dieterich'sche Verlagsbuchhandlung, 1903.

The Qur'ān. Translated by Yusuf Ali. Kansas City: Manat International, 1998.

al-Rāzī, Aḥmad ibn Ḥamdān Abū Ḥātim. *A'lām al-Nubuwwa (The Proofs of Prophecy).* Translated by Tarif Khalidi. Provo: Brigham Young University Press, 2011.

Ṣā'id, Abū al-Qāsim. *Kitāb Ṭabaqāt al-Umam. Livre des catégories des nations.* Translated by Régis Blachère. Paris: Larose, 1935.

al-Sijistānī, Abū Sulaymān Muḥammad. *Muntakhab Ṣiwān al-Ḥikma wa-Thalāth Rasā'il.* Edited by 'Abd al-Raḥmān Badawī. Tehran: Intisharāt-i-Bunyad-i-Farhang-i-Irān, 1974.

al-Sijistānī, Isḥāq ibn Aḥmad Abū Ya'qūb. *Kitāb al-Yanābī'*. Edited by Mustafa Ghalib. Beirut: al-Maktab al-Tijārī, 1965.

al-Sijistānī, Isḥāq ibn Aḥmad Abū Ya'qūb. *The Wellsprings of Wisdom: A Study of Abū Ya'qūb al-Sijistānī's* Kitāb al-Yanābī', *including a Complete English Translation with Commentary and Notes on the Arabic Text*. Translated and edited by Paul E. Walker. Salt Lake City: University of Utah Press, 1994.

al-Tawḥīdī, 'Alī ibn Muḥammad Abū Ḥayyān. *al-Muqābasāt*. Edited by M. T. Ḥusayn. Baghdad: Maṭba'at al-Irshād, 1970.

al-Tawḥīdī, 'Alī ibn Muḥammad Abū Ḥayyān, and Abū 'Alī Miskawayh. *The Philosopher Responds: An Intellectual Correspondence from the Tenth Century*. 2 vols. Edited by Bilal Orfali and Maurice A. Pomerantz. Translated by Sophia Vasalou and James E. Montgomery. New York: New York University Press, 2019.

al-Ṭūsī, Naṣīr al-Dīn. *The Nasirean Ethics* (*Akhlāq-i Nāṣirī*). Translated by G. M. Wickens. London: George Allen & Unwin Ltd., 2011.

Wakelnig, Elvira, trans. *A Philosophy Reader from the Circle of Miskawayh: Text, Translation and Commentary*. Cambridge: Cambridge University Press, 2014.

Woerther, Frédérique, ed. *La Summa Alexandrinorum: abrégé arabo-latin d l'Éthique à Nicomaque d'Aristote, édition critique, traduction française et introduction*. Leiden: Brill, 2020.

Secondary Sources

Adamson, Peter. *The Arabic Plotinus: A Philosophical Study of the 'Theology of Aristotle'*. London: Duckworth, 2002.

Adamson, Peter. 'Al-Kindī and the Mu'tazila: Divine Attributes, Creation, and Freedom'. *Arabic Sciences and Philosophy* 13, no. 1 (2003): 45–77.

Adamson, Peter. '*Plotinus Arabus* and *Proclus Arabus* in the *Harmony of the Two Philosophers* Ascribed to al-Fārābī'. In *Reading Proclus and the Book of Causes*. Vol. 2, *Translations and Acculturations*, edited by Dragos Calma, 182–97. Leiden: Brill, 2021.

Agamben, Giorgio. 'On Potentiality'. In *Potentialities: Collected Essays in the History of Philosophy*, 177–84. Stanford: Stanford University Press, 1999.

Ahmed, Shahab. *What Is Islam? The Importance of Being Islamic*. Princeton: Princeton University Press, 2015.

Akasoy, Anna. 'The Arabic and Islamic Reception of the *Nicomachean Ethics*'. In *The Reception of Aristotle's Ethics*, edited by Jon Miller, 85–106. Cambridge: Cambridge University Press, 2013.

Akasoy, Anna, and Alexander Fidora, eds. *The Arabic Version of the* Nicomachean Ethics. Leiden: Brill, 2005.

Albertini, Tamara. 'Reintroducing Islamic Philosophy: The Persisting Problem of Smaller Orientalisms'. In *The Oxford Handbook of World Philosophy*, edited by Jay L. Garfield and William Edelglass, 387–96. Oxford: Oxford University Press, 2010.

Al Jallad, Nader. 'A Lexicological Study of Friendship in Arabic'. *Transletters: International Journal of Translation and Interpreting* 2 (2018): 49–62.

Alon, Ilai. 'Fārābī's Funny Flora: *Al-Nawābit* as "Opposition"'. *Arabica* 37, no. 1 (1990): 56–90.

Al Qurtuby, Sumanto. 'The Islamic Roots of Liberation, Justice, and Peace: An Anthropocentric Analysis of the Concept of *Tawḥīd*'. *Islamic Studies* 52, no. 3–4 (2013): 297–325.

Alshaar, Nuha A. *Ethics in Islam: Friendship in the Political Thought of al-Tawḥīdī and His Contemporaries*. New York: Routledge, 2014.

Anderson, Benedict. *Imagined Communities: Reflections on the Origins and Spread of Nationalism*. New York: Verso Publications, 1998.

Appiah, Kwame Anthony. *Cosmopolitanism: Ethics in a World of Strangers*. New York: W. W. Norton & Company, 2006.

Arendt, Hannah. *Men in Dark Times*. New York: Harcourt, Brace and Company, 1955.

Arendt, Hannah. *The Origins of Totalitarianism*. London: George Allen & Unwin Ltd., 1951.

Ashfaq, Muhammad. 'Islamic Philosophy of Benevolence (*Al-Iḥsān*) and Aesthetic Reflection: A Study of Sūrah al-Raḥmān'. *Journal of Islamic Theology* 1, no. 2 (2013): 1–11.

Azadpur, Mohammad. *Reason Unbound: On Spiritual Practice in Islamic Peripatetic Philosophy*. Albany: State University of New York Press, 2011.

Baker, Gideon. 'Cynical Cosmopolitanism'. *Theory and Event* 21, no. 3 (2018): 607–26.

Bakhsh, Alireza Omid. '*The Virtuous City*: The Iranian and Islamic Heritage of Utopianism'. *Utopian Studies* 24, no. 1 (2013): 41–51.

Balibar, Étienne. *Secularism and Cosmopolitanism*. New York: Columbia University Press, 2018.

Balty-Guesdon, M.-G. 'Le *Bayt al-Ḥikma*'. *Arabica* 39 (1992): 131–50.

Baracchi, Claudia. *Aristotle's Ethics as First Philosophy*. Cambridge: Cambridge University Press, 2008.

Baracchi, Claudia. *Friendship: The Future of an Ancient Gift*. Bloomington: Indiana University Press, 2023.

Baracchi, Claudia. *Of Myth, Life, and War in Plato's* Republic. Bloomington: Indiana University Press, 2002.

Baracchi, Claudia. 'The Shining and the Hidden: Notes on Politics and Solitude from the "Greek Prophets" to al-Fārābī'. In *Aristotle and the Arabic Tradition*, edited by Ahmed Alwishah and Josh Hayes, 214–33. Cambridge: Cambridge University Press, 2015.

Bausani, Alessandro. *Un filosofo laico del Medioevo musulmano: Abu Bakr Muhammad Ibn Zakariyyā Rāzī.* Rome: Instituto di Studi Islamici, 1981.

Benardete, Seth. *Plato's* Laws*: The Discovery of Being.* Chicago: University of Chicago Press, 2000.

Benveniste, Émile. *Dictionary of Indo-European Concepts and Society.* Chicago: University of Chicago Press, 2016.

Berman, L, V. 'Ibn Rushd's *Middle Commentary* on the *Nicomachean Ethics* in Medieval Hebrew Literature'. In *Multiple Averroes*, edited by Jean Jolivet, 287–321. Paris, 1978.

Berman, L. V. 'The Revised Hebrew Translation of Averroes' *Middle Commentary on the Nicomachean Ethics*'. *The Jewish Quarterly Review* 57 (1967): 104–20.

Berti, Enrico. *La philosophia del 'primo' Aristotele.* Milan, 1997.

Black, Antony. *The History of Islamic Political Thought: From the Prophet to the Present.* Edinburgh: Edinburgh University Press, 2011.

Black, Deborah. *Logic and Aristotle's* Rhetoric *and* Poetics *in Medieval Arabic Philosophy.* Leiden: Brill, 1990.

Bloch, Ernst. *Avicenna and the Aristotelian Left.* Translated by Lauren Goldman and Peter Thompson. New York: Columbia University Press, 2018.

Bobonich, Christopher. *Plato's Utopia Recast: His Later Ethics and Politics.* Oxford: Oxford University Press, 2002.

Brague, Remi. *The Legend of the Middle Ages: Philosophical Explorations of Medieval Christianity, Judaism, and Islam.* Translated by Lydia G. Cochrane. Chicago: University of Chicago Press, 2009.

Brecht, Bertolt. 'An Die Nachgebornen ("To Posterity")'. In *Modern German Poetry (1910–1960)*, edited and translated by Michael Hamburger, 227–33. New York: Grove Press, 2002.

Brill, Sara. *Aristotle on the Concept of Shared Life.* Oxford: Oxford University Press, 2020.

Brisson, Luc. 'Polis as *Kosmos* in Plato's *Laws*'. In *Cosmos in the Ancient World*, edited by Phillip Sidney Horky, 122–41. Cambridge: Cambridge University Press, 2019.

Brown, Jonathan A. C. *Slavery and Islam.* London: Oneworld Publications, 2019.

Brunkhorst, Hake. *Solidarity: From Civic Friendship to a Global Legal Community*. Cambridge, MA: Massachusetts Institute of Technology Press, 2005.

Burns, Daniel E. 'Alfarabi and the Creation of an Islamic Political Science'. *The Review of Politics* 78, no. 3 (2016): 365–89.

Burrell, David B. *Knowing the Unknowable God: Ibn Sina, Maimonides, Aquinas*. South Bend: University of Notre Dame Press, 1986.

Butterworth, Charles E. 'Alfarabi's Goal: Political Philosophy, Not Political Theology'. In *Islam, the State, and Political Authority*, edited by Asma Afsaruddin, 53–74. New York: Palgrave Macmillan, 2011.

Butterworth, Charles E. 'Al-Fārābī's Statecraft: War and the Well-Ordered Regime'. In *Cross, Crescent, and Sword: The Justification and Limitation of War in the Western and Islamic Tradition*, edited by J. Johnson and J. Kelsay, 79–100. New York: Greenwood Press, 1990.

Butterworth, Charles E. 'What Might We Learn from al-Fārābī about Plato and Aristotle with respect to Lawgiving?'. *Mélanges de l'Université Saint Joseph* 61 (2008): 471–91.

Campanini, Massimo. 'Alfarabi and the Foundation of Political Theology in Islam'. In *Islam, the State, and Political Authority*, edited by Asma Afsaruddin, 34–52. New York: Palgrave Macmillan, 2011.

Campanini, Massimo. *An Introduction to Islamic Philosophy*. Edinburgh: Edinburgh University Press, 2008.

Carone, Gabrielle-Roxana. *Plato's Cosmology and Its Ethical Dimensions*. Cambridge: Cambridge University Press, 2005.

Chérif, Mustapha. *Islam & the West: A Conversation with Jacques Derrida*. Translated by Teresa Lavender Fagan. Chicago: University of Chicago Press, 2008.

Colmo, Christopher A. *Breaking with Athens: Alfarabi as Founder*. Lanham: Lexington Books, 2005.

Cooperson, Michael. *Al-Ma'mun: The Revival of Islam*. London: Oneworld Publications, 2005.

Corbin, Henry. *History of Islamic Philosophy*. New York: Routledge, 2006.

Corbin, Henry. *Trilogie Ismaélienne*. Lagrasse: Verdier, 1994.

Crone, Patricia. 'Al-Fārābī's Imperfect Constitutions'. *Mélanges de l'Université Saint Joseph* 57 (2004): 191–228.

Curzer, Howard. *Aristotle and the Virtues*. Oxford: Oxford University Press, 2015.

Daiber, Hans. 'Humanism: A Condition Common to Both Islam and Europe'. *Filozofija i Društvo* 24, no. 1 (2013): 293–310.

Daiber, Hans. *Islamic Thought in the Dialogue of Cultures: A Historical and Biographical Survey*. Leiden: Brill, 2012.

Daiber, Hans. 'The Ismailite Background of Fārābī's Political Philosophy: Abū Ḥātim ar-Rāzī as Forerunner of Fārābī'. In *From the Greeks to the Arabs and Beyond*, vol. 2, 338–46. Leiden: Brill, 2021.

Dallmayr, Fred. *Being in the World: Dialogue and Cosmopolis*. Lexington: University of Kentucky Press, 2013.

D'Ancona, Cristina. '"Arisṭū 'inda l-'Arab", and Beyond'. In *Aristotle and the Arabic Tradition*, edited by Ahmed Alwishah and Josh Hayes, 11–29. Cambridge: Cambridge University Press, 2015.

D'Ancona, Cristina. 'The *Theology* Attributed to Aristotle: Sources, Structure, and Influence'. In *The Oxford Handbook of Islamic Philosophy*, edited by Khaled El-Rouayheb and Sabine Schmidtke, 8–29. Oxford: Oxford University Press, 2017.

D'Ancona, Cristina. 'The *Timaeus* Model for Creation and Providence: An Example of Continuity and Adaptation in Early Arabic Philosophical Literature'. In *Plato's Timaeus as Cultural Icon*, edited by Gretchen J. Reydams-Schils, 206–37. Notre Dame: University of Notre Dame Press, 2003.

Davidson, Herbert A. *Alfarabi, Avicenna, Averroes, on Intellect: Their Cosmologies, Theories of the Active Intellect, and Theories of Human Intellect*. Oxford: Oxford University Press, 1992.

Davis, Garry. *My Country Is the World: Adventure of a World Citizen*. New York: Putnam, 1961.

Derrida, Jacques. *The Death Penalty*. Vol. 1. Translated by Geoffrey Bennington, Marc Crépon, and Thomas Dutoit. Chicago: University of Chicago Press, 2014.

Derrida, Jacques. 'Faith and Knowledge: The Two Sources of "Religion" at the Limits of Reason Alone'. In *Religion*, edited by Jacques Derrida and Gianni Vattimo, 1–78. Stanford: Stanford University Press, 1998.

Derrida, Jacques. *Hospitality*. Vol. 1. Translated by S. E. Burt. Chicago: University of Chicago Press, 2023.

Derrida, Jacques. 'Hostipitality [Seminar]'. In *Acts of Religion*, edited and translated by Gil Anidjar, 338–420. New York: Routledge, 2002.

Derrida, Jacques. *Monolinguism of the Other or the Prosthesis of Origin*. Translated by Patrick Mensah. Stanford: Stanford University Press, 1998.

Derrida, Jacques. *On Cosmopolitanism and Forgiveness*. Translated by Mark Dooley. New York: Routledge, 2001.

Derrida, Jacques. *Politics of Friendship*. Translated by George Collins. London: Verso, 1997.

Derrida, Jacques. *Rogues: Two Essays on Reason*. Translated by Pascale-Anne Brault and Michael Naas. Stanford: Stanford University Press, 2005.

Derrida, Jacques. 'The Time of the King'. In *Given Time I: Counterfeit Money*, translated by Peggy Kamuf, 6–33. Chicago: University of Chicago Press, 1992.

Derrida, Jacques. 'Une hospitalité à l'infini'. In *Manifeste pour l' hospitalité*, edited by Mohammed Seffahi, 197–206. Grigny: Paroles d'aube, 1999.

Derrida, Jacques, and Anne Dufourmantelle. *Of Hospitality*. Translated by Rachel Bowlby. Stanford: Stanford University Press, 2000.

Diagne, Souleymane Bachir. *Open to Reason: Muslim Philosophers in Conversation with the Western Tradition*. New York: Columbia University Press, 2018.

Dobbs-Weinstein, Idit. 'Aristotle on the Natural Dwelling of the Intellect'. In *The Bloomsbury Companion to Aristotle*, edited by Claudia Baracchi, 297–310. London: Bloomsbury, 2013.

Druart, Thérèse-Anne. 'Al-Farabi, Emanation, and Metaphysics'. In *Neoplatonism and Islamic Thought*, edited by Parviz Morewedge, 127–48. Albany: State University of New York Press, 1992.

Druart, Thérèse-Anne. 'What Does Music Have to Do with Language, Logic and Rulership? Al-Fārābī's Answer'. In *The Origin and Nature of Language and Logic: Perspectives in Medieval Islamic, Jewish, and Christian Thought*, edited by Nadja Germann and Steven Harvey, 193–212. Turnhout: Brepols, 2020.

El-Bizri, Nader. 'The Microcosm/Macrocosm Analogy: A Tentative Encounter between Graeco-Arabic Philosophy and Phenomenology'. In *Islamic Philosophy and Occidental Phenomenology on the Perennial Issue of Microcosm and Macrocosm*, vol. 2, edited by Anna-Theresa Tymieniecka, 3–23. Dordrecht: Springer, 2002.

Endress, Gerhard. 'The Circle of al-Kindī: Early Arabic Translations from the Greek and the Rise of Islamic Philosophy'. In *The Ancient Tradition in Christian and Islamic Hellenism*, edited by Gerhard Endress and Remke Kruk, 43–76. Leiden: Research School CNWS, 1997.

Eslami, Seyyed Mohsen, and Alfred Archer. 'The Cautionary Account of Supererogation'. *The Philosophical Quarterly* (2024): 1–24, https://doi.org/10.1093/pq/pqae017.

Euben, Roxanne. *Journeys to the Other Shore: Muslim and Western Travelers in Search of Knowledge*. Princeton: Princeton University Press, 2006.

Ezzaher, Lahcen E. *Three Arabic Treatises on Aristotle's* Rhetoric*: The Commentaries of al-Fārābī, Avicenna, and Averroes*. Carbondale: Southern Illinois University Press, 2015.

Fakhry, Majid. *Al-Fārābī: Founder of Islamic Neoplatonism*. Oxford: Oneworld, 2002.

Fakhry, Majid. *A History of Islamic Philosophy*. New York: Columbia University Press, 1983.

Fraenkel, Carlos. 'Theocracy and Autonomy in Medieval Islamic and Jewish Philosophy'. *Political Theory* 38, no. 3 (2010): 340–66.

Fraenkel, Carlos. *Philosophical Religions from Plato to Spinoza*. Cambridge: Cambridge University Press, 2012.

Galston, Miriam. *Politics and Excellence: The Political Philosophy of Alfarabi*. Princeton: Princeton University Press, 1990.

Galston, Miriam. 'A Re-examination of al-Fārābī's Neoplatonism'. *Journal of the History of Philosophy* 15 (1977): 13–32.

Gauthier, René-Antoine, and Jean-Yves Jolif, eds. *Aristote. L'èthique à Nicomaque*. 2 vols. Louvain: Publications universitaires, 1970.

Ginsberg, Allan. *Cosmopolitan Greetings: Poems, 1986–1992*. New York: HarperCollins, 1994.

Gluck, Andrew. 'The King in His Palace: Ibn Gabirol and Maimonides'. *The Jewish Quarterly Review* 91, no. 3–4 (2001): 337–57.

Goldin, Owen. 'Conflict and Cosmopolitanism in Plato and the Stoics'. *Apeiron* 44, no. 3 (2011): 264–86.

Goodman, Lenn E. 'Friendship in Aristotle, Miskawayh, and al-Ghazālī'. In *Friendship East and West: Philosophical Perspectives*, edited by Oliver Leaman, 164–91. London: Routledge, 1995.

Goodman, Lenn E. *Islamic Humanism*. Oxford: Oxford University Press, 2003.

Griffith, Sidney H. *The Church in the Shadow of the Mosque: Muslims and Christians in the World of Islam*. Princeton: Princeton University Press, 2008.

Groff, Peter S. 'Cultivating Weeds: The Place of Solitude in the Political Philosophies of Ibn Bājja and Nietzsche'. *Philosophy East and West* 70, no. 3 (2020): 699–739.

Guidi, M., and R. Walzer. 'Studi Su al-Kindi'. In *Uno Scritto Introduttivo allo Studio di Aristotele*, 375–419. Rome: Reale Accademia Nazionale dei Lincei, 1940.

Gutas, Dimitri. 'The "Alexandria to Baghdad" Complex of Narratives: A Contribution to the Study of Philosophical and Medical Historiography among the Arabs'. *Documenti e studi sulla tradizione filosofica medievale* 10 (1999): 155–93.

Gutas, Dimitri. 'Fārābī i. Biography'. *Encyclopaedia Iranica*. www.iranicaonline.org/articles/farabi-i.

Gutas, Dimitri. *Greek Thought, Arabic Culture: The Graeco-Arabic Translation Movement in Baghdad and Early 'Abbāsid Society (2nd–4th/8th–10th Centuries)*. London: Routledge, 1998.

Gutas, Dimitri. 'The Meaning of *Madanī* in al-Fārābī's "Political Philosophy"'. *Mélanges de l'Université Saint Joseph* 57 (2004): 259–82.

Gutas, Dimitri. 'The Starting Point of Philosophical Studies in Alexandrian and Arabic Aristotelianism'. In *Theophrastus of Eresus: On His life and Work*, vol. 2, edited by William W. Fortenbraugh, 115–23. New Brunswick: Transaction Books, 1985.

Gutas, Dimitri. 'The Study of Arabic Philosophy in the Twentieth Century'. *British Journal of Middle Eastern Studies* 29, no. 1 (2002): 5–25.

Hadad, Samir. *Derrida and the Inheritance of Democracy*. Bloomington: Indiana University Press, 2013.

Hadreas, Peter. 'εὔνοια: Aristotle on the Beginning of Friendship'. *Ancient Philosophy* 15 (1995): 393–402.

Hall, Joshua M. 'Alfarabi's Imaginative Critique: Overflowing Materialism in *Virtuous Community*'. *South African Journal of Philosophy* 34, no. 2 (2015): 175–92.

Harvey, Steven. 'Did Alfarabi Read Plato's *Laws*?'. *Medioevo Rivista di Storia della Filosofia Medievale* 28 (2008): 51–68.

Harvey, Steven. 'Leo Strauss's Developing Interest in Alfarabi and Its Reverberations in the Study of Medieval Islamic Philosophy'. In *The Pilgrimage of Philosophy: A Festschrift for Charles E. Butterworth*, edited by Rene M. Paddags, Waseem El-Rayes, and Gregory A. McGrayer, 60–83. South Bend: Saint Augustine Press, 2019.

Harvey, Steven. 'The Place of the Philosopher in the City according to Ibn Bājjah'. In *The Political Aspects of Islamic Philosophy: Essays in Honor of Muhsin S. Mahdi*, edited by Charles Butterworth, 199–233. Harvard: Harvard University Press, 1992.

Harvey, Steven, and Frédérique Woerther. 'Averroes' *Middle Commentary* on Book I of the *Nicomachean Ethics*'. *Oriens* 42 (2014): 254–87.

Hayes, Josh. 'The Arabic Reception of the *Nicomachean Ethics*'. In *Aristotle and the Arabic Tradition*, edited by Ahmed Alwishah and Josh Hayes, 200–13. Cambridge: Cambridge University Press, 2015.

Hayes, Josh. 'Configurations of Shame from Ancient Greece to Medieval Islam'. In *Cultures of Shame*, edited by Cecilia Mun, 60–79. New York: Routledge, 2023.

Hayes, Josh. 'Cosmopolitanism in the Medieval Arabic and Islamic World'. In *The Edinburgh Critical History of Middle Ages and Renaissance Philosophy*, edited by Andrew LaZella and Richard A. Lee Jr., 217–33. Edinburgh: Edinburgh University Press, 2020.

Hayes, Josh. 'Al-Fārābī's Phenomenology of the Political Imagination'. *The Iranian Yearbook of Phenomenology*, vol. 1.1, edited by Jahangir Moeini Alamdari and Hamid Malekzadeh, 63–84. 2022. https://doi.org/10.22034/IYP.2020.239888.

Hayes, Josh. 'A Politics to Come: Benevolence and the Nature of Friendship in Aristotle's Ethics'. *Epoché: A Journal for the History of Philosophy* 23, no. 2 (2019): 399–411.

Hayden, Patrick. 'Albert Camus and Rebellious Cosmopolitanism in a Divided World'. *Journal of International Political Theory* 9, no. 2 (2013): 194–219.

Hegel, G. W. F. *Hegel's Phenomenology of Spirit.* Translated by A. V. Miller. Oxford: Oxford University Press, 1977.

Heidegger, Martin. *Basic Concepts of Aristotelian Philosophy.* Translated by Robert D. Metcalf and Mark B. Tanzer. Bloomington: Indiana University Press, 2009.

Heller-Roazen, Daniel. *The Inner Touch: Archaeology of a Sensation.* Cambridge, MA: Massachusetts Institute of Technology Press, 2007.

Hourani, George. *Islamic Rationalism: The Ethics of 'Abd al-Jabbār.* Oxford: Clarendon, 1971.

Huntington, Samuel P. *The Clash of Civilizations and the Remaking of the World Order.* New York: Simon & Shuster, 1996.

Husserl, Edmund. *The Crisis of European Sciences and Transcendental Phenomenology.* Translated by David Carr. Evanston: Northwestern University Press, 1970.

Ilievski, Viktor. 'The Demiurge and His Place in Plato's Metaphysics and Cosmology. In *Time and Cosmology in Plato and the Platonic Tradition,* edited by Daniel Vázquez and Alberto Ross, 44–77. Leiden: Brill, 2002.

Ishanoğlu, Ekmeleddin. *The Abbasid House of Wisdom: Between Myth and Reality.* New York: Routledge, 2023.

Izutsu, Toshiko. *Ethico-religious Concepts in the Qur'ān.* Montreal: McGill-Queen's University Press, 2002.

Jaeger, Werner. *Aristotle: Fundamentals of the History of His Development.* Translated by R. Robinson. Oxford: Oxford University Press, 1967.

Janos, Damien. 'Al-Fārābī's (d. 950) *On the One and Oneness*: Some Preliminary Remarks on Its Structure, Contents, and Theological Implications'. In *The Oxford Handbook of Islamic Philosophy,* edited by Khaled El-Rouayheb and Sabine Schmidtke, 101–28. Oxford: Oxford University Press, 2017.

Janos, Damien. *Method, Structure, and Development in al-Fārābī's Cosmology.* Leiden: Brill, 2012.

Jaspers, Karl. *The Origin and Goal of History.* Translated by M. Bullock. London: Routledge and Kegan & Paul, 1953.

Johansen, Thomas Kjeller. *The Powers of Aristotle's Soul.* Oxford: Oxford University Press, 2012.

Jomaa, Katrin A. *Ummah: A New Paradigm for a Global World.* Albany: State University of New York Press, 2021.

Kant, Immanuel. *The Critique of Pure Reason.* Translated by Norman Kemp Smith. New York: Macmillan & Co, 1965.

Kant, Immanuel. *Perpetual Peace and Other Essays.* Translated by Ted Humphrey. Indianapolis: Hackett, 1983.

Kars, Aydogan. *Unsaying God: Negative Theology in Medieval Islam.* Oxford: Oxford University Press, 2019.

Kearney, Richard. 'Desire of God'. In *God, the Gift, and Postmodernism,* edited by John Caputo and Michael Scanlon, 112–45. Bloomington: Indiana University Press, 1999.

Kearney, Richard, and Kascha Semonovitch, eds. *Phenomenologies of the Stranger: Between Hostility and Hospitality.* New York: Fordham University Press, 2011.

Kennedy-Day, Kiki. *Books of Definition in Islamic Philosophy.* New York: Routledge, 2014.

Khadduri, Majid. *The Islamic Conception of Justice.* Baltimore: Johns Hopkins University Press, 1984.

Khalidi, Muhammad Ali. 'Al-Fārābī on the Democratic City'. *British Journal for the History of Philosophy* 11, no. 3 (2003): 379–94.

Khalidi, Tarif. *Arabic Historical Thought in the Classical Period.* Cambridge: Cambridge University Press, 1994.

Klein, Yaron. 'Imagination and Music: *Takhyīl* and the Production of Music in al-Fārābī's *Kitāb al-mūsīqī al-kabīr*'. In *The Imaginary in Classical Arabic Poetics,* vol. 2, edited by Geert Jan van Gelder and Marlé Hammond, 179–95. Oxford: Oxbow, 2008.

Klosko, George. 'The Nocturnal Council in Plato's *Laws*'. *Political Studies* 36, no. 1 (1988): 74–88.

Kochin, Michael S. 'Weeds: Cultivating the Imagination in Medieval Arabic Political Philosophy'. *Journal of the History of Ideas* 60, no. 3 (1999): 399–416.

Kraemer, Joel L. 'Alfarabi's *Opinions of the Virtuous City* and Maimonides' *Foundations of the Law*'. In *Studio Orientalia memoriae D. H. Baneth dedicate,* edited by J. Blau, S. Pines, M. J. Kister, and S. Shaked, 107–53. Jerusalem: Magnes Press, Hebrew University, 1979.

Kraemer, Joel L. *Humanism in the Renaissance of Islam: The Cultural Revival during the Būyid Age.* Leiden: Brill, 1986.

Kraemer, Joel L. 'The *Jihād* of the *Falāsifa*'. *Jerusalem Studies in Arabic and Islam* 10 (1987): 288–324.

Kraemer, Joel L. *Philosophy in the Renaissance of Islam: Abū Sulaymān al-Sijistānī and His Circle.* Leiden: Brill, 1986.

Laks, André. *Plato's Second Republic: An Essay on the* Laws. Princeton: Princeton University Press, 2022.

Lambton, Ann. *State and Government in Medieval Islam.* Oxford: Oxford University Press, 1981.

Lameer, Joep. *The Arabic Version of al-Ṭūsī's* Nasirean Ethics. Leiden: Brill, 2015.

Largier, Niklaus. *Diogenes der Kyniker. Exempel, Erzählung, Geschichte in Mittelalter and Früher Neuzeit.* Tübingen: Max Niemeyer Verlag, 1997.

L'Arrivee, Robert. 'Discrimination and Violence in Alfarabi's *Virtuous City*: A Response to Alireza Omid Bakhsh'. *Utopian Studies* 25, no. 2 (2014): 432–49.

Lemoine, Rebecca. *Plato's Caves: The Liberating Sting of Cultural Diversity.* Oxford: Oxford University Press, 2020.

Lewis, Bernard. *The Crisis of Islam: Holy War and Unholy Terror.* New York: Random House, 2004.

Lewis, V. Bradley. 'The Nocturnal Council and Platonic Political Philosophy'. *History of Political Thought* 19, no. 1 (1998): 1–20.

Llewelyn, John. *The Middle Voice of Ecological Conscience: A Chiasmic Reading of Responsibility in the Neighborhood of Levinas, Heidegger, and Others.* New York: St. Martin's Press, 1991.

Loevy, Katharine. 'Al-Farabi's Images'. *Epoché: A Journal for the History of Philosophy* 21, no. 1 (2016): 67–84.

Loevy, Katharine. 'Literary Resistance to the Philosophy of Slavery: Al-Farabi and the "Ikhwan Al-Safa"'. *Philosophy and Literature* 44, no. 2 (2020): 237–54.

Long, Anthony, and David Sedley, eds. *The Hellenistic Philosophers.* 2 vols. Cambridge: Cambridge University Press, 1987.

Long, Christopher. *Aristotle on the Nature of Truth.* Cambridge: Cambridge University Press, 2011.

López-Farjeat, Luis Xavier. 'Al-Fārābī's Psychology and Epistemology'. *The Stanford Encyclopedia of Philosophy.* Edited by Edward N. Zalta. https://plato.stanford.edu/entries/al-farabi-psych/.

López-Farjeat, Luis Xavier. 'The Language of Non-human Animals in al-Fārābī and Avicenna'. In *The Origin and Nature of Language and Logic: Perspectives in Medieval Islamic, Jewish, and Christian Thought,* edited by Nadja Germann and Steven Harvey, 73–192. Turnhout: Brepols, 2020.

Mahdi, Muhsin S. 'Alfarabi'. In *The History of Political Philosophy,* edited by Leo Strauss and Joseph Cropsey, 206–27. Chicago: University of Chicago Press, 1987.

Mahdi, Muhsin S. *Alfarabi and the Foundations of Islamic Political Philosophy.* Chicago: University of Chicago Press, 2001.

Mahdi, Muhsin S. *Ibn Khaldūn's Philosophy of History: A Study in the Philosophic Foundation of the Science of Culture.* London: George Allen & Unwin Ltd., 1957.

Makari, George. *Of Fear and Strangers: A History of Xenophobia.* New York: W. W. Norton & Company, 2021.

Makdisi, George. *The Rise of Humanism in Classical Islam and the Christian West.* Edinburgh: Edinburgh University Press, 1990.

Mamdani, Mahmood. *Citizen and Subject: Contemporary Africa and the Legacy of Late Colonialism.* Princeton: Princeton University Press, 2018.

Mansfeld, Jaap. *Prolegomena: Questions to be Settled before the Study of an Author or a Text.* Leiden: Brill, 2004.

Marder, Michael. *The Philosopher's Plant: An Intellectual Herbarium.* New York: Columbia University Press, 2014.

Marlow, Louise. *Hierarchy and Egalitarianism in Islamic Thought.* Cambridge: Cambridge University Press, 1997.

Martin, Richard, Mark Woodward, and Dwi S. Atmaja, eds. *Defenders of Reason in Islam: Mu'tazilism from Medieval School to Modern Symbol.* London: Oneworld Publications, 1997.

Mattila, Janne. *The Eudaimonist Ethics of al-Fārābī and Avicenna.* Leiden: Brill, 2022.

McCoy, Marina. *Plato on the Rhetoric of Philosophers and Sophists.* Cambridge: Cambridge University Press, 2008.

McGee, Martin. 'Pierre Claverie and the Truth That Unites Us'. *The Tablet,* 5 August 2021. www.thetablet.co.uk/features/2/20416/pierre-claverie-and-the-truth-that-unites-us#google_vignette.

Melamed, Abraham. *The Philosopher-King in Medieval and Renaissance Jewish Political Thought.* Albany: State University of New York Press, 2003.

Mian, Ali Altaf. 'Love in Islamic Philosophy'. In *The Routledge Handbook of Love in Philosophy,* edited by Adrienne Martin, 395–408. New York: Routledge, 2018.

Mian, Ali Altaf. 'Muslim Political Philosophy and the Affective Turn: Farabi on Language, Affect, and Reason'. *Journal of Shi'a Islamic Studies* 4, no. 1 (2011): 47–70.

Monocal, Maria Rosa. *The Ornament of the World: How Muslims, Jews, and Christians Created a Culture of Tolerance in Medieval Spain.* Boston: Backbay Books, 2002.

Morewedge, Parviz. 'The Neoplatonic Structure of Some Islamic Mystical Doctrines'. In *Neoplatonism and Islamic Thought,* edited by Parviz Morewedge, 50–75. Albany: State University of New York Press, 1992.

Morrow, Glenn R. 'The Demiurge in Politics: The *Timaeus* and the *Laws*'. *Proceedings and Addresses of the American Philosophical Association* 27 (1953–4): 5–23.

Morrow, Glenn R. *Plato's Cretan City: A Historical Interpretation of the* Laws. Princeton: Princeton University Press, 1963.

Mufti, Malik. *The Art of Jihad: Realism in Islamic Political Thought.* Albany: State University of New York Press, 2019.

Najjar, Fauzi M. 'Democracy in Islamic Political Philosophy'. *Studia Islamica* 51 (1980): 107–22.

Namazi, Rasoul. *Leo Strauss and Islamic Political Thought.* Cambridge: Cambridge University Press, 2022.

Nasr, Seyyed Hossein. *An Introduction to Islamic Cosmological Doctrines.* Albany: State University of New York Press, 1978.

Neria, Chaim Meir. 'Al-Fārābī's Lost Commentary on the Ethics: New Textual Evidence'. *Arabic Sciences and Philosophy* 23, no. 1 (2013): 69–99.

Netton, Ian Richard. *Allāh Transcendent: Studies in the Structure and Semiotics of Islamic Theology, Philosophy, and Cosmology*. London: Routledge, 1995.

Netton, Ian Richard. *Al-Fārābī and His School.* London: Routledge, 1992.

Netton, Ian Richard. *Muslim Neoplatonists: An Introduction to the Thought of the Brethren of Purity (Ikhwān al-Ṣafā').* London: Routledge, 2002.

Netton, Ian Richard. 'A Tale of Three Cities: Al-Fārābī and the Path to Perfection'. In *Islamic Philosophy and Theology*, vol. 2, edited by Ian Richard Netton, 89–107. New York: Routledge, 2007.

Nussbaum, Martha C. *Cosmopolitanism: A Noble but Flawed Ideal.* Cambridge, MA: Harvard University Press, 2019.

Nusseibeh, Sari. 'To Justice with Love'. In *Comparative Philosophy without Borders*, edited by Arindam Chakrabarti and Ralph Weber, 175–204. London: Bloomsbury, 2015.

Obiedat, A. Z. 'Friendship in Arabic: Its Synonyms, Etymologies, and Transformations'. In *Friendship in Islamic Ethic and World Politics*, edited by Mohammad Jafar Amir Mahallati, 49–68. Ann Arbor: University of Michigan Press, 2019.

Ogden, Stephen. *Averroes on the Intellect: From Aristotelian Origins to Aquinas' Critique.* Oxford: Oxford University Press, 2021.

O'Gorman, Ned. 'Aristotle's "Phantasia" in the *Rhetoric*: "Lexis", Appearance, and the Epideictic Function of Discourse'. *Philosophy & Rhetoric* 38, no. 1 (2005): 16–40.

Oklopcic, Zoran. *Beyond the People: Social Imaginary and Constituent Imagination.* Oxford: Oxford University Press, 2018.

O'Meara, Dominic J. *Cosmology and Politics in Plato's Later Works*. Cambridge: Cambridge University Press, 2017.

O'Meara, Dominic J. *Platonopolis: Platonic Political Philosophy in Late Antiquity*. Oxford: Oxford University Press, 2003.

Orwin, Alexander. 'Can Humankind Deliberate on a Global Scale? Alfarabi and the Politics of the Inhabited World'. *American Political Science Review* 108, no. 4 (2014): 830–9.

Orwin, Alexander. 'Democracy under the Caliphs: Alfarabi's Unusual Understanding of Popular Rule'. *The Review of Politics* 77, no. 2 (2015): 171–90.

Orwin, Alexander. *Redefining the Muslim Community: Ethnicity, Religion, and Politics in the Thought of Alfarabi*. Philadelphia: University of Pennsylvania Press, 2017.

Paolucci, Anne. 'Exile among Exiles: Dante's Party of One'. *Mosaic* 8, no. 3 (1975): 117–25.

Parens, Joshua. 'Escaping the Scholastic Paradigm: The Dispute between Strauss and His Contemporaries about How to Approach Islamic and Jewish Medieval Philosophy'. In *Encountering the Medieval in Modern Jewish Thought*, edited by James A. Diamond and Aaron W. Hughes, 203–28. Leiden: Brill, 2012.

Parens, Joshua. *An Islamic Philosophy of Virtuous Religions: Introducing Alfarabi*. Albany: State University of New York Press, 2006.

Parens, Joshua. *Metaphysics as Rhetoric: Alfarabi's Summary of Plato's* Laws. Albany: State University of New York Press, 1995.

Pellegrin, Pierre. 'Natural Slavery'. Translated by E. Zoli Filotas in *The Cambridge Companion to Aristotle's Politics*, edited by Marguerite Deslauriers and Pierre Destrée, 92–116. Cambridge: Cambridge University Press, 2013.

Peters, Francis E. *Aristoteles Arabus: The Oriental Translations and Commentaries on the Aristotelian Corpus*. Leiden: Brill, 1968.

Pogge, Thomas. 'Cosmopolitanism and Sovereignty'. *Ethics* 103, no. 1 (1992): 48–75.

Poirié, Francoise. *Emmanuel Levinas (Qui êtes-vous?)*. Lyon: La Manufacture, 1987.

Polansky, Ronald. *Aristotle's* De Anima. Cambridge: Cambridge University Press, 2007.

Raffa, Guy P. 'Dante's Poetics of Exile'. *Annali d'Italianistica* 20 (2002): 73–87.

Reisman, David C. 'Al-Fārābī and the Philosophical Curriculum'. In *The Cambridge Companion to Arabic Philosophy*, edited by Peter Adamson and Richard Taylor, 52–71. Cambridge: Cambridge University Press, 2005.

Rescher, Nicholas. 'Al-Kindī's Epistle on the Concentric Structure of the Universe'. In *Studies in Arabic Philosophy*, edited by Nicholas Rescher, 1–14. Pittsburgh: University of Pittsburgh Press, 1968.

Richter, Daniel S. *Cosmopolis: Imagining Community in Late Classical Athens and the Early Roman Empire*. Oxford: Oxford University Press, 2011.

Robineau, Jean-Manuel. *The Dangerous Life and Ideas of Diogenes the Cynic*. Translated by Malcolm DeBevoise. Oxford: Oxford University Press, 2023.

Romm, James S. *The Edges of the Earth in Ancient Thought: Geography, Exploration, and Fiction*. Princeton: Princeton University Press, 1992.

Rosenthal, E. I. J. *Political Thought in Medieval Islam: An Introductory Outline*. Cambridge: Cambridge University Press, 1958.

Rosenthal, Franz. 'The Stranger in Medieval Islam'. *Arabica* 44 (1997): 35–75.

Roth, Wolff-Michael. 'Solidarity and Responsibility, Ontologically (Categorically)'. *Mind Culture, and Activity* 16 (2009): 1–12.

Roy, Oliver. *The Failure of Political Islam*. Translated by Carol Volk. Cambridge, MA: Harvard University Press, 1998.

Rudolph, Ulrich. 'Reflections on al-Fārābī's *Mabādi' ārā' ahl al-madīna al-fāḍila*'. In *The Age of Alfarabi: Arabic Philosophy in the Fourth/Tenth Century*, edited by Peter Adamson, 1–14. London: Warburg Institute, 2008.

Sachedina, Abdulaziz. *The Islamic Roots of Democratic Pluralism*. Oxford: Oxford University Press, 2001.

Said, Edward. *Orientalism*. New York: Pantheon Books, 1978.

Sallis, John. *Ethicality and Imagination: On Luminous Abodes*. Bloomington: Indiana University Press, 2022.

Schürmann, Reiner. *Broken Hegemonies*. Translated by Reginald Lilly. Bloomington: Indiana University Press, 2003.

Segev, Mor. *Aristotle on Religion*. Cambridge: Cambridge University Press, 2017.

Shaker, Anthony F. *Reintroducing Philosophy: Thinking as the Gathering of Civilization*. Wilmington: Vernon Press, 2021.

Shedai, Fadlou. *Philosophies of Music in Medieval Islam*. Leiden: Brill, 1995.

Siddiqui, Mona. *Hospitality and Islam: Welcoming in God's Name*. New Haven: Yale University Press, 2015.

Smith, William, ed. *Dictionary of Greek and Roman Biography and Mythology*. London: Spottiswoode, 1844.

Steiris, Georgios. 'Al-Fārābī's Ecumenical State and Its Modern Connotations'. *Skepsis: A Journal of Philosophy and Interdisciplinary Research* 22, no. 3 (2012): 253–61.

Stern, Samuel Miklos. *Aristotle on the World State*. Columbia: University of South Carolina Press, 1970.

Stern, Samuel Miklos. 'Notes on al-Kindī's Treatise on Definitions'. *Journal of the Royal Asiatic Society* 91, no. 1-2 (1959): 32-43.

Stone, Gregory B. 'Dante and the *Falasifa*: Religion as Imagination'. *Dante Studies* 125 (2007): 133-56.

Stone, Gregory B. *Dante's Pluralism and the Islamic Philosophy of Religion.* New York: Palgrave Macmillan, 2006.

Strauss, Leo. *The Argument and Action of Plato's* Laws. Chicago: University of Chicago Press, 1975.

Strauss, Leo. 'Farabi's Plato'. In *Louis Ginzberg: Jubilee Volume on the Occasion of His Seventieth Birthday*, edited by Saul Lieberman, Alexander Marx, Shalom Spiegel, and Solomon Zeitlin, 357-93. New York: The American Academy of Jewish Research, 1945.

Strauss, Leo. 'How Fārābī Read Plato's *Laws*'. In *What Is Political Philosophy? And Other Studies*, 134-54. Chicago: University of Chicago Press, 1959.

Strauss, Leo. *Persecution and the Art of Writing.* Westport: Greenwood Press, 1973.

Strauss, Leo. 'Some Remarks on the Political Science of Maimonides and Farabi'. Translated by Robert Bartlett. *Interpretation* 18, no. 1 (1990): 3-30.

Streetman, Craig. 'If It Were God Who Sent Them . . . Aristotle and al-Fārābī on Prophetic Vision'. *Arabic Sciences and Philosophy* 18 (2008): 211-46.

Sweeney, Michael J. 'Greek Essence and Islamic Tolerance: Al-Farabi, Al-Ghazali, Ibn Rushd'. *Review of Metaphysics* 65, no. 1 (2011): 41-61.

Sweeney, Michael J. 'Philosophy and *Jihād*: Al-Fārābī on Compulsion to Happiness'. *Review of Metaphysics* 60, no. 3 (2007): 543-72.

Tamer, Georges. *Islamische Philosophie und Die Krise der Moderne: Das Verhältnis von Leo Strauss zu Alfarabi, Avicenna, und Averroes.* Leiden: Brill, 2001.

Tannous, Jack. *The Making of the Medieval Middle East: Religion, Society, and Simple Believers.* Princeton: Princeton University Press, 2020.

Taylor, Charles. *Modern Social Imaginaries.* Durham: Duke University Press, 2023.

Taylor, Richard C. 'A Critical Analysis of the Structure of the *Kalām fī mahd al-khair* (*Liber de Causis*)'. In *Neoplatonism and Islamic Thought*, edited by Parviz Morewedge, 11-40. Albany: State University of New York Press, 1992.

Took, John. *Dante.* Princeton: Princeton University Press, 2020.

Treanor, Brian. 'Putting Hospitality in Its Place'. In *Phenomenologies of the Stranger: Between Hostility and Hospitality*, edited by Richard Kearney and Kascha Semonovitch, 49-66. New York: Fordham University Press, 2011.

Urvoy, Dominique. *Ibn Rushd (Averroes).* London: Routledge, 1991.

Vagelpohl, Uwe. 'The *Rhetoric* and *Poetics* in the Islamic World'. In *Aristotle and the Arabic Tradition*, edited by Ahmed Alwishah and Josh Hayes, 76–91. Cambridge: Cambridge University Press, 2015.

Vallat, Philippe. *Fārābī et l'école d'Alexandrie: Des prémisses de la connaissance à la philosophie politique*. Paris: Vrin, 2004.

Vallat, Philippe. 'Principles of the Philosophy of State'. In *The Routledge Companion to Islamic Philosophy*, edited by Richard C. Taylor and Luis Xavier López-Farjeat, 337–45. London: Routledge, 2016.

Van Ess, Josef. *Theologie und Gesellschaft im 2. And 3. Jarhhundert Hidschra*. 6 vols. Berlin: De Gruyter, 1991–5.

van Koningsveld, P. S. 'Greek Manuscripts in the Early 'Abbāsid Empire: Fiction and Facts about Their Origin, Translation, and Destruction'. *Bibliotheca Orientalis* 55, no. 3–4 (1998): 345–71.

Vasalou, Sophia. *Moral Agents and Their Deserts: The Character of Mu'tazilite Ethics*. Princeton: Princeton University Press, 2008.

Vasalou, Sophia. *Virtues of Greatness in the Arabic Tradition*. Oxford: Oxford University Press, 2019.

Wakelnig, Elvira. 'Greek Sages on the *Tawḥīd*: Ancient Philosophy in Accord with the Islamic Doctrine of the Oneness of God'. *Studeo graeco-arabica* 5 (2015): 205–45.

Walbridge, John. *God and Logic in Islam: The Caliphate of Reason*. Cambridge: Cambridge University Press, 2010.

Walker, Paul. E. *Early Philosophical Shiism: The Ismaili Neoplatonism of Abū Ya'qūb al-Sijistānī*. Cambridge: Cambridge University Press, 1993.

Walzer, Richard. 'Aspects of Islamic Political Thought: Al-Fārābī and Ibn Xaldūn'. *Oriens* 16 (1963): 40–60.

Walzer, Richard. 'Al-Fārābī's Theory of Prophecy and Divination'. In *Greek into Arabic: Essays on Islamic Philosophy*, edited by Richard Walzer, 206–19. Cambridge, MA: Harvard University Press, 1962.

Walzer, Richard. 'New Studies on Al-Kindi'. In *Greek into Arabic: Essays on Islamic Philosophy*, edited by Richard Walzer, 175–205. Cambridge, MA: Harvard University Press, 1962.

Warf, Barney. 'Nationalism, Cosmopolitanism, and Geographical Imaginations'. *Geographical Review* 102, no. 3 (2012): 271–92.

Watt, John W. 'The Syriac Aristotelian Tradition and the Arabic Baghdad Philosophers'. In *Ideas in Motion in Baghdad and Beyond: Philosophical and Theological Exchanges between Christians and Muslims in the Third/Ninth and Fourth/Tenth Centuries*, edited by Damien Janos, 7–43. Leiden: Brill, 2016.

Westerink L. G. *Anonymous Prolegomena to Platonic Philosophy*. Amsterdam: North-Holland, 1962.

Woerther, Frédérique. 'Averroes' Goals in the Paraphrase (Middle Commentary) of Aristotle's *Nicomachean Ethics*'. In *Interpreting Averroes*, edited by Matteo Di Giovanni and Peter Adamson, 218–36. Cambridge: Cambridge University Press, 2018.

Woerther, Frédérique. 'Al-Fārābī and the Didascalia'. In *Aristotle and the Arabic Tradition*, edited by Ahmed Alwishah and Josh Hayes, 96–104. Cambridge: Cambridge University Press, 2015.

Wolfson, Harry Austryn. *The Philosophy of the Kalam*. Cambridge, MA: Harvard University Press, 1976.

Zargar, Cyrus Ali. *The Polished Mirror: Storytelling and the Pursuit of Virtue in Islamic Philosophy and Sufism*. London: Oneworld Publications, 2017.

Index

EU Authorised Representative:
Easy Access System Europe Mustamäe tee 50, 10621 Tallinn, Estonia
gpsr.requests@easproject.com

Printed and bound by CPI Group (UK) Ltd, Croydon, CR0 4YY
29/09/2026
02224981-0007